T0330148

A Research Agenda for Real Estate

Elgar Research Agendas outline the future of research in a given area. Leading scholars are given the space to explore their subject in provocative ways, and map out the potential directions of travel. They are relevant but also visionary.

Forward-looking and innovative, Elgar Research Agendas are an essential resource for PhD students, scholars and anybody who wants to be at the forefront of research.

Titles in the series include:

A Research Agenda for Social Innovation
Edited by Jürgen Howaldt Christoph Kaletka and Antonius Schröder

A Research Agenda for Multilevel Governance
Edited by Arthur Benz, Jörg Broschek and Markus Lederer

A Research Agenda for Space Policy
Edited by Kai-Uwe Schrogl, Christina Giannopapa and Ntorina Antoni

A Research Agenda for Event Impacts
Edited by Nicholas Wise and Kelly Maguire

A Research Agenda for Urban Tourism
Edited by Jan van der Borg

A Research Agenda for Manufacturing Industries in the Global Economy
Edited by John R. Bryson, Chloe Billing, William Graves and Godfrey Yeung

A Research Agenda for Global Higher Education
Jeroen Huisman and Marijk van der Wende

A Research Agenda for Real Estate
Edited by Piyush Tiwari and Julie T. Miao

A Research Agenda for Real Estate

Edited by

PIYUSH TIWARI

Professor of Property, Faculty of Architecture, Building and Planning, The University of Melbourne, Australia

JULIE T. MIAO

Associate Professor of Property and Economic Development, Faculty of Architecture, Building and Planning, The University of Melbourne, Australia

Elgar Research Agendas

Cheltenham, UK • Northampton, MA, USA

Published by
Edward Elgar Publishing Limited
The Lypiatts
15 Lansdown Road
Cheltenham
Glos GL50 2JA
UK

Edward Elgar Publishing, Inc.
William Pratt House
9 Dewey Court
Northampton
Massachusetts 01060
USA

A catalogue record for this book
is available from the British Library

Library of Congress Control Number: 2022931263

This book is available electronically in the **Elgar**online
Economics subject collection
http://dx.doi.org/10.4337/9781839103933

ISBN 978 1 83910 392 6 (cased)
ISBN 978 1 83910 393 3 (eBook)

Printed and bound by CPI Group (UK) Ltd, Croydon, CR0 4YY

Contents

Figures

Tables

Contributors

Ashish Gupta has over 20 years of experience in the real estate profession and academia. He worked for eight years with Jones Lang LaSalle in consulting, valuation, investments and capital markets. Subsequently, he headed real estate practices in India within wealth management for Aditya Birla Money and Bajaj Capital. Currently, he is Associate Professor and Director – Research & Consulting at RICS School of Built Environment, Amity University Noida. He is a qualified architect, housing planner, MBA (finance) with a PhD in Built Environment. He has published papers in various international journals and has research interests in real estate investment, development and urban land and housing issues. He is a Fellow member of Royal Institution of Chartered Surveyors (RICS); a professional trainer; and an assessor, counsellor and auditor for RICS Assessment of Professional Competence (APC).

Huiying (Cynthia) Hou is an Assistant Professor in the Department of Building Service Engineering, The Hong Kong Polytechnic University. Her main research interests lie in facilities management, real estate development and management, heritage adaptive reuse and management.

Anna Hurlimann is an Associate Professor of Urban Planning at the Faculty of Architecture Building and Planning at the University of Melbourne Australia. Anna's teaching and research interests focus on environmental planning, with a particular focus on planning for climate change. Anna is the lead chief investigator of an Australian Research Council Grant titled Integrating Climate Change Adaptation and Mitigation In Built Environments 2020–2023, which is investigating the integration of climate change action across built environment sectors including urban planning, property, construction, architecture, landscape architecture and urban design. Anna is a member of Planners for Climate Action, and a lead author for the third assessment report on climate change and cities.

Godwin Kavaarpuo is an urban planner, real estate professional and PhD Researcher in Property at the Faculty of Architecture, Building and Planning, the University of Melbourne. He has consulted for local and international organisations including the African Development Bank, the Centre for Affordable Housing Finance, and real estate developers, mainly in Ghana. His doctoral research investigates housebuilding innovation adoption from transaction costs economics and Austrian entrepreneurial theories. Godwin's teaching and research focus on sustainable real estate development and investment, proptech, affordable housing and policy.

Hyung Min Kim is a Senior Lecturer (ongoing position) at the Faculty of Architecture, Building and Planning, The University of Melbourne. He was a full-time Lecturer at RMIT University (Melbourne, Australia) and Xian Jiaotong-Liverpool University (Suzhou, China). He completed his PhD at The University of Melbourne supported by an Australian competitive scholarship Endeavour Postgraduate Award. His teaching and research activities focus on urban development, land policy, and international planning studies. His research findings have appeared in prestigious peer-reviewed international journals including *Progress in Planning, Cities, Habitat International, International Development Planning Review*, and *Land Use Policy*.

Xiang Li is an Assistant Professor in the Department of Urban Planning, School of Architecture and Civil Engineering at Xiamen University. His research interests lie in urban redevelopment, policy mobility and institutional reform, urban governance and urban politics in China. He received his PhD from the Faculty of Architecture, Building and Planning at the University of Melbourne. His PhD research focuses on participatory urban redevelopment policies and their implications on power relations in Shenzhen, China. Xiang has been working on a research agenda which brings out China's rich and nuanced materials for innovative theorisation in urban studies. He has been active in pursuing the research agenda, fund raising and publications.

Xuqing Li holds a Master of Property degree from the University of Melbourne. She has worked as a property manager since 2020. Her main expertise includes real estate asset management, operation budgeting, lease contract management and communication.

Mike McDermott has over 40 years' real estate valuation and valuation-related experience in the public and private sectors, both nationally and internationally. Internationally, and mainly in Africa and Asia, Mike has consulted on land policy, legislation and administration matters in general, and on facilitating fit-for-purpose land valuations in opaque markets in particular, for the last 28 years. Mike's master's degree was on addressing complex social issues, and his doctoral thesis was on addressing wicked valuation problems in the developing world. His recent major works include *Wicked Valuations* (2018, Routledge), the UN-HABITAT/GLTN policy guide on the valuation of unregistered land (2018, lead author), and the UN-HABITAT/GLTN manual on implementing that policy (2021, co-author).

Julie T. Miao is an Associate Professor of Property and Economic Development at the University of Melbourne and also an honorary Research Fellow at Shanghai Jiaotong and Henan Universities, China. Dr Miao obtained her PhD in economic geography and planning from University College London. Her research has been developed along two innovative fields on the 'intrapreneurial state' (entrepreneurship within the public sectors) and 'innovation-space' (interface between housing, labour and the knowledge economy). She has published widely on these themes and conducted policy research for various public institutions.

Jyoti Shukla is a Lecturer in Property at the University of Melbourne. During the course of her academic training as an architect, urban planner, and real estate professional, Jyoti developed an interest in those negatively impacted by developmental activities due to the loss of land and property rights and later conducted a PhD on this topic. In her latest book, *Functionings of Land*, Jyoti applies the economic theory of 'capability' to understand the wellbeing of those who are dispossessed of their land. In complementary work, Jyoti is working towards designing a 'resilient compensation mechanism' for those affected by natural and man-made disasters in Australia, India, and Japan. Jyoti also works on institutional aspects of housing markets. In a co-authored book, *Development Paradigms for Urban Housing in BRICS Countries*, she has identified the aspects of institutional arrangements that cause housing markets to fail.

Eileen Sim is a Teaching Fellow in property at the University of Melbourne, Australia with an educational background in Property, Accounting and Finance. She is a workplace specialist and has a PhD from studying the adoption of Activity Based Working offices, a type of innovative workplace. Her research focuses on increasing employees' acceptance of innovative workplaces through the way organisations accept and implement them. Her research approach utilises a combination of theories and concepts from the field of Corporate Real Estate and Psychology. Her main research focus is Corporate Real Estate and Innovative Workplace acceptance.

Djordje Stojanovic has been a Senior Lecturer at the University of Melbourne, Faculty of Architecture, Building and Planning since June 2019. Previously, he was an Associate Professor at the University of Belgrade and founder of 4of7 Architecture. He has been an ARB certified architect in the UK since 2001. He holds a PhD from the University of Belgrade, a Master of Science degree from London School of Economics and a Master of Architecture degree from the

Architectural Association. His research interests include design innovation in collective housing and architectural design of communal spaces.

Raghu Dharmapuri Tirumala is a Senior Lecturer at the Faculty of Architecture, Building and Planning at the University of Melbourne. Raghu's research focuses on public, private partnerships in infrastructure, project and property finance, and managing the transformation of cities. Raghu holds a PhD in Built Environment, MBA in Marketing and Finance and Bachelor of Technology in Mechanical Engineering. Previously, he was the Professor and Director at RICS School of Built Environment (Noida, India), and was the CEO of Infrastructure Development Corporation (Karnataka) Limited in Bangalore, India. Raghu has partnered with various governments, multi-lateral agencies, international development organisations and private sector clients in the urban infrastructure, property, integrated transportation, tourism, energy, commercial and industrial infrastructure sectors. Raghu has authored numerous policy documents and research reports.

Piyush Tiwari is Professor of Property at the University of Melbourne, Australia. Prior to his current position he was Director of Policy at Infrastructure Development Finance Company (IDFC), India. He has held positions at the University of Aberdeen, UK, HDFC, India and the University of Tsukuba, Japan. His research interests include housing economics and mortgages, commercial real estate investment and valuation, land economics and financing infrastructure in developing countries. He is a member of the International Land Measurement Standards Committee which is engaged in writing standards for land measurement.

Georgia Warren-Myers has a PhD in Property Valuation and is an Associate Professor in the Faculty of Architecture, Building and Planning at the University of Melbourne. Her core focus investigates the relationships between value, valuation and industry practice, and climate related risk and sustainability in the built environment. Specific areas of study examine: climate-related physical risks to property and implications for professional practice and property markets; sustainability rating tools and emissions profiles and the effects on markets and stakeholder behaviours; and challenges related to housing affordability and identifying opportunities for development. Dr Warren-Myers' research has important connections with industry and her involvement in various professional bodies in the development of standards, guidelines and tools for the property industry.

Hao Wu is a Senior Lecturer in Property at the Faculty of Architecture, Building and Planning, the University of Melbourne. He is an expert in real estate markets and valuation, property rights and land and urban (re)development in China, Australia and the Asia-Pacific region.

1 Introduction to *A Research Agenda for Real Estate*

Piyush Tiwari and Julie T. Miao

Introduction

A book with the title *A Research Agenda for Real Estate* seems to promise that it will review all past research that has been conducted on real estate and will list all topic areas and questions for which answers are still illusive. If that is the expectation, we are sure to disappoint you. The approach to real estate research is multifaceted. Several generations of property economists in academia and the profession have been conducting quantitative research on the important aspects of real estate transactions, valuation, development, investment and finance. The last three decades has also seen the emergence of qualitative and quantitative research on aspects of corporate real estate management using theories from management science.

When we look at the history of real estate research, early research in real estate focused on examining the urban population patterns and urban land values (Weber, 1899; Hurd, 1903). A boost to real estate research came with the formal launch of the field of urban land economics in the 1920s. The collection of data and analysis using quantitative methods to understand many aspects of real estate business and urbanisation, as exemplified in early treatise of land values by Hoyt (1933), provided a foundation for subsequent research and development of real estate as an academic field. The oldest journal that addressed questions related to real estate is *Land Economics*, founded in 1925 (with the title *Journal of Land and Public Utility Economics*). In its first issue, Richard T. Ely identified four areas of interest for researchers in the field of land economics: land use, land ownership, valuation of land and taxation of land (Ely, 1925). Ely identified topics that had promise for research. These topics included: optimal allocation for land uses, optimal utilisation of agricultural land, optimal urban land development, housing policy, transportation and comprehensive city planning, land tenure, financial return on real estate investment, the relationship between construction cost and production of income, financialisation of land and the impact of taxation on economic

1

activity and use of land (Roulac et al., 2005). This set the pace for a long list of inquiries into real estate ownership, use, values, development, financing and various other aspects of this huge economic sector. This research has also been complemented by the understanding of real estate use, investment and development activities and processes from an institutional economics perspective.

Roulac et al. (2005) conducted an analysis of topics that have been researched from 1925 to 1999 based on publication in *Land Economics*. With each decade, the complexity of topics being researched increased. The 1920s saw research on topics such as real estate as public utility and tenure decisions. While these continued to be the focus during the 1930s, housing policy and real estate cycles emerged as themes for research. Housing policy and public housing received far more attention during the 1940s and 1950s. During the 1960s, additional research topics, reflecting urban challenges of the time, such as urban blight, location decisions, land use controls and urban development processes were added. While real estate as public utility continued to be the focus of a large part of research during the 1970s, land use controls and market structure also became the focus of attention. The 1990s' leading topic of research was valuation/appraisal theory. Environmental value also emerged as a theme for research (Roulac et al., 2005).

The rapid expansion of real estate as an academic field and research occurred from the mid-1980s onwards with the formation of academic real estate societies and the emergence of journals that were dedicated to publishing real estate research, such as the *Journal of Real Estate Research* (JRER) and the *Journal of Real Estate Finance and Economics* (JREFE). These journals complemented the oldest real estate journal, *Real Estate Economics* (REE) which was founded in 1973. Dombrow and Turnbull (2004) examined the areas of real estate research that witnessed significant activity during 1988–2001, as evidenced through publication in REE and JREFE. The most researched areas during this period were mortgages, commercial property and appraisal. Research on housing markets remained important, as it had been in past decades, but interest in commercial property and mortgages increased due to the availability of new data and advances in financial theory. The primary geographic concentration of research in these journals was the United States.

Real estate research in Europe gained momentum after the formation of the European Real Estate Society in 1994. A major European real estate journal that was founded in 1984 is the *Journal of Property Research*. The other two major European journals are the *Journal of Property Investment and Finance* and the *Journal of European Real Estate Research*, which was created in 2008. Other real estate related journals are *Housing Studies* and *Urban Studies*. Three main research areas for European property researchers have been valuation, housing, and investment and portfolio management (Hoesli, 2016).

In 2001, Newell et al. (2002) conducted a survey to identify research priorities for Australian institutional property investors and academics. The focus of Newell et al. (2002) was to identify topics within the property finance domain. The role of property in a mixed asset portfolio, portfolio risk management, measurement of property performance and diversification within portfolios emerged as key research priorities. These priorities were similar to what Worzala et al. (2002) identified for the US except that, in the US, technological factors affecting portfolios and international property in a portfolio were also becoming prominent areas for research compared with in Australia. Newell et al. (2002) also identified specific property topics. These were the impact of capital flows in and out for property markets, the role of indirect property in mixed asset portfolios, listed property trusts as a proxy for mixed asset portfolios, diversification within a mixed asset portfolio and forecasting methodologies (Newell et al., 2002). These topics were far broader than those researchers in the US were pursuing, such as property sales and exit strategies, the effect of asset management fees in property portfolios, the existence and predictability of property cycles, and diversification – economic vs geographic vs property type (Worzala et al., 2002). Newell et al. (2004) examined the research priorities of institutional property investors and academics in Germany and the UK. The role of real estate in a mixed asset portfolio was a top area of research in the UK. In addition, UK research priorities included analysis of macroeconomic factors that affect real estate, and real estate and portfolio risk management. For Germany, with its bank-dominated financial system and vehicles such as open-ended real estate funds for investment in real estate, the top research priority was real estate and portfolio risk management. In addition, performance measures for real estate and the role of international real estate in a portfolio were becoming important.

The review of real estate research in Asia by Chau (1998) identified cross-section analysis of housing markets as the key focus. A focus on policy issues has been another characteristic of research on Asia. A lack of data resulted in studies that were either theoretical or were based on case studies. Research on emerging markets (such as mainland China) was largely descriptive. Chau (1998) suggested in his review that the future direction of real estate research in Asia would include analysis of the impact of fiscal, monetary, land, housing and immigration policies on tenure choice. Further, development of financial markets, such as Hong Kong, and the availability of data would lead to studies related to the mortgage market and securitisation. Prior to 1998, time series data on Asian markets were limited. Chau (1998) opined that the availability of time series data would facilitate the analysis of dynamics of various real estate sub-sectors. With the internationalisation of property markets, portfolio analysis of Asian real estate would also become an important area of research. Research over the next 20 years after Chau (1998) presented his review indicates that most of the aspects he had mentioned attracted considerable attention in research. Newell (2020) revisited research opportunities in Asia and argued that Asia now constitutes 28% of the global real estate investment market. The availability of high-quality data from various sources on a number of Asian markets provides opportunities for new research at the micro and macro levels (Newell, 2020). Research related to alternative real estate assets, sustainability, development sites, and infrastructure present opportunities for researchers focusing on Asian markets (Newell, 2020).

While the real estate research topics that have been pursued during 2000–2020 or even before are still relevant, and the research along these beaten paths continues to hold interest and add to the literature, there is a distinction. With the availability of data and development of researchers, research on real estate markets such as in developing Asia, Central and Eastern Europe and Africa is also emerging.

In *A Research Agenda for Real Estate*, we take a fresh look into the key emerging issues for real estate research. There is no doubt that the choice of topics is constrained by the selection of contributing authors and their areas of interest. We have not tried to be comprehensive either in the coverage of possible themes for research or in the geographical location of researchers, as that would be a tall expectation to meet. But what we have tried to do is to bring to the table a set of issues that are contemporary concerns and have the potential to generate interest from researchers for their future research. The other important aspect that we have tried to distinguish from other attempts to identify real estate research topic areas is to bring together a team of multidisciplinary authors who are looking at real estate from their primary disciplinary focus, be it planning, property or economics. This provides an important departure from past studies, which have confined themselves to look at real estate questions that real estate researchers are engaged in. We hope that this will expand the horizon of the real estate research agenda beyond what is already being considered within the discipline.

There are 12 chapters following this introduction, organised under the following three parts.

Part I concentrates on disruptive changes in, and surrounding, the real estate sector. Many of these changes are derived from technological revolutions and have had impacts on how we perceive and use space. Dealing with changes in the real estate industry has not been a strength nor a key focus of orthodox approaches within real estate studies. The broadening of the mainstream of real estate economics discussions with the development of an institutional perspective by scholars such as Graaskamp (1992), Healey (1991), Keogh and D'Arcy (1999) has gradually unveiled the mechanisms, processes, actors involved in, and challenges of responding to changes in general, and new technologies in particular, in the real estate sector. Focusing on the operational environment of the housebuilding sector, Ball (1999) for example, pointed out that the prevalence of sub-contracting, risk-aversion of the financial sector, skill speciality and labour shortage, were some of the main factors causing poor innovation and productivity performance in the industry. Much has changed since the writings of the above scholars both within the sector and its context. The development of real estate brokerage and investment vehicles and their readiness to adopt new technologies have a ripple effect on both property demand and supply (Saiz, 2020). Users now have broader choices and platforms in their hunt for space and are also becoming more imaginative and demanding of the space configurations, building materials and sustainable performance. Since many changes are emerging and are implicit, with their short and long-term impacts still unfolding, we see a necessity to compose a section addressing this topic.

Value is a permanent concern for the real estate industry. Part II focuses on this theme by reflecting upon the meaning of value, risks and investment behaviours. Mainstream real estate economic analysis interprets 'value' as the present worth of future benefits arising from the ownership of the property, which is embodied in, but not necessarily equal to, market price (Brueggeman & Fisher, 2018). Exogenous demand and supply dynamics play a crucial role in determining a property's value. Hedonic theory, in comparison, argues that the value of a property is determined endogenously by its quality and its immediate environment and amenity. Institutional economics further brings in subjective factors in deciding a property's value, as individuals attach different meanings and utilities to their belongings. Given the considerable challenge in incorporating individual preferences, a market-transaction based value definition dominates current literature. Subsequently, investment decision-making and risk analysis also primarily depart from an analysis of market transactions and tend to focus on those factors contributing most directly to capital gains and cash flows. Our edited volume intends to broaden such a narrow perspective on value by introducing the multifaceted functions of assets and the various actors involved in the value-generating process. We also recognise the urgency to update the standard techniques used in investment and risk analyses in order to operationalise a broader definition of value and to be more responsive to the sustainable development agenda. A cross-disciplinary and cross-sector dialogue could be beneficial in achieving such a goal.

Since our understanding of the changes and values of the real estate industry calls for a context-embedded approach, Part III turns to institutions explicitly. It is widely agreed that institutional settings frame and constrain behaviours and decision-making in the real estate industry domestically (Ball, 2006) and internationally (Seabrooke et al., 2008; Tiwari & White, 2010). Governments and public policies are also important components of the operational environment for the real estate industry (Adams et al., 2008). In liberal markets, governments mainly assume the roles of regulators and facilitators of the market. Zoning and planning, for example, can provide clarity regarding property development and investment opportunities in liberal market economies but there is also variety in local, let alone national, planning 'cultures' (Valler & Phelps, 2017) that impact the realisation of value in real estate development. In developmental markets, as represented by China and Singapore, governments often intervene more directly in the functioning of the real estate sector (Cao, 2015; Haila, 2015). It is therefore expected that the role of governments will not be completely rolled-back as has been argued by the neoliberal doctrine, but will be diversified in the future. Moreover, foreign actors have become important forces in shaping domestic built environments, in particular the real estate sector, as globalisation deepens (Rogers & Koh, 2017). International 'hot money', while actively seeking risk diversification and/or higher returns, is profoundly framing our property landscape, especially in global cities (Fadeyi et al., 2021). These phenomena, while not completely new, call for fresh examination from both conceptual and empirical perspectives when increasing numbers of developing countries and regions are becoming active in the international real estate arena.

Book structure

Following this introduction, we have 12 chapters, grouped into three parts, which shed light on various valuable research directions for real estate, both as an industry and as a discipline. Multidisciplinary perspectives are brought together in intellectual and provocative dialogues on the future of the industry.

Part 1 opens up the conversation on mega changes happening or emerging in the real estate sector. Many of these changes are rather disruptive to established norms, practices and standards. Yet they also provide Schumpeterian moments of 'creative destruction', which revolutionises the economic structure from within, incessantly destroying the old models and creating new ones. In Chapter 2, Tiwari and Shukla summarise three prominent disruptors on the real estate market, including demographic disruption, globalisation disruptions and technological disruptions. The demographic disruption, associated with the rise of the millennial population, has led to a significant growth of sharing alternatives for assets that were traditionally owned. Stojanovic in Chapter 5 elaborates this phenomenon further. Globalisation disruptions are aroused by the growth of footloose capital into a range of assets, with the real estate sector emerging as one of the largest recipients of international capital. The prevalence of global investment instruments, such as crowdsourcing, have facilitated this process. This process has tampered ideological and institutional barriers across different countries, a topic that is picked up again in Chapter 11 by Kim. For technological disruptions, Tiwari and Shukla have usefully distinguished between those endogenous to the property sector, or the so-called PropTech; and those exogenous to the sector. For the former, smart buildings, real estate fintech and the sharing economy are identified as the major disruptors that not only influence how space is designed and utilised but also the valuation of properties. For the latter, blockchain emerges as a key invention that enables frictionless and secure transactions between parties without the need for intermediation. Its adoption in the property sector could potentially lead to cost and time efficiency as the real estate market is notoriously encumbered with intermediaries. All these disruptions invite new ways of thinking and new challenges for the sector going forward. These include, for example, the robustness of technology platforms, regulation frameworks, growing uncertainties in risks and returns, and the cyclical movement of the market itself.

Miao follows up the discussion on technological disruptions in Chapter 3. Drawing insights from urban studies, planning and geography, Miao interprets the effects of a knowledge-based development worldwide in the property sector, from micro- to macro-level. At the micro, labour market level, Miao highlights the emergence of the creative class who earn with their creativity and 'big ideas'. These creative workers are portrayed as preferring bespoke living embedded in an organic and indigenous street-level culture. In parallel to this trend is the casualisation of labour contracts and the extension of working activities well beyond the traditional office spaces. Both trends challenge the established real estate design, construction and management practices, as seen by the growing adoption of innovative workplaces discussed by Sim in Chapter 4. However, the scale and scope of their impacts are yet to be ascertained. On the sector level, Miao discusses the impact of new technologies, especially the information and communication technologies (ICT), on the construction, consumption and service activities of the property sector. It is noted that adoption of ICT has been relatively slow in the construction sector. The lack of conclusive evidence on the added value of ICT is partially to blame; whereas the potentially higher transaction costs involved, as discussed by Kavaarpuo in Chapter 13, is another important underlining barrier. At the macro-level, Miao explores the interfaces between urban configurations and property dynamics starting with the debates on monocentric and polycentric urbanisation processes. Miao suggests that high-tech sectors are prone to a dispersed concentration and prefer a mixed use configuration. Yet in-depth and ideally comparative studies are called for to further qualify and ground many of these stylised facts.

Focusing on the trend towards greater flexibility in working and living in modern society, Sim and Stojanovic elaborate changes happening in the office (Chapter 4) and residential (Chapter 5) sectors. In reviewing the evolution of office workplaces, Sim points out an increased adoption of innovative, non-territorial, workplaces, such as Co-location, Activity Based Working (ABW), Self-owned Desks and Hot-desking, which offer more collaborative spaces, improve productivity through a larger work setting variety and increased real estate cost efficiency. In particular, her argument on the preference of talent in using ABW due to the resulting higher autonomy, flexibility and productivity echoes that of Miao in her discussion of the creative class. In reflection, Sim emphasises that the advancement in technological devices has been the most influential factor in enabling third generation offices. Future transdisciplinary research into the integration of technology in building services is required to reveal how innovative office workplaces are keeping up with the advancement of technology and how well they are integrated.

Similarly, in studying the phenomenon of housing sharing in Chapter 5, Stojanovic calls for interdisciplinary research and intersectoral collaboration to improve financial, legal and planning mechanisms, enabling advanced housing solutions. In this chapter, Stojanovic identifies six formats of housing sharing, which are (1) Short-term Rental, which is a key component of the emergent sharing economy as discussed by Tiwari and Shukla in Chapter 2; (2) the Private Rented Sector, which is sustained and escalated with the development of information and communication technologies, especially digitally mediated peer-to-peer platforms; (3) Co-living, which is often privately managed and delivered, combining informal workspaces and recreational facilities with dwelling space. Echoing Miao, Stojanovic points out a renewed interest in this form of housing is stimulated by its appeal to knowledge workers, whose employment is usually sessional and often requires relocations from one city to another; (4) Co-housing, where private dwellings are combined with communal facilities. Users often participate in the design process and management of the communal spaces; (5) Self-development housing groups;

and (6) Cooperatives. With copious formats of new ownership, development, management, and investment potentials emerging, Stojanovic rightly calls for further inquiries into 'hybrid housing tenures' that go beyond the duality of customary homeownership and rental tenures.

Part II discusses another important topic in the property sector: values, risks and finance. Shukla and McDermott's chapter invites a critical rethink of the theory of value and standard appraisal practices in 'non-standard' contexts, such as when the land is not registered; when land is acquired compulsorily; and when there are multiple stakeholders with varying levels of claims. To fully comprehend the plural value of land/property and to approach equitable distribution of resources across members of the society, the authors suggest using the theoretical framework of 'capability' as an alternative to capture values that are perceived as important to an individual's wellbeing, both monetary and non-monetary. Specifically, the authors identify ten fundamental functionings of land that are generally valuable to landowners/users across the globe. The importance of these functionings varies depending on the social-economic status of an individual. Their conceptual reasoning helps to distinguish those 'objectively' valuable functionings that are tradable between buyers and sellers, and those 'subjective functionings' that are context specific, extensive and often hard to put a price tag on, making them difficult, if at all possible, to be fully comprehended in current appraisal practice. Their exploration poses further questions, such as how to incorporate variations in rights and duties under different systems of property rights, and whether 'capability theory' can be used to identify and measure the social benefits of public projects.

In Chapter 7, Gupta and Tiwari highlight the value of transiting towards a circular economy in the real estate sector. These authors, quoting figures from McKinsey, estimate that there will be a US$1.6 trillion additional productivity gain if the construction sector catches up with the global economy using circular economy principles. They emphasise that real estate businesses will need a strong vision, and societal, regulatory, and economic initiatives to change their inherent linear operation mindset of take-make-sale-dispose. It is also important to implement circular principles throughout the industry and project lifecycle. This would mean evaluating various phases of value addition across the lifecycle of a project, for example the land stage, market research and feasibility, design and planning, financing, construction and project management, lease, operation and maintenance, extended life and end-of-life salvage value extraction.

In Chapter 8, Warren-Myers and Hurlimann touch upon the issue of 'value' from the perspective of risks. In particular, their concern is the limited research on the impacts of climate change in the real estate sector. Five key challenges and associated research agendas have been identified: (1) a need for detailed understanding of climate change implications on real estate at local scales; (2) a need to understand the climate change impacts across the diversity of the real estate sector; (3) a need for an increase in the quality, reliability and sharing of data on climate change and its implications; (4) a need to consider the life cycle of greenhouse gas emissions and to understand the drivers and levers to generate mainstream change across the real estate industry; and (5) a need to anticipate the type of adaptive action and level of action required to future-proof property assets. Summative information is provided regarding climate change risks and how they are translated to loss and value implications for real estate, and the variegated barriers to take climate change actions in the property and construction sectors. This chapter calls for actions in the real estate sector to adapt and adjust to climate change, in order to avoid becoming the frog in the cooking pot. The authors nonetheless emphasis that there will not be a uniform approach and therefore extensive research is required to identify a variety of, and often unique, pathways and solutions to the challenges.

Tirumala in Chapter 9 also discusses risks but does so from an investment perspective at the confluence of real estate and infrastructure. The similarities and differences between real estate and infrastructure have been a topic of interest to many researchers, particularly from the investment perspective. It is noted that the risk-return profile of the global infrastructure assets is substantially different from that of global equities and real estate, hence international financial investors have started looking at infrastructure as a separate asset class from the late 2000s as a means of achieving diversification benefits. There is also a wide and emerging range of research possibilities at the interface between these two sectors. These possibilities include: (1) financialisation and internationalisation, a topic that has been briefly discussed in Chapter 2 and is revisited by Kim in Chapter 11; (2) land value capture and land-based financing, which is in need of both conceptual and practical revisits, as discussed by Shukla and McDermott in Chapter 6; (3) the roles and influences of different stakeholders across the project life cycle, as well as how the advising community, the asset managers, and the Big Four management consulting firms influence the project structures or the policy landscape; and (4) greater regional diversity, especially with the rise of emerging markets in Asia and Africa. Building upon these, Tirumala concludes that a future research agenda for property needs to make a shift from considering these two sectors independently to a more holistic, integrated theme by/for a larger group of researchers.

Part III moves beyond sector-specific discussions to examine the institutional contexts and stakeholders that shape the operation of the real estate industry. Li, Wu and Hou's study on the engagement of local community in the Alphington Paper Mill project in Chapter 10 offers a micro-scale case study that speaks broadly to the local communities' role and involvement in brownfield redevelopment. Although in the literature, community support has often been identified as one of the variables that has a strong impact on brownfield project success, the authors point out that a clear extent to which local communities are involved in a brownfield project process is often ignored. Taking a grounded evaluation approach, the authors conducted face-to-face interviews and questionnaire surveys among community members and developers to understand locals' experience of the project and the perceived effects. Survey results show a gap between self-stated awareness and self-stated involvement due to a lack of effective knowledge, participation obstructions and motivational issues. This echoes the theoretical discussion of Shukla and McDermott in that 'subjective functionings' of public projects are hard to define, even for impacted actors. This leads Li, Wu and Hou to call for effective means to engage active learning in local communities to allow their meaningful participation in urban redevelopment.

In Chapter 11, Kim discusses the trend, opportunities and challenges associated with the growing real estate foreign direct investment (FDI). Kim categorises the current literature on real estate FDI into four thematic approaches. First, studies have paid attention to the rationale of international real estate investments from an investment performance perspective, a theme also covered by Tirumala in Chapter 9. Second, key actors, such as transnational investors and real estate advisory service providers, have been a focal point due to their significant influence on this trend. Third, studies on the interface between city reconfiguration and international real estate investment activities have been growing noticeably. Fourth, institutional changes, both as causes and results of transnational real estate industries, are drawing attention. While the scopes of exploration on real estate FDI are expanding rapidly, Kim still notices several major gaps that call for further research. These include data issues, the diverse investment activities involved, the complex legal matters associated with land transactions, and the escalation and vulnerability of property prices. Challenges and advancements in these matters are illustrated with real estate FDI in Vietnam.

China is another emerging economy that has attracted a large volume of real estate FDI. Li in Chapter 12 presents a detailed case study of China's effort to promote real estate development. For Li, the latest economic transformation in Chinese cities through participatory governance represents a second wave of neoliberalisation that follows the first wave of marketisation in the 1980s. The first wave was characterised by land monetisation and property-led development initiated through top-down reformative policies and collective actions to meet the goals of urban modernisation and economic growth. In this process, the real estate sector had been identified as one of the growth pillars. However, such an absolute growth-focused development regime had ignored a large proportion of what Shukla and McDermott identified as the 'subjective functionings' of land, resulting in widespread contestations and social conflicts. In response, a participatory institutional reform was launched in the 2000s, involving significant changes in the property rights regime, a new land transfer approach and new procedures for interest distribution. Yet, through multiple case studies, Li notices that the participatory governance structure in China is merely an ostensible policy change to address practical issues of urban (re)development rather than an overturning of the entire authoritarian institutional and political complex. Li's chapter concludes with a call for the worldwide recalibration of the neoliberalism mindset and implicitly warns of an over-enthusiasm among international investors towards China's hot real estate market.

In the context of Sub-Saharan Africa, the final chapter in this volume, contributed by Kavaarpuo, presents a critical reflection of the reluctance with regard to innovation adoption and diffusion in housing developments – a phenomenon also noticed in Chapter 3. A literature review on extant works diagnosing the problem of reluctant innovation in housing delivery has led Kavaarpuo to conclude that most studies have no explicit theoretical underpinnings and/or lack cogent explanations for developers' decisions to adopt innovative house-building technologies. To fill this gap, Kavaarpuo proposes a shift of analytical focus to the micro-unit by drawing insights from the transaction cost theory. Four key barriers are highlighted: first, innovation processes are idiosyncratic transactions with non-zero transaction costs. Second, the trade gains from economic transactions depend on the efficacy of intentionally designed governance mechanisms, which however is not guaranteed. Third, innovation choices are satisficing instead of maximising and may be emotionally rather than logically evaluated. Bounded rationality and dispersed information make complex contracts inevitably incomplete. Fourth, innovations are specific assets with more severe uncertainties relative to business-as-usual housing products and processes. All these barriers also add new insights into understanding the relatively low climate change adaption and mitigation innovations in the real estate sector, as discussed in Chapter 8.

Put together, what are the major lessons shared across the chapters and key agenda setting questions proposed by our contributors? Without overgeneralising, we can distil three mega issues facing the property sector going forward.

First, there is a need to critically debate, and rethink, many of the taken-for-granted theories and practices in the property sector. These include, for example, the fundamental cost–return analysis, the standard property appraisal concepts and formulations, and investment portfolio models. This need, in turn, is caused by changing socio-economic contexts and emerging trends, such as broader community participations in development, a greater emphasis on a fair compensation and social responsibility, the shifting demands triggered by the rise of the millennial population and the creative class, and the current COVID-safe requirements and health considerations.

Second, there is a consensus among all contributors for the need of more interdisciplinary research and intersectoral collaborations. Insights from disciplines such as finance, design, planning, geography, environmental science and international relations, etc., could enrich both the ontology and epistemology of our property discipline in order to solve the complex challenges facing the real estate sector, and future-proof its healthy development, especially for a post-pandemic comeback and for a sustainable and inclusive growth in line with the United Nations' Sustainable Development Goals.

Third, although real estate activities are still predominantly locally based, cross-border capital and labour circulations have penetrated, and are increasingly influencing, the functions and dynamics of the local property market. On the one hand, we still perceive market fragmentations that are profoundly shaped by regional social, economic and institutional divides. On the other, there are growing co-movements among global real estate markets and harmonisation across property practices, standards and regulations. Moreover, there are many universal, long-term challenges, such as climate change and social disparities, that need coordinated actions across countries and sectors, including the real estate industry, to mitigate, to prevent and to adapt to. It is expected that issues that lie across the local and global, short-term and long-term, sector-specific and all-mankind spectrums will increase and hence call for innovative and holistic solutions.

References

Adams, D., Watkins, C., & White, M. (2008). *Planning, Public Policy and Property Markets*. Oxford: Blackwell.

Ball, M. (1999). Chasing a Snail: Innovation and Housebuilding Firms' Strategies. *Housing Studies, 14*(1), 9–22.

Ball, M. (2006). *Markets and Institutions in Real Estate and Construction*. Oxford: Blackwell.

Brueggeman, W. B., & Fisher, J. D. (2018). *Real Estate Finance & Investments* (16th ed.). New York: McGraw-Hill Education.

Cao, J. A. (2015). *The Chinese Real Estate Market: Development, Regulation and Investment*. London and New York: Routledge.

Chau, K. W. (1998). Real Estate Research in Asia – Past, Present and the Future. *Journal of Asian Real Estate Society, 1*(1), 1–16.

Dombrow, J., & Turnbull, G. (2004). Trends in Real Estate Research, 1988–2001: What's Hot and What's Not. *Journal of Real Estate Finance and Economics, 29*(1), 47–70.

Ely, R. T. (1925). Research in Land and Public Utility Economics. *The Journal of Land and Public Utility Economics, 1*(Jan.), 1–11.

Fadeyi, O., McGreal, S., McCord, M., & Berry, J. (2021). Capital Flows and Office Markets in Major Global Cities. *Journal of Property Investment & Finance, 39*(4), 298–322.

Graaskamp, J. A. (1992). Institutional Constraints on, and Forces for, Evaluation of Appraisal Precepts and Practices. *Journal of Property Valuation and Investment, 10*(3), 603–618.

Haila, A. (2015). *Urban Land Rent: Singapore as a Property State*. Chichester: Wiley.

Healey, P. (1991). Models of the Development Process: A Review. *Journal of Property Research, 8*(3), 219–238.

Hoesli, M. (2016). Real Estate Research in Europe, Working Paper 16-40, Swiss Finance Institute, archive ouverte UNIGE, http://archive-ouverte.unige.ch/.

Hoyt, H. (1933). *One Hundred Years of Land Values in Chicago: The Relationship of the Growth of Chicago to the Rise in its Land Values*. Chicago: The University of Chicago Press.

Hurd, R. M. (1903). *Principles of City Land Values*. New York: Record and Guide.

Keogh, G., & D'Arcy, E. (1999). Property Market Efficiency: An Institutional Economics Perspective. *Urban Studies, 36*(13), 2401–2414.

Newell, G. (2020). The Need for More Research on the Asian Real Estate Markets. *Journal of Property Investment and Finance, 39*(1), 3–8.

Newell, G., Acheampong, P., & Worzala, E. (2002). Property Research Priorities in Australia. *Pacific Rim Property Research Journal, 8*(2), 127–139.

Newell, G., Worzala, E., McAllister, P., & Schulte, K.-W. (2004). An International Perspective on Real Estate Research Priorities. *Journal of Real Estate Portfolio Management, 10*(3), 161–170.

Rogers, D., & Koh, S. Y. (2017). The Globalisation of Real Estate: The Politics and Practice of Foreign Real Estate Investment. *International Journal of Housing Policy, 17*(1), 1–14.

Roulac, S. E., Dotzour, M. O., Cheng, P., & Webb, J. R. (2005). Evolving Research Priorities: The Contents of Land Economics. *Land Economics, 81*(4), 457–476.

Saiz, A. (2020). Bricks, Mortar, and Proptech: The Economics of IT in Brokerage, Space Utilization and Commercial Real Estate Finance. *Journal of Property Investment & Finance, 38*(4), 327–347.

Seabrooke, W., Kent, P., & How, H. H.-H. (Eds.) (2008). *International Real Estate: An Institutional Approach.* Oxford: Blackwell.

Tiwari, P., & White, M. (2010). *International Real Estate Economics.* London: Palgrave Macmillan.

Valler, D., & Phelps, N. A. (2017). Framing the Future: On Local Planning Cultures and Legacies. *Planning Theory & Practice, 19*(5), 698–716.

Weber, A. F. (1899). *The Growth of Cities in the Nineteenth Century: A Study of Statistics.* New York: Macmillan.

Worzala, E., Gilliland, D., & Gordon, J. (2002). Real Estate Research Needs of the Plan Sponsor Community. *Journal of Real Estate Portfolio Management, 8*(1), 65–78.

PART I

Disruptive changes: technologies and spaces

2 Market disruptions and the future trends in real estate: what do we not know?

Piyush Tiwari and Jyoti Shukla

Introduction

The last two decades have seen phenomenal changes in the way property is developed, invested, owned and used. A number of market disruptors have changed the face of the real estate market. The latest impact has been that of COVID-19, an exogenous shock, that has changed the way people live, commute, work and socialize. While the industry has been discussing for a long time working from home and its impact on offices, hospitality and e-commerce as well as on retail, the centrifugal force of COVID-19 brought that discussion forward and, overnight, everything shifted towards working from home and retailing through online channels supported by technology. This chapter examines the impact of three significant market disruptors on real estate markets and the challenges they pose: demographic disruption caused by the rise of the millennial population; disruptions due to the globalization of footloose capital, such as crowdfunding; and technological (or PropTech) disruptors and the consequential reduction in the power of traditional institutions and regulators. The last two decades have seen significant literature examining how changes in consumer preferences, globalization and technology are impacting development, investment, financing, ownership and the use of real estate (Tiwari and White, 2010, 2014). There still are numerous questions that remain unanswered, which will be discussed in this chapter and which form an agenda for future research.

This chapter discusses the following two questions:

1. What market disrupters are affecting the real estate market?
2. How is the real estate market adapting to the changes in human behaviour consequential to such disruptions?

The rest of the chapter is structured as follows. The next section discusses the three major disruptors that have a profound impact on real estate markets – demographic shift, globalization and technology. This is followed by a more detailed discussion on technological disruptors, both endogenous and exogenous to the real estate domain in the subsequent two sections. The third section discusses endogenous technological disrupters or PropTech and its components. The section will also highlight key questions related to the impact of PropTech for which answers are still emerging, and these form the agenda for future research. The fourth section briefly discusses blockchain technology, as an exogenous technological disrupter, and its current and potential impact on the real estate market. The concluding section summarizes these discussions.

Market disruptors

Three market disruptors that are impacting consumer behaviour and attitude towards asset use, ownership, investment and financing are demographics, globalization and technology. This section briefly discusses the nature of these disruptors and their impact on the real estate market.

Demographics: the rise of millennials

The last two decades have seen the rise of millennials – a population cohort that was born between 1980 and the mid-1990s, who would now be around 30 to 40 years of age. Millennials entered the workforce ten years ago and comprise about 1.8 billion people worldwide, or 23% of the global population (Figure 2.1) (MSCI, 2020). Millennials are highly educated. More than 25% of millennials have an education that is higher than secondary education (MSCI, 2020). This is different from previous generations where, relatively, fewer had post-secondary qualifications. The millennial population is not evenly distributed and a large proportion of them, roughly one billion, live in Asia, particularly in the emerging markets of China (327 million millennials) and India (333 million millennials) as per the United Nations World Population Prospects of 2019 (Figure 2.2).

Owing to their higher level of education compared with previous generations, millennials are far more technology savvy. The millennial generation coincided with the peak of the technology revolution, which makes them comfortable with the adoption and use of technology. The other important aspect of the millennial generation is that more women than men have postsecondary

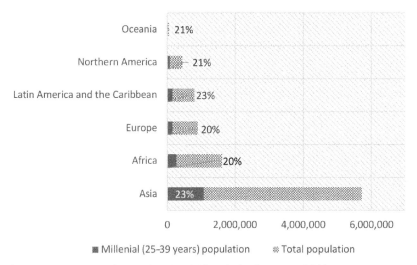

Source: Authors; *United Nations World Population Prospects 2019*

Figure 2.1   Share of millennials in the global population

Source: Authors; *United Nations World Population Prospects 2019*

Figure 2.2   Country-wise distribution of millennials (persons in thousands)

education. One implication of higher education among women is that a major segment of the population, which in the past had stayed out of the workforce, is entering the job market. Women are actively contributing to work from grass-roots to the highest levels in public and private sectors. This is delaying their family formation and childbearing, and consequently family sizes are becoming smaller (MSCI, 2020). Another aspect of millennials that is different from previous generations is that they have less certain or clear career development paths and are far more prone to risk taking in their career choices. Millennials embrace new ideas more easily than their predecessors and are excited about trying new things. The values that millennials espouse are individualistic with a significant focus on entertainment.

Millennials' life stage without family commitment has impacted on savings, their inheritance motives, consumption pattern and travel behaviour and all these are changing their attitudes towards ownership of real estate and location to live. The preference to own assets among millennials is low and they are more inclined towards renting. This has led to a significant growth of several sharing alternatives for assets that were traditionally owned. Airbnb and ShareDesk are some examples of sharing economy-based platforms that have emerged over the last 12 years. Growth in internet-based technologies have facilitated the development of such platforms (Baum, 2014). The high cost of owning an asset has also shifted the preference towards renting. The political instability that has given rise to entrepreneurship and has given power to many companies, and the social change that is largely driven by the values of millennials have contributed to the rise of the sharing economy (Baum, 2014).

Globalization

The second disruptor is globalization. Globalization manifests itself at three levels – economic, political and social (Table 2.1). Economic globalization has led to growth in trade in goods and services and the rise of transnational enterprises. It has also led to growth in the flow of capital.

A number of institutions at the national and organization level have facilitated economic globalization. Economic globalization is also changing consumer preferences and is leading to universalization of consumer preferences. E-commerce and the rise of online retailing platforms such as Amazon or Alibaba have further disintegrated the walls of localized consumer preferences. We have seen huge international capital flows into a range of assets and one of the largest recipients of international capital is real estate. Real estate used to be a local asset, but now global investors are investing in this asset class which is far from their place of residence. What it has done for the real estate market

Table 2.1   Manifestation of globalization

	National	Organization	Personal
Economic	Actions by states to promote economic transfers • World Trade Organization • The North American Free Trade Agreement • Association of Southeast Asian Nations • International Monetary Fund • European Union	Actions by businesses and trade organizations to promote international economic transfers • Transnational Corporations • International Financial Reporting Standards • Foreign participation in capital markets	Personal actions that involve international transactions • Universalization of consumer preferences • International tourism • Demand for imported goods
Political	Actions by states to consolidate policies based on ideology, security • United Nations • North Atlantic Treaty Organization • African Union	Actions by institutions to achieve political or ideological goals • Greenpeace	Personal actions to meet political or ideological ends through lobbying • Amnesty International
Social	Actions by states to find common ground on ethnic/religious basis • Arab League • Islamic Council	Actions by institutions to bring about cross-cultural understanding • International Olympic Committee • Universitas 21 • Association of Pacific Rim Universities	Personal actions that result in better international understanding • CNN • Multilingualism • Immigration

Source: Lake (1997)

is that, on the ownership side, it has delinked the real estate market from the economy of a country because the capital can flow freely from anywhere. This has impacted cycles in property markets. Cities such as New York, London, Los Angeles, Paris and Berlin were the initial attractors of international capital but now cities in the emerging economies, such as Mumbai or Shanghai, are also attracting huge amounts of foreign capital.

The second manifestation of globalization is in political processes where the ideologies across different countries are aligning to some extent. There are impacts at the organization as well as personal level. The concern for sustainability is shared widely across the globe. The activism for human rights is also a global phenomenon. At the real estate market level, the legal institutions of property rights, taxation, leasing and capital transactions have become much more convergent than what they were half a century ago.

The third process of globalization is social. The values and beliefs that the societies have a reason to uphold is becoming aligned. This is leading to changes in national, organization and personal attitudes. An example is the campaign against the use of child labour, which has resulted in denouncing goods produced using child labour. This has forced countries to actively develop laws to protect the rights of children. The rise of media (print, visual and social) has further assisted in the alignment of values and beliefs across various cultures. Recognition of customary land rights internationally is gaining importance in property exchange (Tiwari et al., 2020).

Technology has enabled globalization, and social media such as Facebook are important carriers of ideas across borders.

Technology

Technology has emerged as a major disruptor of formal institutional structures. It has transferred power from centralized institutions to consumers and suppliers by creating a structure where the regulation of activities of consumers and suppliers is becoming challenging. An interesting aspect of current trends is that when the demographics, globalization and technology collide, it creates a unique pattern of activities. This is being observed in the real estate markets as well. Some of the technologies that are affecting real estate markets are endogenous to real estate, and have been created for and by the real estate market. Other technologies, which are exogenous, have profound impacts on real estate markets and institutions but are not meant specifically for the real estate sector. There are a number of examples: Airbnb is a technological revolution impacting the hospitality industry. Another example is WeWork, which is a coworking platform that has changed the way we work. With technology enabled, and flexible spaces for work and collaboration, WeWork has revolutionized the design and supply of office spaces. PropTiger is an India-based PropTech company for the listing of properties for rent or sale. Argus is a data-driven software technology that has eased the way information can be converted into a decision-making tool.

There are also technologies that are exogenous to real estate and are not created for or by the real estate market but are impacting it. One of the biggest nightmares today for property developers is the evolution or the development of autonomous cars, which will make the ownership of cars redundant. Aurora is a startup company that is developing autonomous car technology and has collaborated with Toyota, a leading car manufacturer, in this endeavour. There are planning requirements to provide car parking spaces in a newly constructed building in proportion of the office or residential space that the building provides. If autonomous cars become the norm, parking spaces in existing buildings may become redundant. Many of these parking spaces cannot be converted for any other use easily, owing to their low ceiling heights and slopes. The parking space can't be demolished and rebuilt easily as the rest of the building stands on this parking space.

The second important development exogenous to the real estate market is the development of online payment technology, which has revolutionized e-commerce. This has made huge chunks of retail space dysfunctional, and a large proportion of commerce, as we have seen during the COVID-19 time, is happening through online channels. This is only going to grow as we move forward.

The third technological development that is exogenously developed and is going to be the biggest disruptor is the blockchain. Blockchain technology is already showing promising signs and is breaking down barriers that had hindered transactions across various sectors including real estate.

It is important at this stage to distinguish PropTech from Fintech, or the technology that is used in capital markets and finance (Baum, 2014).

There are three major components of PropTech: (i) smart real estate or smart buildings; (ii) real estate Fintech, which to some extent overlaps with Fintech but are the technologies that are used in real estate, for example online mortgage apps, or leasing apps or property buying and selling apps; and (iii) the shared economy. Some parts of the shared economy are outside of the PropTech space, for example Uber or Ola, which are transportation solutions. There is a part of the shared economy that is emerging and developing fast, for example Airbnb or WeWork and similar other platforms, which form part of PropTech. PropTech is a global phenomenon (Braesemann and Baum, 2020) and a number of firms have emerged across almost all parts of the world. Major concentrations of the PropTech industry are in California, the US east coast, Western Europe (in particular the UK), and metropolitan areas in Asia (Delhi, Shanghai, Beijing, Seoul, Singapore) (Braesemann and Baum, 2020). O'Grady

(2019) presents a PropTech map for Australia, which lists 188 PropTech companies in 2019. Similar other maps have been prepared for different countries. There is a huge number of companies which have emerged in the last ten years that relate to the sharing economy, residential market listings, sales and marketing, hospitality and others.

Endogenous technological disruptors – PropTech and its components

The extent of the impact of PropTech on real estate market activity is a question that has received significant attention in research. This section does not attempt to provide a comprehensive literature review but presents a selective review with the aim of setting an agenda for future research.

Read (2019) argues that human behaviour and innovation are intertwined, both shaping each other. With that premise, Read (2019) asks three questions: how does real estate development follow or anticipate human behaviour? How will real estate evolve to accommodate future innovation and consumer demand? Will real estate continue to become more service oriented? Consumers will continue to pay a premium for amenities and services. Developers will have to be willing to pay more for design to create demand for the finished product. The question that will become important is how should developers anticipate future trends in consumer behaviour? Read (2019) argues that industry disrupters such as Airbnb, WeWork and e-commerce are a response to consumer demand for more power, with changing preferences requiring flexibility, integration with technology and globalization. Literature confirms that companies are increasingly using real estate to attract high-quality talent. In addition, an alignment of real estate and business strategy enabled by technology is impacting how space is designed and utilized (Green et al., 2017). The ability to be nimble and adaptable, sharing spaces between different business functions and working groups, and opportunities to balance work and life are becoming important determinants in space design (Green et al., 2017). Residential design is also changing as digital technologies have reduced the need for space that earlier was occupied by books or DVDs. This has shrunk the space requirements in an apartment by 10–15% (Read, 2019). A similar trend is also being observed for office space requirements (Zhai, 2017).

The impact of PropTech is also being felt on the valuation of properties. In the US, there are examples where retail Real Estate Investment Trusts (REITs) have traded at significant discounts to net asset value (NAV) due to the dominance of e-commerce. Airbnb generates an income from tourism for a residential property and, when revenue forms the basis of valuation, it can lead to misunderstanding of values (Raboj, 2019). The question that arises for researchers is how to assess the impact of PropTech on the design, ownership, use and investment in existing assets? Would owners of these assets repurpose and reposition them? Developers usually take risk based on their expected future demand for properties. The nature of risks associated with asset classes is also changing. For example, Airbnb not owning the physical assets protects the company from liabilities associated with owning physical buildings, such as deterioration, real estate taxes, and capital market risks. This is different from traditional hotel assets. The question for research is how to price these risks and how to value these new assets as both residential property and hotel asset valuation approaches seem inadequate.

In the following discussion, three components of PropTech, their impact on real estate markets and the emerging issues that require research attention are discussed.

Smart buildings

There are two aspects of smart buildings – buildings that use PropTech and buildings that are required for PropTech such as data centres. Smart buildings use a range of technology such as sensors or actuators together with activity data so that the data can be analysed and utilized to find out which operation can run more efficiently. There are a number of reasons why investors and developers are investing in smart buildings. Most important is that it saves them operation costs as these buildings are energy efficient (Baum, 2014). These buildings also impact on the wellbeing of occupants and enhance productivity of the users of these spaces (Baum, 2014). The research question, whether these buildings attract higher rent and/or value, is still unanswered. Also, while smart buildings are viewed as energy efficient, their use increases the demand for another asset class called data centres, which themselves are highly energy intensive and often require captive power.

Real estate fintech and crowdfunding

The second component of PropTech is real estate fintech. Real estate fintech supports transactions in real estate, for example through crowdfunding. Crowdfunding is the practice of funding a venture by raising small amounts of money from a large number of people, usually via the internet (Vogel and Moll, 2014).

Early crowdfunding in real estate was in the form of debt on small residential properties. This innovation happened because, despite the development of capital markets, innovations in finance such as the development of financial derivatives and securitization, and deregulation of the banking industry, access to finance has been subjected to stringent due diligence of investors. In addition, the national capital market and banking regulations and the requirements of the international regulatory framework for banks developed by the Basel committee, have further constrained access to finance, particularly for less financially capable buyers. Given that property is a lumpy investment, the potential buyer base has been limited. For example, a homeowner who wants to buy a property may need a mortgage but may at times be unable to access desired levels of funding. Through crowdfunding, they can reach out to small and medium investors to raise equity. Of course, any gains from property, whether it be a capital gains or rental income, would be shared among different equity partners but this mechanism reduces the cash flow risk that a debt poses due to lenders' first claim on cash flows.

Crowdfunding has emerged as a platform for funding ventures by raising money from a sizeable group of individuals (Cohen, 2016). Although crowdfunding has a long history for social and charitable causes, as a mechanism for raising capital for companies it became a platform after a legislation entitled Jumpstart Our Business Startups (JOBS) Act was signed in 2012 in the US (Cohen, 2016). This permitted small firms to raise capital without having to register with the US Securities and Exchange Commission (SEC). In a short span of time, the crowdfunding platform has evolved to raise equity, mezzanine capital and large debt for commercial and multifamily property investments (Vogel and Moll, 2014).

In terms of due diligence of sponsors, crowdfunding platforms follow similar processes as traditional investment management companies and the funds that sponsors aim to raise through crowdfunding should only form a part of their overall requirements (Vogel and Moll, 2014). Transparency, access to small and medium investors, lower transaction fees, enhanced reporting and accountability are some of the advantages that crowdfunding platforms offer (Vogel and Moll, 2014). There are disadvantages as well, such as lack of investor expertise, potentially unrealistic projections by crowdfunding platforms and lack of personal relationship with sponsor and project (Vogel and Moll, 2014). Fundrise, Realty Mogul, Realty Shares and iFunding are some examples of crowdfunding platforms through which debt and equity investment has been made in commercial property.

There are concerns over regulations around crowdfunding that can ensure transparency and ethical considerations and guarantee scalability and sustainability as a business model.

Sharing economy

The third component of PropTech is the sharing economy, also referred to as 'collaborative consumption' or 'excess economy'. The underpinning economic philosophy for a 'sharing economy' is that space and capital goods are better utilized when shared among multiple users. This is because many of the assets that companies or households own are used only for a part of the time. One could capitalize on the time when an asset is not being used by sharing it with others on a rental arrangement. The underlying drivers of a sharing economy are "access to communication technologies, increased trust and social acceptance of online exchanges and sharing, recognition of the existing inefficiencies and the savings those models can deliver to consumers, and flexible working patterns" (Le Jeune, 2016). Younger generations show more of these trends and form the most active users of sharing businesses.

The growth of sharing businesses is fast paced. Le Jeune (2016) in their study present statistics, based on literature, that show the share of Airbnb in the global lodging supply was about 5% in 2020. The share of crowdfunding at 1–2% of bank lending is small. However, the projected growth is exponential and by 2020 the volume of crowdfunding was likely to reach $90 billion. Of course, COVID-19 would have impacted some of these projections but they are still substantial.

Airbnb

Residence sharing platforms such as Airbnb have created opportunities for homeowners to profit from the underused space in their houses by renting on a short term basis in a low-overhead, asset-light model. Think of a hotel chain; if it plans to increase supply it will be expensive as it would need to buy/develop a property for hotel use. It will also be time consuming. However, Airbnb can cheaply increase (or decrease) the supply overnight. Airbnb doesn't have any physical assets, which protects the company from any liabilities. There is no depreciation cost or real estate taxes. Also, there is no capital market risk as it is an asset light model which has expanded in the last ten years.

What are the conditions for such kinds of products or models to emerge? First, a widely distributed source of demand is needed – exactly the kind we had in the hospitality industry where there was a demand for short stay hospitality.

Second, we also need a diverse and widely distributed heterogeneous source of rooms across different locations, cities and countries. Third, there shouldn't be any dominant or efficient mechanism for bringing demand and supply together. The hotel industry is very inefficient in its use of platforms for bookings and cancellations, which is not centralized. All these conditions are necessary, and Airbnb met these conditions. This is reflected in Airbnb performance statistics. There are over 150 million users of Airbnb worldwide. Six guests check in to Airbnb properties every second and the average nightly rate is $185 with an average stay of 4.3 nights. What is interesting is that 54% of Airbnb guests are female and 58% of booking guests are millennials. The average yearly revenue in 2018 was US$3.6 billion and the Airbnb company valuation was about US$38 billion. This, of course, after COVID, has plummeted significantly but is still a substantial valuation for a data-based company.

What is Airbnb doing to the traditional housing market? A study by Barron et al. (2019) published in *Harvard Business Review* indicates that a 1% increase in Airbnb listings increases the rents in the rental housing market by 0.018% and house prices by 0.026%. Moreover, Airbnb listings are increasing at the rate of 44% each year. The net increase of Airbnb on the housing market is a 5% increase in rents and 8% increase in house value on a yearly basis. The results also indicate that zip codes where there are higher owner-occupancy rates are not affected by Airbnb. Another study, by Garcia-Lopez et al. (2019), analysed the impact of Airbnb on housing rents and transaction prices in Barcelona. They found that rents have increased by 1.9% and prices by 5.3% as a consequence of Airbnb. What is noteworthy in their results is that neighbourhoods in the top decile of Airbnb activity have seen rents rise by 7% and transaction price increases by 19%. The consequence of such increases is worsening housing affordability in cities where the short-term tourist population is high. However, the impact of Airbnb activities may not be as harmful as is presumed to the hotel industry. According to Coyle and Yeung (2016), "Airbnb reduces the demand by budget tourists for hotels, which can however then charge a higher price to other travellers whose demand is less price-elastic. Hotels would then enjoy a higher average daily rate but might or might not enjoy higher revenue, depending on the relative change in price and quantity."

Nevertheless, Airbnb is affecting the housing market through re-allocation of housing stock to hospitality use. There are a number of regulatory questions that arise with the growth of Airbnb, such as their impact on the collection of taxes, neighbourhood disadvantages from an increase in visitor numbers, and possible safety issues (Coyle and Yeung, 2016). There are questions that are becoming important for planning – how to regulate this industry that is totally unchecked but has a profound impact on the built environment? And property – what is the valuation for Airbnb, and should it be valued as property or should it be valued as a business?

Coworking

The second sharing economy model is the coworking model. Coworking models have been in existence for many years in some form or other since 1959. Figure 2.3 presents the evolution of the coworking model. Early models were in the form of incubators which were spaces available for rent with the objective of stimulating commerce by grouping together small businesses. Later incarnations of incubators also provided business assistance and financing opportunities. Incubator models continued for a very long time. In 1999, 40 years after the early incubators, a new type of model emerged for co-working, the innovation centre. Innovation centres provided office space and services for young companies, generally tech startups, for commercialization of innovation and entrepreneurship. By the early or mid-2000s, the accelerator model emerged – programming-based workplaces which are designed to help startup companies grow more rapidly by providing them with technical and educational assistance, mentoring and network opportunities, and workspaces. Then came the coworking centre, which was a revolutionary idea. Coworking centres were membership-based, interdisciplinary spaces where workers and startup companies could locate. The focus of these centres was on flexibility in terms of space and time use, as well as the services that the coworking companies provided. WeWork is the poster boy of the coworking model. Recently, WeWork has been in trouble because the model that the coworking companies had adopted was untenable, particularly during an economic downcycle. On the liability side, the WeWork model has long term leases, while on the asset side their tenancies are on a short-term basis, as short as maybe one month to three months. Thus, there exists an asset-liability mismatch. While WeWork models generated good revenue during the healthier phase of the economy, problems are surfacing during the economic slowdown when vacancy rate and lease-up costs are high.

Business strategies of companies in a shared economy space

An important area for research is the business strategies used by companies in a shared economy space to expand their business. Analysing coworking companies' strategies, Zhai (2017) identified that these companies create and leverage from economies of scale. This helps them in negotiating better services for their members and also benefits coworking companies through cost savings. Coworking companies also have used profit sharing arrangements with landlords in negotiation for a free rent period, tenant improvement allowance, and reduced deposit (Zhai, 2017). Coworking companies have also attempted to standardize workflows for new developments, as this allows them to quickly scale up. Coworking companies do not have large initial capital requirements and their financing sources and costs differ at different stages and with different sizes of assets under management. From a profitability point of view, the focus of these companies is on revenue generation rather than cost control (Zhai, 2017). These points raise a number of issues for research, such as the impact of business strategies adopted by shared economy companies on the formation of market structure, the potential for their scalability, their resilience during different phases of the economic cycle, their capital structure and risk.

There are also questions that relate to the property business models that have emerged as a result of the shared economy. There are two types of coworking models. First, there is where the technology firm is an intermediary or broker (such as Airbnb) of short-term space leasing and does not control capital assets (Baum, 2014). These firms rely on customer feedback. The second model is the operator model where the company also directly or indirectly controls capital assets (Baum, 2014). Both these models have different risks. The first model faces regulatory risk while the second has commercial risk for the company. The membership-based space renting model that WeWork uses can be compared with traditional leasing, with leases of five years duration that office property occupiers have. Risk in real estate comprises systematic and idiosyncratic risk. The systematic risk for a property is the lease risk. Hotels have the shortest lease length and therefore the highest systematic risk. From that perspective, coworking models have a similarity to hotels, but a difference between coworking companies and hotels is that coworking companies are still obligated to make the rent payments to the landlord, whereas hotel companies only have to manage operating costs and service any debt. In that sense, coworking companies are highly leveraged and carry much larger risk than hotels. This raises the questions of whether the coworking model is sustainable and how these companies would manage business cycle risk?

Zhai (2017) presented a summary of WeWork models with different risk-return profiles that have emerged over time (refer to Figure 2.4):

- The lease model is highly risky because there are significant upfront costs and, in the initial periods when the business is looking for more clients or more tenants, there are some significant negative initial cash-flows. For owners of these spaces there are minimal risks as their cash flows are certain, as coworking companies pay them rent irrespective of whether they are able to lease to clients or not.

- The joint venture model offers high return and low risk for the coworking business. In a joint venture, owners of space and the coworking company share the risk as well as return. The large investment is by the property owners and a smaller investment is from the coworking company.
- The third model is the management model, in which the capital and operational investment is made by the property owners and coworking companies have the management contract to operate and manage the property.
- There are some emerging coworking business models, such as the franchising model. This is similar to hotels where all the investment in asset and operation is by the owners and the owner also pays royalties to the coworking company to use their brand. The risk (particularly reputation risk) for the coworking company is high as the operation is not managed by the coworking company but the returns are also high as capital investment is negligible.
- Another emerging model is the owner-operator model. In this model, a coworking company owns properties rather than leasing them from another landlord. The risk and return for this model are high.

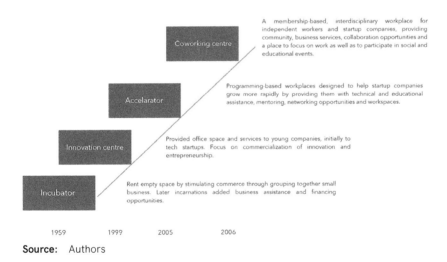

Source: Authors

Figure 2.3   History of coworking models

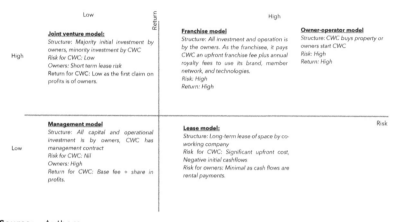

Source: Authors

Figure 2.4   Coworking company operating models

Given the challenges that the WeWork model has faced, a number of coworking companies are considering office development and investment in the traditional sense: a developer builds the property, which is sold to an investor who then leases it to tenants using coworking service-based models. The challenge that arises is whether landlords/investors should lease the space to blue-chip tenants, as is done traditionally, who are willing to lease space for a longer period and are valued more highly by the market, or lease to coworking companies who provide service-based, short-term leases to startup entrepreneurs. The blue-chip company has credit strength, which will support a high valuation for the income stream, WeWork has weaker cash flow but a strong appeal to a valuable source of emerging tenants (Baum, 2014). Many landlords are preferring to lease their properties to coworking companies because they see that the future is moving in a direction where tenants will require shorter leases.

An important question of investigation is what are the challenges for the coworking companies model? On the other hand, tenants need flexibility and want short term leases. What does it mean for the property and planning professions? And how to value the coworking companies? Are they data companies or hotels or service-businesses, or real estate companies? Considering the high risk, why are developers and investors considering investing in coworking companies?

Exogenous technological disrupter – blockchain

Another technology-led innovation is Blockchain, which is finding its application in various sectors including finance. Blockchain technology is bound to revolutionize the real estate market as well. Frictionless and secure transactions between parties without the need for intermediation, transparency between parties, the increased use of digital currency and smart contracts are features of blockchain (Baum, 2014). In simple terms, according to Euromoney (2021) "blockchain is a technology that's essentially a digital Ledger of transaction that is duplicated and distributed across the entire network or computer system on the blockchain". This allows execution of a transaction without an intermediary. This would suit perfectly well the real estate market where any transaction involves many intermediaries – lawyers, financiers, agents, transaction advisors, analysts, government agencies, etc. Blockchain could eliminate many of these intermediaries as it will allow direct transactions from one party to another. This would not only be cost efficient but also time efficient.

Researchers have investigated the possibilities of the application of blockchain technology to replace inefficient practices, particularly related to land acquisition and land records (Mintah et al., 2020). Blockchain could provide an alternative to the international property Stock Exchange, which is one of the platforms through which units in properties are bought and sold. In a blockchain, the distributed ledger holds the history of a transaction of an asset, or a title, and it develops a digitally secure identifier for a proposed transaction. It offers the ability to transfer assets in new ways. Secure, efficient and smart contracts are some of the major impacts of blockchain. Transparency between transactors along with faster transactions and lower costs are some of the benefits of blockchain technology.

There are examples of the utilization of blockchain technology in the real estate sector. The Swedish Land Registry, the tech firms ChromaWay, Kairos Future and the Telia Company have investigated the possibilities of using blockchain technology for real estate transactions. BitFury and the Estonian government are working together to secure land titles over a private network, using the bitcoin blockchain for validation. ConsenSys and the Dubai government are developing blockchain strategies for public services and smart city connectivity. Ubitquity, Velox.RE and Propy are developing the blockchain for title deed transparency and cross-border transactions of high end residential real estate. Deloitte Netherlands, the City of Rotterdam and Cambridge Innovation Centre are developing a blockchain application for recording lease agreements.

These examples are only growing in number and the range of applications in real estate markets.

Conclusion

This chapter presents a summary of real estate market disrupters that are making it harder to predict future demand for space, its nature, ownership and rental formats, and valuation methods. Changing housing preferences of millennials; globalizing economies and foreign investments in the real estate market; and technological innovations within and outside the real estate domain are highlighted as three important disrupters to the real estate market.

The chapter pays particular attention to technological disrupters, which are fast evolving by circumventing contemporary regulations and institutional arrangements of owning, renting, financing, and investing in property. Both endogenous and exogenous technological innovations are creating new opportunities for the real estate domain while also posing challenges to the contemporary institutions that are struggling to accommodate these changes. Discussions in this chapter highlight key questions of investigation that property research could take on. These would result in the development of theories, institutions and industry to keep pace with the fast-changing technological world.

Sharing economy

While the earlier generation of technology disruptors (such as Google, Facebook, Amazon) faced federal regulatory scrutiny, the shared economy enterprises are shaped by local regulations such as zoning codes, insurance mandates, hotel licensing regimes and so on (Davidson and Infranca, 2016). Most platforms that comprise a shared economy rely for their value proposition on urban conditions. Urban regulatory regimes that skew the supply of urban amenities have resulted in sharing economy firms exploiting the situation by filling in demand for, say, alternative accommodation to hotel rooms (Davidson and Infranca, 2016). City characteristics such as density, proximity, amenities and specialization enable a sharing economy. A critical mass of providers and consumers is necessary for a sharing economy to flourish.

The confrontation between sharing economy enterprises and local governments is not just shaping the sharing economy and local regulatory responses but is also impacting real estate development and land use, as sharing economy entrepreneurs seek new configurations of use and ownership. The sharing economy is pushing local governments to be transparent about the rationale for public intervention and to demonstrate the link between regulations and their intended outcomes. While regulatory strategies of local governments have become an important area of development due to the emergence of the sharing economy, an important aspect of how the sharing economy will transform urban governance and the shape of cities is yet to be understood (Davidson and Infranca, 2016). This definitely would be an agenda for further research.

SEI (2020), in their report on the future of real estate investing ask the following questions, which have an impact on investment decisions: "Will shared mobility fundamentally reformat how communities are (or should be) designed? Will co-living take root beyond its current niches? Are intergenerational living arrangements among strangers realistic? What binds communities when all products and services can be delivered?" (SEI, 2020, p. 20). Answering these questions would require further research.

Regarding WeWork business models, an important question of investigation is what are the challenges for the coworking companies model? From the point of view of a landlord, the question that they face is whether they should lease their space to WeWork or a blue-chip company? Alternatively, should landlords launch their own coworking operations? Answering these questions would require research in various business models, property and non-property institutions and property market characteristics. On the other hand, tenants need flexibility and want short term leases. What does it mean for the property and planning professions? How can coworking companies be valued? Are they data companies or hotels or service-businesses, or real estate companies? Considering the high risk, why are developers and investors considering investing in coworking companies?

It is acknowledged that real estate is becoming a more data-driven industry which will give larger corporations an advantage over smaller firms that have less technology at their disposal (Read, 2019). In addition, data is the backbone of a shared economy and further research is required to understand the role of data in the transformation of the real estate market. For example, WeWork uses sensor technology to monitor the usage of space inside each of its locations. Data from these sensors can help monitor a building's usage more efficiently.

PropTech entrepreneurs have argued that the impact of PropTech on the real estate market would be its digitalization and globalization. Digitalization of the real estate market would be driven by data. Analysing 7000 PropTech firms, Braesemann and Baum (2020) find that PropTech is a global phenomenon with data analytics technologies at the core of the network of property technologies. They argue that to benefit from efficiency gains arising from digitalization, users and owners would need to be aware of the value of data that they are generating while buying, renting and managing real estate. Key questions are: how is data transforming real estate from a black box into an institutional asset class? What impact does big data have on the market competition as data becomes concentrated and in the hands of firms with large balance sheets?

Real estate fintech and crowdfunding

Crowdfunding (debt and equity) is fast emerging as a source of capital for less financially capable buyers as it reduces the deal size for an investor and also spreads the investment risk widely. The regulation and impact of crowdfunding on regulated investment management business is unclear. There are also questions that relate to the crowdfunding platform itself – its technological requirements, profitability, transparency, risks, particularly arising from liquidity and speed of execution, reporting requirements to investors, ethical considerations, scalability and sustainability as a business model, which require further research.

Blockchain technology

As discussed earlier, blockchain is being explored in property, although its use is still in its nascent stages. The question that blockchain poses for research is what risk distributed ledgers pose for established real estate market architectures and practices, as it has the potential for new services and applications to emerge. The other question will be what systems, processes, national and international regulations and governance would be required to ensure longevity of the blockchain? An important area for research is the social impact of distributed ledger technology. Can blockchain technology reduce transaction and search cost, and overcome the challenges associated with land acquisition and title registration, particularly where land title is customary? Would blockchain result in new models of land administration or more broadly land management, which has less of a role for state institutions? Several startups have emerged within the distributed ledger technology ecosystem that propose fractional home ownership to enable low earners to part-own and accrue ownership and as a novel financial portfolio for the wealthy (Gürgüç and Learney, 2020). The social impact of such models on households and the built environment would need examination.

Other questions that relate to the fundamental nature of property assets and market characteristics would also be important for research. Would technology remove the problem of physical deterioration and obsolescence of real assets? Given that the supply side of property is controlled by planning and zoning regulations, which are highly price inelastic, how would supply respond to the changes in demand? Unintended consequences of the rise of Airbnb on the rental housing market in terms of the rental housing shortage and rise in rents are already being seen in some cities. Another question would be: can PropTech disrupt property cycles? Unitization of property due to PropTech may make valuation machine-generated. Shorter and more complex leases will make properties harder to value. There are significant questions for research on valuation approaches and processes. Online marketplaces for real assets will bring in real time pricing and enhanced volatility. The risk of the asset will rise. Property will behave more like a risky equity and less like a bond due to shorter leases and operational real estate (Baum, 2014). The question for research is would unitization and real-time pricing make the property asset more like equities than bonds? Would the balance sheet of borrowers and lenders become unstable? Property is an illiquid asset with a risk of abortive expenditure. How would crowdfunding, blockchain and online secondary market platforms impact the transaction cost and the risk of abortive expenditures?

References

Barron, K., Kung, E. and Proserpio, D. (2019). When Airbnb listings in a city increase, so do rent prices. *Harvard Business Review*. Available at https://hbr.org/2019/04/research-when-airbnb-listings-in-a-city-increase-so-do-rent-prices.

Baum, A. (2014). *PropTech 3.0 the Future of Real Estate*. University of Oxford Research, www.sbs.oxford.edu.

Braesemann, F. and Baum, A. (2020). *PropTech: Turning Real Estate into a Data-driven Market?* (Working Paper). Oxford Future of Real Estate Initiative, Said Business School, University of Oxford.

Cohen, J. (2016). *A Study on the History and Functionality of Real Estate Crowdfunding*. Joseph Wharton Scholars. Available at http://repository.upenn.edu/joseph_wharton_scholars/19.

Coyle, D. and Yeung, T.Y. (2016). *Understanding Airbnb in Fourteen European Cities*. Mimeo.

Davidson, N.M. and Infranca, J.J. (2016). The sharing economy as an urban phenomenon. *Yale Law and Policy Review*, 34, 215–279.

Euromoney (2021). What is Blockchain? Euromoney Learning. Available at https://www.euromoney.com/learning/blockchain-explained/what-is-blockchain (accessed 26 April 2021).

Garcia-Lopez, M., Jofre-Monseny, J., Mazza, R.M. and Segu, M. (2019). *Do Short-term Rental Platforms Affect Housing Markets? Evidence from Airbnb in Barcelona* (IEB Working Paper 2019/05). Munich Personal RePEc Archive.

Green, M., Spritzer, J., Chagani, E. and Mashian, S. (2017). 34th Annual Cornell Real Estate Conference recap. *Cornell Real Estate Review*, 15(1), 36–39. Retrieved from: http://scholarship.sha.cornell.edu/crer/ vol15/iss1/13.

Gürgüç, Z. and Learney, R.M. (2020). A dual model of ownership. *Front Blockchain*, 3, 30.

Lake, T.J. (1997). Globalization's effects on corporate real estate decision making. *Research Bulletin No. 13*, The IDRC Foundation.

Le Jeune, S. (2016). *The Sharing Economy*. Schroder Investment Management Limited, London.

Mintah, K., Baako, K.T., Kavaarpuo, G. and Otchere, G.K. (2020). Skin lands in Ghana and application of blockchain technology for acquisition and title registration. *Journal of Property, Planning and Environmental Law*, 12(2), 147–169.

MSCI (2020). *Millennials: Demographic Change and the Impact of a Generation*. MSCI.

O'Grady, R. (2019). Australian PropTech Ecosystem Map. *PropTech Now*. Available at https://www.proptechnow.com.au/2019/09/australian-proptech-ecosystem-map/ (accessed 26 April 2021).

Raboj, D. (2019). The impact of Airbnb platforms on Romanian real estate market. *Bulletin UASVM Horticulture*, 76(2), 245–249.

Read, W.S. (2019). *The Evolution of Dirt: Real Estate in the Age of Disruption*. The University of Texas at Austin.

SEI (2020). *The Future of Real Estate Investing*. SEI.

Tiwari, P. and White, M. (2010). *International Real Estate Economics*. Palgrave Macmillan.

Tiwari, P. and White, M. (2014). *Real Estate Finance in the New Economy*. Wiley Blackwell.

Tiwari, P., Stillman, G. B. and Yoshino, N. (2020). *Equitable Land Use for Asian Infrastructure*. Asian Development Bank Institute.

United Nations, Department of Economic and Social Affairs, Population Division (2019). *World Population Prospects 2019: Highlights*. United Nations.

Vogel Jr., J.H. and Moll, B.H. (2014). Crowdfunding for real estate. *Real Estate Finance Journal*, Summer/Fall Issue, 5–16.

Zhai, W. (2017). *A Study of the Co-working Operating Model* (Thesis). Massachusetts Institute of Technology.

3 Interface of property and knowledge-based economic development

Julie T. Miao

Introduction

For the last two centuries, economic growth had been primarily understood through the lens of neo-classical economic theory, which focused on three factors of inputs: land, labour and capital. Technology, knowledge and education were considered as marginal, if not incidental, parameters of production (Knight, 1995). Starting from the fourth Kondratiev long wave, underpinned by electronics innovations, and increasingly so in the unfolding of the fifth long wave led by information and communication technologies (ICT), it has become apparent that knowledge in and of itself is sufficiently important to deserve recognition as a fourth factor of production. A knowledge-based economy, i.e., the part of the economy where organisations generate wealth by utilising knowledge specialism in their workforce, has been argued as the foundation for a nation and region's competitive advantage, and underpins sustainability, employment, health and other political objectives that are related to wellbeing and inclusive growth (OECD, 2015). Its prevalence has, in many cases, been accompanied by a concomitant decline in traditional manufacturing activity, and the replacement of physical commodity production by more abstract forms of production in the format of information, ideas, and creativity. Although some scholars hence advocate a 'world of flows' (Castells, 1996) and supermodernity (Augé, 1995), many have noticed a paradoxical reinforcement of some regions and cities in the fighting for knowledge assets and retaining competitiveness (Asheim et al., 2006; Boschma & Fritsch, 2009; Fan & Scott, 2003).

The ongoing transformation of world economies from manufacturing to service-based and then to knowledge-based, innovation-driven activities has important implications for economic structures, for the organisation of economic activities, and for cities at large. The rising importance of a knowledge-based development model has exerted pressure on industrial restructuring in developing countries such as China and India. The Chinese government, for example, has had a national campaign to transform 'made-in-China' towards 'create-in-China' running since the 2000s. In India, 100 smart cities have been identified as the seedbeds for new technologies and innovations. Of course, at the industry level, the speed and scale of technology adoption differs noticeably. The property sector, the focus of this book, has been notoriously resistant to changes. Ball (2003) pointed out that such immunity to innovation results from the inherent industrial structure and market position of this sector, including:

- A network of interrelationships, and in particular, the wide use of sub-contracting to solve information asymmetry problems, which in turn, 'encourages standardisation of work tasks and simple, easily repeatable, dwelling designs, so that tasks can be broken down into uniform sub-contracts and assessed more easily' (Ball, 2003, p. 904).
- A tendency for developers to combine land development and construction activities to strengthen their monopolistic position in the local market. Such monopolistic position, in turn, defers the necessity for change.
- Financial actors play an important role in determining organisational structures and products in the property sector. Bankers and large institutional funders are risk averse by nature (although financial innovations such as various property derivatives are emerging more prominently now). They would further defer innovative practice and products by adding extra conditions in their funding requirement.

Despite these constraints, Miao (2019) argues that more and more developers are recognising the importance of new/high technologies, partially pulled by their reduced costs and associated risks, and partially pushed by customers seeking tech-enabled real estate products. Literature on how new technologies, such as ICT, have gradually transformed the property sector has grown rapidly since the new century (Dixon et al., 2005), but there is still a lack of systematic review on the impact of the knowledge economy on the whole spectrum of property activities.

This chapter aims to fill this gap by offering a holistic review on the interfaces between a knowledge-based economic growth and the property activities (Figure 3.1). Systematic analyses will be organised on the micro-level (space users; next section), sector-level (property industry; third section), and the urban-level (built environment, fourth section). The final section summarises the main findings and suggests further directions of research.

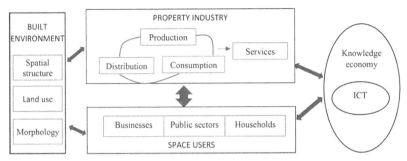

Source: The author

Figure 3.1   A holistic view of the interfaces between knowledge
economy and the property development activities

New divisions of labour and the property market

It is not possible, in one chapter, to review all the changes that have occurred
in the workplace since the early 1990s. Two key trends will be briefly described
here. First, the types of work that require creativity and 'big ideas' have been
increasing at such a speed and scale that a new class – the so-called 'creative
class' (Florida, 2002) and 'symbolic analysts' (Reich, 1992) – is emerging.
Second, many young generations are faced with new types of contract and
employment experience that differ from those that prevailed prior to the early
1990s (Shearmur, 2017). Both changes have substantial implications on the
property market as discussed below.

Starting with Florida's creative class thesis, for many commentators, its
importance lies in offering an alternative way of theorising the relationship
between job market and labour market. While the traditional location theory
pays attention to the relative distance to markets and raw materials, and the
agglomeration theory emphasises the importance of the labour pool, shared
facilities, and networking (Parr, 2002; Phelps, 2009), they share the same logic:
companies decide their location first, which then attracts labour to follow.
The creative class thesis, on the contrary, argues that 'the old mode of people
moving to follow jobs is turned on its head' (Baris, 2003, p. 42), as new ideas,
carried by these footloose 'creative workers', have become the key drivers
of economic growth and competitiveness. The built environment plays an
important role in attracting these creative workers, who 'are drawn to stimulating and experiential creative environments. They gravitate to the indigenous

street-level culture found in Soho, Greenwich Village, and parts of Brooklyn and [New] Jersey' (Florida, 2005, p. 164). These places often boast a lively sub-cultural scene, an exciting and participatory 'look and feel' (Helbrecht, 2004), and a wide availability of public spaces for business but also spontaneous encounters and interactions.

Miao (2020) and Lawton et al. (2013) nonetheless, rightly pointed out that the thesis on creative class merely offers a romanticised and sometimes ambiguous reference to the housing market, even though housing is part of the 'urban authenticity'. Among the few empirical studies that have explored their connections, findings are polarised between two viewpoints. On the one hand, creative class seems to prefer established urban neighbourhoods in city centres, initially attracted by cheap rent and later by the 'feel' of this place – as opposed to 'monolithic' and 'organised' suburbia (Whyte, 1956). On a finer grained level of housing styles and street morphology, the creatives prefer bespoke, personalised housing (Musterd & Ostendorf, 2004) that are adjacent to, or not far from, an 'organic and indigenous street-level culture', where

> certain streets lined with a multitude of small venues. These may include coffee shops, restaurants and bars, some of which offer performance or exhibits along with the food and drink; art galleries; bookstores and other stores; small to mid-sized theatres for film or live performance or both; and various hybrid spaces. (Florida, 2002, pp. 182–183)

On the other hand, many empirical studies have failed to identify the urban orientation of creative class and its unique housing taste. Tomaney and Bradley (2007) for example, noticed that the 'top end' housing – large size on bigger plots that are often found in a middle-class residential suburbs – was still more attractive to creative professionals. In Dublin, Murphy and Redmond (2009) noticed a high dissatisfaction of creative workers with the cost of living in the city. It seems that the traditional decision-making role in housing consumption, i.e., finding the optimal point between income constraints and housing attributes, still holds true. Nonetheless, meticulous studies on the creative class's housing consumption behaviour, assisted with better definitions and methodologically approaches, are still needed.

On the changing work experience, Friedman (2014, p. 171) described that:

> A growing number of American workers are no longer employed in 'jobs' with a long-term connection with a company but are hired for 'gigs' under 'flexible' arrangements as 'independent contractors' or 'consultants', working only to complete a particular task or for defined time and with no more connection with their

employer than there might be between a consumer and a particular brand of soap or potato chips.

This casualisation of labour contracts has resulted in an intense pressure on workers. Hence, their workday extends well beyond traditional hours (Boltanski & Chiapello, 2005) and their working activities are performed in all types of location – at home, in an office, in airport lounges, in cafes and in parks. This means that separation between work, live and leisure – in terms of spaces needed – is blurring (Schieman & Young, 2010). The traditional office blocks, designed with formal divisions of individual working desks, meeting rooms, and executive offices, that are fit for the purpose of full-time employment and clear job hierarchies, are therefore under the threat of being out of date. Two counter trends are emerging. On the one hand, large companies have been seeking to concentrate their 'brains' in mega R&D campuses, such as the Technocentre of Renault in Paris, the 'Googleplex' headquarters of Google in Mountain View, and the Alibaba 'airspace' in Hangzhou. Apple has built its 'Apple Campus 2' in Cupertino, which can host over 12,000 employees in a single circular building (Moriset, 2014, p. 5).

On the other hand, there has been a surge of non-traditional office spaces in the forms of coworking spaces and work cafés around the world. These spaces are designed to support mainly micro-enterprises, self-employed and freelance workers, who do not need/cannot afford formal office spaces yet still find it beneficial to have interactions with like-minded fellows. According to the 2019 data of deskwanted (a portal dedicated to coworking), there were 6500 coworking spaces across 168 countries, which host more than 12,000 member spaces.[1] This represents an increase of 160% compared with 2013. Special services provided by many coworking spaces include: 24/7 access, free parking, catering and child-care.[2] The impact of coworking on the office market, however, is understudied. Preliminarily, Wilson (2019) reported the impact on lease structure (from long-term, 5–10 years, to short-term, monthly based); risk-return profile (coworking spaces yield 2–3 times more per square foot than traditional workspace offerings, but their flexible lease structure also means higher risks for landlords), and competition (especially on the sub-market of smaller office units). More rigorous studies are urgently needed to clarify and quantify the impact of non-traditional office spaces, such as coworking, on the mainstream commercial property market.

ICT revolution and the property industry

In mature economies, the real estate sector normally contributes a substantial proportion of business assets and fixed investment. In the UK, for example, private sector commercial property represented 34% of total business assets (Dixon et al., 2005). Technology revolutions, especially ICT and the ubiquitous internet coverage, have significant impacts on the property industry. Some of the key questions that have emerged are: if ICT improves efficiency in space use and output, will this reduce or shift the demand for real estate in certain sectors (i.e., retail, office and industry)? Where will new demand for spaces be? Will future supplies be reconfigured by new technologies so differently that they accelerate the depreciation of existing assets?

As ICT and related technologies are penetrating into the whole production cycle of the property sector, a comprehensive analysis covering its whole production value chain is needed. This chapter focuses on three activities: construction, consumption, and service.

Research on the interactions between ICT and the property construction sector has primarily focused on two topics: one is the impact of adopting ICT on sector productivity, and the other is concerned with the factors influencing the wider adoption of ICT in this industry.

For the former, Ruddock (2006) noticed a lag between investment in ICT and economic benefits. Molnár et al. (2007) further added that such a lag ranges between two and five years. This complicated the task of identifying the economic and institutional impacts of ICT, as shown by the controversial findings in earlier literature. Lehr and Lichtenberg (1999) for example, recorded positive evidence for ICT-associated productivity improvement, whereas David (1990) warned that there might be a negative effect resulting from the delayed effect of ICT investment on productivity gains and its dependence on network externalities. More nuanced analysis was conducted later. These analyses include those examining the impact of ICT on particular stages or tasks involved in the construction process, and those seeking insights from the perceived value of adopting ICT among shareholders. Vasista and Abone (2018), for example, outlined six stages of project life cycle management and nine project management knowledge areas, and identified that building information model software such as AutoDesk, virtual reality, CAD, and group collaboration technologies have increasingly been applied in different stages of the construction life cycle and fulfilled different tasks. From the users' perspective, Jacobsson and Linderoth (2012) reported that 'improved quality of work' was perceived to be impacted the most from ICT adoption. But significant differences could be distilled among offsite managers, onsite managers and foremen, with the former showing the highest engagement with ICT and the latter the least. In the context of Nigeria, Owolabi and Olufemi (2018) noted that wastage control, lower operational expenses and less paper work were the top three perceived benefits of adopting ICT. They also pointed out that the size of company influenced the adoption rate most significantly. Here, it seems that some systematic differences might exist between developed and developing countries, between occupation categories and between the scale of the company. Comparative studies are therefore highly desirable to explore these hidden factors further.

Although the tested and perceived benefits of adopting ICT are substantial, many scholars noticed a relatively low adoption rate in the construction industry compared with other industries. Ruddock (2006) reported that, in the UK, the construction sector had the lowest turnover spent on IT (0.4%) compared with manufacturing (1.5%), retailing (1.6%) and finance (6.6%). Construction also featured the lowest IT usage rate (0.4%) among retailing (1.0%), architectural activities (2.4%), real estate letting (7.9%) and all industries (1.0%). This necessitates studies to identify the factors influencing its adoption. Using Orlikowski's (1992, p. 409) institutional properties framework, Jacobsson and Linderoth (2010) argued that the project-based operational structure was one of the most distinguishable characteristics of the construction industry, which also defined its other features, such as local-based competitions and lack of standardisations. All these features, according to the authors, had held back the use of ICT in the production process.

Moving to ICT's impact on consumer behaviours, it is worth noting that different products and sub-markets are affected differently. In terms of the products, 'those goods of which consumers have a good knowledge before purchase or whose characteristics can easily be summarised online tend to be most suited to online sales' (Dixon et al., 2005, p. 227). In this regard, property products are still more immune to online transactions due to their uniqueness in locations and attributes. Consumers would typically prefer seeing the property and the neighbourhood physically before making decisions. The capital-intensive nature of property transactions also adds to the cautiousness of space users. However, most property developers and sales agencies have a web presence these days for marketing purposes and to attract the interest of their 'loyal customers' once they have established a strong brand and market recognition.

The impact of e-commerce on the retail sector has also been widely discussed and debated. Verdict, a British-based retail analyst, showed that UK online retail sales totalled £4.9 billion in 2003, accounting for 1.9% of total retail expenditure, and representing a 36% increase compared with that in 2002. Similarly, in the US, online sales accounted for 1.9% of total retail sales, worth $55 billion in 2013 according to the data from the US Department of Commerce (Dixon et al., 2005, p. 228). The share of e-commerce sales has steadily increased worldwide. The UK was the world's third largest e-commerce market by 2017. Its online share of retail sales reached 16.8% in 2017 with a total value of £586 billion (Statista, 2020a). In the US, the online share of total US retail sales has grown from 4.6% in the fourth quarter of 2010 to 11.4% by the fourth quarter of 2019, an increase of 148%, and amounted to over $158 billion (Statista, 2020b). Nonetheless, the hype over e-commerce and the argument on the death of retail stores in the late 1990s might be overblown. As evidenced by Farrag et al. (2010), shopping remains an important part of households' social activities, whose function extends considerably beyond selling and buying, towards a leisure pursuit and social gathering. It embodies our contemporary identities such as class, ethnicity, gender and generation (Jackson & Holbrook, 1995).

Altierre Corporation (2018) further broke down the 2017 retail sales in the US by industrial categories. It noticed that e-commerce sales recorded the highest in GAFO[3] with an approximately 26% share of total transactions. This was followed by Motor Vehicle & Parts, which only derived 3.5% of its total transactions from online sales. Online consumption of property is almost non-existent. Therefore, it seems the traditional department stores, where GAFO are the main selling items, are facing severe challenges. As a counter-measure, we are seeing more and more shopping malls being designed with mixed functions (catering, shopping, cinemas, etc.), family-friendly facilities, and open-plan layouts to make shopping an enjoyable experience. However, how much design could contribute to a return premium still needs to be explored further.

In property services, real estate agencies have long embraced online marketing channels and data management software. Now they are increasingly using other high technologies such as big data and virtual reality in market analysis and marketing. Piletic (2017) for example, identified the following areas where big data will make substantial impacts on the service of the property market, including:

• Appraisals: the tremendous data storage and analysis capacity of Big Data technologies enable a more accurate and quicker estimate of properties when the transaction values of neighbouring properties in a particular

area are stored in the database and an evaluation algorithm is already pro-
grammed in the software.

- Finance: with a big volume of cases and records of transactions and default
rate, Big Data offers financial institutions greater insights on risk analysis
of any asset on the agenda.
- Money laundering prevention: Big Data can provide suspicious activity
analysis and can alert the concerned owners at the right time.
- Targeted marketing: it is now a common practice to keep a record of customers' details when they are viewing a particular property or surfing property websites. Powerful data management and analysis software are then
used to generate trends regarding the preference of a particular gender, age
or geographical area. Property agencies can then avail themselves of this
opportunity to find the best suitable properties for a particular buyer or for
marketing suitable properties among potential buyers.
- Insurance analytics: small areas or larger geographical locations can be
analysed with Big Data to determine what kind of coverage people would
need.

Augmented reality (AR) is another top-notch invention that gives a real picture
of an imaginary world and stimulates consumption by potential buyers. Unlike
virtual reality that creates a complete artificial environment, AR reproduces
the real-world environment by using automated sensors, such as sound, GPS
data, video and graphics available on the computer. Agencies and customers
can layer new information (such as adding furniture in a house or railway
station that is going to be built) on the top of it. It has been used by the industry
to create 3D models of commercial properties during the blueprint stage. For
customers, AR provides the opportunity to thoroughly overview the property
without even visiting the location physically. They can also see virtual designs,
interiors and even make changes to the existing environment with a few clicks
(Khanna, 2018). Because AR is still new to the property sector, there are few
studies discussing its added value and/or damages to the sector. Judge and
Brown (2018) nonetheless, pointed out that the popularity of Pokémon Go[4]
has harmed residential properties by increasing nuisance, trespass and noise
in the neighbourhood, and hence heightened the argument for the 'right not
to be mapped'.

Property dynamics and urban configurations

This section borrows insights from the writings of David Harvey (1982, 1989,
2006) in discussing the interface between property market dynamics and urban

configurations. For Harvey (2001, pp. 23–24), 'the production, reproduction and reconfiguration of space have always been central to understanding the political economy of capitalism'. A 'spatial fix', where geographical expansion and restructuring are used to resolve capitalism's inner crisis, is therefore a temporary solution. Technology revolutions including ICT, have stimulated new organisations and forms of productions, which are competing for spaces with the traditional ones. Property demand and supply, as derived from economic activities, are also undergoing a noticeable transformation worldwide. This section will examine the various spatial formats and urban morphologies in support of high-tech growth.

Starting with the debates on monocentric, polycentric, and dispersal urban forms, the classic Chicago school of urbanism offered a monocentric urban expansion model with specialised zones radiating from the urban core. A modernisation of this theory was offered by Paul Krugman (1993, 1999), which focuses on how a self-organising spatial principle of the agglomeration economy plays an important role in consolidating some urban and regional centres while missing out others. High-tech sectors and innovation intensive industries, according to Acs (2002), have a higher inclination for concentration due to their needs for sharing tactic information. This monocentrism view, however, was challenged by postmodern urbanism studies (Aring, 1999; Garreau, 1991; Kling et al., 1995), which argue that economic activities tend to disperse for space and cost reasons. Suburbs therefore are where new economic activities are happening. Centres of high-tech growth are often found on the edge of cities where the availability of open spaces, lesser organisational redcaps and cheaper property costs are all luring factors.

Polycentrism is somewhere in between: it refuses the dominance of one single urban centre, but also believes that urbanism cannot disperse infinitely and irregularly. Instead, scholars argue that there will be dispersal of economic activities which, in turn, will agglomerate in separate, relatively independent centres. Hall and Pain's (2006) work is seminal here. Although Gordon and Richardson (1996) argued that polycentrism was nothing more than an intermediate stage between monocentrism and dispersal, Muñiz and Garcia-López (2010) noticed that knowledge intensive and other employment activities decentralise in a similar way, but the former tends to be more concentrated through the formation of employment sub-centres and therefore follows a polycentric location model. Some of these centres and sub-centres are identified as important nodes of 'global commodity chains', 'world city networks' or 'global production networks' (Neil et al., 2010).

The underlining rational for monocentric and polycentric urbanisation patterns – i.e., external returns of scale and scope – also underpins the popularity of special economic zones, science parks, technology parks and the like. UNESCO identified over 400 science parks worldwide and Miao (2013) reported over 5000 different types of science parks in China in the early 2000s. In the Arabian Peninsula, a survey among knowledge-intensive companies indicated that firms were mainly accumulated around purposely built special zones including Dubai International Financial Centre, Knowledge Village, Internet City, Media City and Jebel Ali free zone. The advantages of being located in these zones include exemption from taxation combined with high quality facilities, infrastructures and maintenance, although it is acknowledged that these specially designed economic zones tend to be disconnected from the rest of the city (Thierstein & Schein, 2008). Gower and Harris (1994), nonetheless, pointed out that the remit of science parks was principally to cater for the needs of small start-up businesses; this means that the typical property features may include:

- Multiplicity of building ownership and tenancy agreements;
- The subdivision of single units into smaller units to accommodate the needs of small businesses;
- A predominance of flexible, short-term leases, or even floor space let on licence;
- A requirement for high levels of management support, both during initial stages and throughout the life of the development; and
- The likely adoption of a restrictive letting policy, i.e., potential tenant/ resident companies may be required to show commitment to research and development activities and manufacturing companies will normally be excluded.

This implies that science parks generally do not feature highly in investors' portfolio. Actually, they might even discourage private investment given the implied higher management costs. How to stimulate greater interests from the private sector and institutional investors through, for example, innovative financial arrangement and/or management structure, is a topic worth exploring further.

Besides these bigger scale spatial configurations, the rise of the high-tech sectors also leaves its mark on the micro, urban morphology level. Social spaces and open spaces, for example, are emphasised as crucial to maximise the opportunities for unplanned encounters and face-to-face meetings (Moriset, 2014). The term 'third place' for example, was coined by Oldenburg (1989) to describe places out of the home and the office where people convene and socialise in a free, informal manner. Oldenburg regards these places as irre-placeable in the production of the urban social fabric. Cafés such as Starbucks, McDonald's restaurants, hotel and airport lounges, the hairdressers or barber shops, are typical third places. With the growth of the creative class (Florida, 2002), the importance of these social spaces has become even more prominent. For the property sector, these third spaces challenge the established boundaries between retail, office, residential and even industry. How to accommodate such hybridity is still an open question.

Mixed land use is another tendency for creative cities. In Yigitcanlar's (2007) review of global knowledge cities, including Austin, US; Helsinki, Finland; Melbourne, Australia; Barcelona, Spain; and Singapore, a shared feature was their weaving of different land uses. The 'Barcelona model' for example, encompasses the essence of complex functions in land uses in order to avoid marginal social zones and functional specialisation (Garcia-Ramon & Albet, 2000). Yet for Grant (2002, p. 71), 'mixed use' had become a mantra in con-temporary planning by the end of the 20th century, whose benefits have been taken for granted. Few questioned its premise or endeavoured to clarify its meaning. What this translates to is a lack of analysis on the intended objectives and appropriate strategies in mixing different uses. Developers sometimes use the term 'mixed use' to gain planning permission, but often end up with what they are familiar with in delivery.

Reflection and further research directions

This chapter has focused on three interfaces between knowledge-based growth and the property sector, including changes in the labour market; adoption of ICT in the sector; and the spatial transformation associated with new formats of production. For each interface, noticeable trends of changes are discussed and major debates explored. There are yet many unanswered questions that are worth following-on explorations.

In examining changes in the labour market, the rise of a creative class whose role involves significant knowledge creation and diffusion was discussed. Although the thesis on creative class emphasises the importance of urban amenities and the built environment (housing and commercial properties should be part of the considerations), empirical evidence is not conclusive. The collective consumption pressure caused by the agglomeration of often highly-paid creative workers would likely squeeze out the normal residences and/or those employees who engage in labour-intensive works (such as key workers). This in turn might aggregate social disparity in areas concentrated with high-tech/creative jobs. More research is needed here. In parallel with the rise of the creative class is the casualisation of contracts and the increase of freelance workers. For them, the boundaries between their work, social lives and travel are becoming increasingly blurred, which calls for a re-think of space design and new functions of properties. The inert nature of the property sector and, to a certain extent, the rigid planning regulations, however, are deferring the prevalence of hybrid places for multifunctional operations. Systematic research is needed to explore the causes and potential solutions to overcome these constraints.

In terms of the adoption of ICT in the property sector, it is not an exaggeration to say that construction has not been one of the pioneers in embracing high-tech inventions. Scholars have tried to identify the potential added-value of ICT adoption for the sector as a whole and for individual projects. The perceived benefits were found to differ between countries and between tasks involved. Comparative studies are therefore desirable to provide a more holistic picture here. Work has also been done to detect the social, economic and institutional factors that hinder the wider usage of ICT in the property sector. It seems that the project-based organisational nature of construction has been one of the major reasons for discouraging the adoption of ICT. The impacts of ICT on the consumption of property products and services are also found to be divergent depending on sub-sectors. High-street retailing is arguably affected the most by online shopping, whereas the transactions of housing and office spaces still often involve face-to-face interactions and physical presence, which nonetheless, are slowly changing as well. It is therefore highly desirable to examine this trend and the emerging marketing practice, and how they impact consumer experience, real estate agencies, and the costs involved in the process.

While looking at the interactions between property market dynamics and spatial configurations, this chapter draws insight from the argument that cities are produced through processes of uneven development caused by cycles of capital accumulation, commodification, biased investment and preference (McFarlane, 2011). The debate between monocentric, polycentric and dispersed urban formats, for example, is a reflection of such geographically uneven development processes. The agglomeration economy which supports higher return is arguably one of the most robust explanations underpinning the persistent concentration of high-tech activities, no matter whether they are located in greenfield spaces, as in the case of Silicon Valley, or in established urban centres, as in the current hype over innovation districts and culture quarters. Yet, as Miao (2017) rightly pointed out, there tends to be a neglect of housing provision and the spatial relations between housing and working spaces in current industrial and economic development policies. Moreover, the current policy enthusiasm over urban centres risks further polarising investment, leaving many suburbs and new towns to struggle to keep their talents and jobs. This leads to further questions on the role of the public sector, and in particular planning, on the strategic thinking about, and balancing of, market forces with social and environmental considerations.

Notes

1. https://coworkinginsights.com/everything-you-need-to-know-about-coworking-in-2019-so-far/
2. https://www.dropbox.com/s/24p6i2vy00btzga/ULTIMATE%20COWORKING%20SPACE%20DATA%20REPORT%20-%20SELECTED%20SLIDES.pdf?dl=0
3. GAFO is the NAICS category that encompasses retailers that deal in the following set of goods: (1) general merchandise retailers; (2) furniture & home furnishings; (3) electronics & appliances; (4) clothing & accessories; (5) sporting goods, hobbies, books, and music; and (6) office supplies, stationery, and gift stores.
4. This is an enhanced digital mapping game in which players participate in a digital scavenger hunt by visiting real-world locations.

References

Acs, Z. J. (2002). *Innovation and the Growth of Cities*. Cheltenham: Edward Elgar Publishing.

Altierre Corporation (Producer). (2018, 22/03/2020). The real impact of e-commerce on retail.

Aring, J. (1999). *Suburbia – Postsuburbia – Zwischenstadt*. Hannover: ARL.

Asheim, T. B., Cooke, P., & Martin, R. (2006). *Clusters and Regional Development: Critical Reflections and Explorations* (Vol. 1). London and New York: Routledge.

Augé, M. (1995). *Non-places: Introduction to an Anthropology of Supermodernity* (J. Howe, Trans.). London: Verso.

Ball, M. (2003). Markets and the structure of the housebuilding industry: An international perspective. *Urban Studies*, 40(5–6), 897–916.

Baris, M. (2003). Review of Richard Florida: The rise of the creative class: And how it's transforming work, leisure, community, and everyday life. *The Next American City*, 1, 42–45.

Boltanski, L., & Chiapello, E. (2005). The new spirit of capitalism. *International Journal of Politics, Culture, and Society*, 18(3/4), 161–188.

Boschma, R. A., & Fritsch, M. (2009). Creative class and regional growth: Empirical evidence from seven European countries. *Economic Geography*, 85(4), 391–423.

Castells, M. (1996). *The Information Age: Economy, Society and Culture*. Malden, US: Blackwell Publishers.

David, P. A. (1990). The dynamo and the computer and dynamo. A historical perspective on the modern productivity paradox. *American Economic Review, 80*(2), 355–361.

Dixon, T., Thompson, B., McAllister, P., Marston, A., & Snow, J. (2005). *Real Estate and the New Economy*. Oxford: Blackwell Publishing.

Fan, C. C., & Scott, A. J. (2003). Industrial agglomeration and development: A survey of spatial economic issues in East Asia and a statistical analysis of Chinese regions. *Economic Geography, 79*(3), 295–319.

Farrag, D., Sayed, I. E., & Belk, R. (2010). Mall shopping motives and activities: A multimethod approach. *Journal of International Consumer Marketing, 22*(2), 95–115.

Florida, R. (2002). *The Rise of the Creative Class*. New York: Basic Books.

Florida, R. (2005). *Cities and the Creative Class*. New York: Routledge.

Friedman, G. (2014). Workers without employers: Shadow corporations and the rise of the gig economy. *Review of Keynesian Economics, 2*(2), 171–188.

Garcia-Ramon, M., & Albet, A. (2000). Pre-Olympic and post-Olympic Barcelona, a model for urban regeneration today? *Environment and Planning A, 32*(8), 1331–1334.

Garreau, J. (1991). *Edge City: Life on the New Frontier*. New York: Doubleday.

Gordon, P., & Richardson, H. W. (1996). Beyond polycentricity: The dispersed metropolis, Los Angeles, 1970–1990. *Journal of the American Planning Association, 62*(3), 289–295.

Gower, S. M., & Harris, F. C. (1994). The funding of, and investment in, British Science Parks: A review. *Journal of Property Finance, 5*(3), 7–18.

Grant, J. (2002). Mixed use in theory and practice: Canadian experience with implementing a planning principle. *Journal of the American Planning Association, 68*(1), 71–84.

Hall, P., & Pain, K. (2006). *The Polycentric Metropolis: Learning from Mega-city Regions in Europe*. London and Sterling, VA: Earthscan.

Harvey, D. (1982). *Limits to Capital*. Oxford: Blackwell.

Harvey, D. (1989). From managerialism to entrepreneurialism: The transformation in urban governance in late capitalism. *Geografiska Annaler. Series B, Human Geography, 71*(1), 3–17.

Harvey, D. (2001). Globalization and the "Spatial Fix". *geographische revue, 2*(1), 23–30.

Harvey, D. (2006). *Spaces of Global Capitalism: Towards a Theory of Uneven Development*. London, UK: Verso.

Helbrecht, I. (2004). Bare geographies in knowledge societies – Creative cities as text and piece of art: Two eyes, one vision. *Built Environment, 30*(3), 194–203.

Jackson, P., & Holbrook, B. (1995). Multiple meanings: Shopping and the cultural politics of identity. *Environment & Planning A, 27*, 1913–1930.

Jacobsson, M., & Linderoth, H. C. J. (2010). The influence of contextual elements, actors' frames of reference, and technology on the adoption and use of ICT in construction projects: A Swedish case study. *Construction Management and Economics, 28*(1), 13–23.

Jacobsson, M., & Linderoth, H. C. J. (2012). User perceptions of ICT impacts in Swedish construction companies: 'It's fine, just as it is'. *Construction Management and Economics, 30*(5), 339–357.

Judge, E. F., & Brown, T. E. (2018). A right not to be mapped? Augmented reality, real property, and zoning. *Laws, 7*(23), 1–23.

Khanna, M. (Producer). (2018, 22/03/2020). How augmented reality would revolution-ise the commercial real estate market?

Kling, R., Olin, S., & Poster, M. (1995). *Postsuburban California: The Transformation of Orange County Since World War Two*. Berkeley, CA: University of California Press.

Knight, R. (1995). Knowledge-based development: Policy and planning implications for cities. *Urban Studies, 32*(2), 225–260.

Krugman, P. (1993). First nature, second nature, and metropolitan location. *Journal of Regional Science, 33*, 129–144.

Krugman, P. (1999). The role of geography in development. *International Regional Science Review, 22*(2), 142–161.

Lawton, P., Murphy, E., & Redmond, D. (2013). Residential preferences of the 'creative class'? *Cities, 31*(2), 47–56.

Lehr, B., & Lichtenberg, F. (1999). Information technology and its impact on produc-tivity. Firm-level evidence from government and private data sources. *Canadian Journal of Economics, 32*(2), 335–362.

McFarlane, C. (2011). The city as assemblage: Dwelling and urban space. *Environment and Planning D: Society and Space, 29*, 649–671.

Miao, J. T. (2013). *The Birth, Evolution and Performance of High-tech Zones in China*. (PhD) London: University College London.

Miao, J. T. (2017). Housing the knowledge economy in China: An examination of housing provision in support of science parks. *Urban Studies, 54*(6), 1426–1445.

Miao, J. T. (2019). *Housing the Creative Sector: A Comparative Study of Paintworks, Bristol and Baltic Triangle, Liverpool*. Glasgow: UK Centre for Housing Evidence.

Miao, J. T. (2020). Getting creative with housing? Liverpool's Baltic Triangle and Bristol's Paintworks compared. *European Planning Studies*. doi.org/10.1080/09654313.2020.1777942.

Molnár, M., Andersson, R., & Ekholm, A. (2007). *Benefits of ICT in the Construction Industry – Characterization of the Present Situation in House-building Processes*. Paper presented at the 24th W78 Conference, Maribor. https://www.lunduniversity.lu.se/lup/publication/402c1b26-e4e5-4e80-a2fc-c3a31eb6a4fa.

Moriset, B. (2014). *Building New Places of the Creative Economy. The Rise of Coworking Spaces*. Paper presented at the 2nd Geography of Innovation International Conference 2014, Utrecht, the Netherlands.

Muñiz, I., & Garcia-López, M.-À. (2010). The polycentric knowledge economy in Barcelona. *Urban Geography, 31*(6), 774–799.

Murphy, E., & Redmond, D. (2009). The role of 'hard' and 'soft' factors for accommo-dating creative knowledge: Insights from Dublin's 'creative class'. *Irish Geography, 42*(1), 69–84.

Musterd, S., & Ostendorf, W. (2004). Creative cultural knowledge cities: Perspectives and planning strategies. *Built Environment, 30*(3), 189–193.

Neil, M. C., Dicken, P., Hess, M., & Yeung, H. W.-C. (2010). Making connections: Global production networks and world city networks. *Global Networks, 10*(1), 138–149.

OECD. (2015). *The Innovation Imperative*. Paris: OECD.

Oldenburg, R. (1989). *The Great Good Place*. New York: Paragon House.

Orlikowski, W. J. (1992). The duality of technology: Rethinking the concept of technol-ogy in organizations. *Organization Science, 3*(3), 398–427.

Owolabi, O., & Olufemi, O. (2018). Effect of the use of ICT in the Nigerian construction industry. *The International Journal of Engineering and Science, 7*(5), 71–76.

Parr, J. B. (2002). Agglomeration economies: Ambiguities and confusions. *Environment and Planning A*, *34*, 717–731.

Phelps, N. A. (2009). From branch plant economies to knowledge economies? Manufacturing industry, government policy, and economic development in Britain's old industrial regions. *Environment and Planning C: Government and Policy*, *27*, 574–592.

Piletic, P. (Producer). (2017, 22/03/2020). Big data in real estate: Staying ahead of the curve.

Reich, R. (1992). *The Work of Nations*. New York: Basic Books.

Ruddock, L. (2006). ICT in the construction sector: Computing the economic benefits. *International Journal of Strategic Property Management*, *10*(1), 39–50.

Schieman, S., & Young, M. (2010). Is there a downside to schedule control for the work-family interface? *Journal of Family Issues*, 31(10), 1391–1414.

Shearmur, R. (2017). The Millennial urban space-economy: Dissolving workplaces and the delocalization of economic value-creation. In M. Moos, D. Pfeiffer, & T. Vinodrai (Eds), *Millennial City* (pp. 61–76). London: Routledge.

Statista (Producer). (2020a, 22/03/2020). E-commerce in the United Kingdom (UK) – Statistics & Facts.

Statista (Producer). (2020b, 22/03/2020). Quarterly share of e-commerce sales of total U.S. retail sales from 1st quarter 2010 to 4th quarter 2019.

Thierstein, A., & Schein, E. (2008). Emerging cities on the Arabian Peninsula: Urban space in the knowledge economy context. *International Journal of Architectural Research*, *2*(2), 178–195.

Tomaney, J., & Bradley, D. (2007). The economic role of mobile professional and creative workers and their housing and residential preferences: Evidence from North East England. *Town Planning Review*, *78*(4), 511–530.

Vasista, T. G., & Abone, A. (2018). Benefits, barriers and applications of information communication technology in construction industry: A contemporary study. *International Journal of Engineering & Technology*, *7*(3), 492–499.

Whyte, W. H. (1956). *The Organization Man*. New York: Simon and Schuster.

Wilson, D. (Producer). (2019, 21/03/2020). What the rise of coworking means for the real estate industry.

Yigitcanlar, T. (2007). *The Making of Urban Spaces for the Knowledge Economy: Global Practices*. Paper presented at the 2nd International Symposium on KNOWLEDGE CITIES: Future of Cities in the Knowledge Economy, Malaysia.

4 Future directions of research in innovative workplaces

Eileen Sim

Introduction

Office workplaces are increasingly gaining attention in the fields of real estate, psychology and health. Office workplaces house organisations' human capital affecting employees' wellbeing and performance. With the rising cost of real estate, organisations are seeking more effective and efficient ways of housing employees and have started to turn to innovative workplaces, specifically Activity Based Working offices. The discussions of this chapter can be separated into two categories that both contribute towards identifying the future potential areas of research in innovative workplaces. First, the history of office workplaces is explored to provide a background on how workplaces have changed over time, the drivers of change and potential future changes. A review of the significant shifts in office workplaces points towards an increased adoption of innovative workplaces, such as Activity Based Working (ABW) offices, to offer more collaborative workspaces, improve productivity through a larger worksetting variety and increase real estate cost efficiency. Therefore, the second half of this chapter discusses the current research on ABW offices to identify areas to be further researched.

History of office workplaces

The history of office workplaces is briefly discussed here to provide a landscape of how office workplaces have changed since the inception and drivers of historical workplace changes, to understand the direction of future changes. Office workplaces can be divided into three generations of offices (Bedford and Tong, 1997, p. 65) and each of these will be discussed in turn.

First-generation office: small private office

Before the 19th century and the industrial revolution, there were few large corporations. Most merchants and self-employed entrepreneurs conducted their work in the marketplace, coffee houses and a room in their own homes (Gatter, 1982). As their business expanded, they started occupying what were early office buildings and primarily took on small private offices (Gatter, 1982; Aronoff and Kaplan, 1995; Bedford and Tong, 1997) resembling hotel rooms or corridor offices (Duffy and Wankum, 1969) designed to reflect solitude. These enclosed rooms are known as First-generation offices, supporting small groups or solo work functions (Bedford and Tong, 1997, p. 65). One major limitation in the First-generation offices was the reliance on natural lighting and ventilation, as electric light fittings and refrigerated air-conditioning only arrived in the 1930s (Gatter, 1982; Sundstrom and Sundstrom, 1986; Aronoff and Kaplan, 1995, p. 29).

Second-generation office: Open-plan office, Bürolandschaft, Action Office

Rapid industrialisation in the Western world resulted in larger scale organisational operations and growth, thus requiring more coordination and control over the growing complexity of information in manufacturing and distribution (Gatter, 1982). This led to the birth of Second-generation offices as there was a surge in office demand for house clerks within the cities (Bedford and Tong, 1997). Additionally, offices provided key decision makers and employees with a place of gathering, interaction, information and equipment (Aronoff and Kaplan, 1995). The growth of offices was described as 'astronomical' in cities across America and Europe with an increase in population and commercial clerks of 78% and 476% respectively in London from 1851 to 1891 (Gatter, 1982).

Open-plan offices emerged to house the large proportion of clerical staff relative to managerial staff. Clerical workers worked in open desks without enclosures arranged in a rectilinear manner which resembled a factory production line or a bull-pen enclosure. The open desks were enclosed by private offices along the building perimeter housing higher-ranked employees or professionals requiring privacy (Sundstrom and Sundstrom, 1986; Bedford and Tong, 1997). The advancement of technology in construction and services also supported Open-plan offices as deep-plan office structures could be constructed and air-conditioning and electric lighting became standard in the 1960s (Gatter, 1982).

Since the Second-generation offices emerged in the manufacturing and industrialisation era, a highly influential management philosophy, the Taylor Scientific Management System, designed to increase productivity in factories, was employed in designing Open-plan offices (Forty, 1986; Kuang, 2009). Management experts studied the clerks' work, broke them down into a series of basic actions and identified the best way of conducting each basic action. The manager would then conduct a time-motion study where clerks were taught the best way of conducting the basic action, how to calculate a norm performance rate to set the basic wage-performance and remunerate staff based on performance (Forty, 1986; Kuang, 2009). The traditional clerk desk with pigeonholes was redesigned to remove inefficiencies, resulting in flat surfaces where drawers only held the tools needed to do the assigned actions and stationery was organised systemically (Forty, 1986).

Open-plan offices were commended for the efficiency in workflow, communication flow, space saved, ease in making layout changes, and excellent supervision, with managers overlooking from their private offices, thus resembling a factory floor (Duffy and Wankum, 1969; Kuang, 2009). Duffy and Powell (1997) sum up the Taylor values as a combination of order, hierarchy, supervision and depersonalisation, where employees were best managed if they were treated as 'unthinking automatons'. Employees resented the Open-plan office because it removed all control, visual and audio privacy, had many distractions and no longer reflected employees' status (Duffy and Wankum, 1969). This provided scope for the introduction of another office workplace.

In the 1960s, the Bürolandschaft, which originated in Germany – 'Office Landscape' in English – was introduced. Distinctive principles incorporated in its design were the team approach, flexibility of its well-serviced space, and modern organisational theory removing hierarchy (Duffy et al., 2013). The Bürolandschaft removed private offices and consisted of large undivided open floor areas with minimal walls, desks arranged at odd angles, and workers arranged based on a communication analysis (Gatter, 1982; Duffy et al., 2013). Flexibility was achieved through the use of standardised, mobile and reasonably light furniture (Duffy and Wankum, 1969; Budd, 2001). Multipurpose 'movable screens' were introduced to deal with issues around privacy, noise, distraction and to allow employees to personalise their movable screens (Duffy and Wankum, 1969, p. 10). However, the Bürolandschaft failed to gain widespread acceptance in America (Budd, 2001) because its openness failed to address noise and privacy and its concept removed status markers and the unrealistic expectations to create an infinite flowing communications network of people (Sundstrom and Sundstrom, 1986; Duffy, 1992).

By 1968, the Action Office, originating in America, started gaining traction (Aronoff and Kaplan, 1995; Laing, 1997). It was intended to deal with the privacy and communication issues of the Bürolandschaft, and featured a modular design and enclosures promoting autonomy and open access (Budd, 2001). A key feature was the ability to hang various elements such as storage units, personal items and work surfaces on the freestanding panels, thus providing employees with an adaptable desk (Gatter, 1982; Laing, 1997). This is also commonly known as the cubicle or the cellular office. It has been highly adopted to date and has been reported to be taken to extremes in some large floor spaces (Stone and Luchetti, 1985; Budd, 2001; Kuang, 2009). Taken to an extreme, the Action Office started being associated with a lack of privacy and interaction (Budd, 2001).

Up to this point, employees had always been assigned their own workspace or 'territory'.

Third-generation office

In the 1970s, the first Third-generation offices were introduced featuring non-territorial offices (Allen and Gerstberger, 1973) but their adoption was far less than the Action Office. The main ideas behind Third-generation offices are the sharing-based model, which removes individual territory for the more efficient use of offices, and the process-based model, which supports a variety of work processes (Bedford and Tong, 1997, p. 65). This concept of the Third-generation office first emerged when IBM experimented with a variety of unassigned worksettings, except for a 'central communicator' who had an assigned station to direct and redirect mail, visitors and calls (Allen and Gerstberger, 1973). Although this transition was a success, where communications increased significantly and employees preferred the non-territorial office over the Second-generation office, IBM decided to remain with their previous territorial office layouts. There are speculations that the non-territorial office was too innovative for its time as the innovation in technology was lagging and unable to support mobility (Stone and Luchetti, 1985). The emergence of superior technology supporting mobility, such as wireless networks and laptops, has resurrected the non-territorial office in recent years.

A non-territorial office can be defined

> ... as a space allocation policy in which individual employees had no personally assigned desk, office, or workstation over an indefinite time period. Employees used whatever space they preferred when they came into the office, and no one person was associated with any particular workspace. (Becker et al., 1994, pp. 28–29)

Individual territory is removed using workplace guidelines to encourage non-territorial behaviour. Over the years, four types of non-territorial offices (Co-location spaces; Activity Based Working; Self-owned Desks; and Hot-desking) have emerged and can be differentiated based on an organisation's exclusive use of desks, individuals' exclusive use of workstations and the variety of worksettings.

Co-location spaces and Activity Based Working (ABW) are similar as individuals do not have exclusive use of desks but differ in that Co-location spaces are shared with several organisations, unlike ABW (Nenonen, 2016). ABW and Self-owned Desks are similar as they are exclusively occupied by one organisation, but Self-owned Desks provide employees with exclusive use of a desk, unlike ABW. With Self-owned Desks, employees are assigned a pedestal desk that they store in a locker at the end of the day alongside their belongings, but the office area and other worksettings are unassigned (Ortony et al., 1987). Whilst the differences between ABW and Hot-desking lack documentation in the academic journals, it is widely agreed by industry practitioners that Hot-desking lacks a large variety of worksettings and is similar to non-territorial Open-plan offices, unlike ABW offices (Veldhoen + Company, no date; Duerksen, 2012). There is much effort put into differentiating between the two due to the negative connotations that have emerged around Hot-desking, see for example, Warner (2013) and Wyllie et al. (2012).

After the 2007 global financial crisis, Hot-desking seemed to gain more traction due to the cost savings offered and its low-cost implementation, as some organisations with suitable technology solutions could introduce the non-territorial guidelines in their existing Open-plan offices and install locker storage. However, Hot-desking offered few benefits besides cost-savings, and organisations started turning to ABW offices that addressed more real estate and employee-related strategic drivers as economies recovered. The purported real estate drivers are that the ABW provides cost-savings, higher space efficiency and utilisation and more real estate flexibility to accommodate organisation changes, such as future spaceless growth (Becker and Steele, 1995; Brunia et al., 2016; Candido et al., 2016). The primary employee-related drivers are that the ABW attracts and retains more talent by providing more autonomy, flexibility and enjoyable workplaces; increases productivity due to the worksetting design that best supports employee activity needs; facilitates knowledge-sharing through superior communication and collaboration (Voordt, 2004; Been et al., 2015; Brunia et al., 2016; Candido et al., 2016); and better aligns with organisational equality values since no employees are assigned desks (Ekstrand, 2016).

There are a few significant shifts from the first to the third generation of work-places with various implications for current and future workplace design. First, there is a shift towards more collaboration and less individualism in the work-place. This implies that there is less individual ownership over worksettings for individual use, such as a desk, and more worksettings supporting collaboration and socialising, with a shift in perception that work is no longer constrained to the desk and meeting rooms. Second, there is a shift towards increasing employees' productivity by providing a large variety of worksettings suited to the large variety of activities conducted in the workplace. Third, there is a shift to offer employees increased flexibility of location and time, which has led to fewer employees being at their office desk at one point in time. The urgent shift in working from home due to COVID-19 is forecast to have lasting impacts, such that partial working from home will be the norm post-COVID-19 (Henry et al., 2020; Lang et al., 2020; Savills, 2020) offering employees more flexibility, as certain activities have been found to be better conducted at home (Lang et al., 2020). This has led to organisations' increased awareness of their inef-ficient real estate due to the low desk utilisation, and a shift towards a more cost-efficient workplace by offering employees unassigned seating. Despite the increased popularity of coworking spaces and working from home, a combi-nation of working from home and organisational office space is required for: a daily routine, mental health, physical health, quality family time, sense of belonging or pride in company, personal growth, work–life balance (Lang et al., 2020).

With these shifts, the adoption of ABW is forecast to increase as it is a work-place exclusively used by a single organisation with a large variety of unassigned worksettings (Warner, 2013; Telsyte, 2015). Therefore, a further discussion on the current research on ABW offices will be presented later.

Drivers of workplace change

From reviewing the history of workplaces, the few drivers for these workplace changes can be classified into: (1) economic factors; (2) social factors; (3) technological developments; and (4) organisational changes (Vos and Dewulf, 1999; Budd, 2001; Petrulaitiene and Tuuli, 2015).

Economic factors

Economic booms create a demand for more offices as employment increases, whereas economic busts push organisations to be more cost-driven in their workplace choices to minimise their real estate expenses. Additionally, the cause of an economic boom may also influence the workplace itself, such as employing management principles from the booming industries, the workplace design and the changes in the type of work and activities to be accommodated at the workplace. With the shift from the manufacturing economy to the service economy and now the knowledge economy (Mawson, 2002), it's not clear how the economy will change further and more research in this area is required to understand the management principles, type of work and activity changes that the workplace should support. The COVID-19 crisis, beginning in late December 2019, has resulted in a global health and economic crisis that has seen government restrictions pushing organisations to urgently promote working from home where possible, and increased unemployment rates due to business closures. Studying organisations' readiness to support working from home, employees' productivity, employees' satisfaction and organisations' response may reveal future workplace changes and organisations' contingency plans should a similar pandemic occur in the future.

Social factors

Social factors also play a role in what employees demand from workplaces, from status symbols to more flexibility regarding time and place, lifestyle, wellbeing, health and the ageing population in some countries, as employees are retiring later (Vos and Dewulf, 1999). There has been a major shift away from treating employees as 'unthinking automatons' (Duffy and Powell, 1997) to providing them with a work environment that promotes thinking in the knowledge economy, to increase employee retention and productivity. Thus, the innovative workplace has to research employees' demands and address them to keep up with their changes.

Technological development

The three primary technological developments are in building construction, building services and technological devices. However, the advancement in technological devices has been the most influential in enabling Third-generation offices owing to the affordability and mobility options enabled through devices such as cordless phones, the internet and computers. These have significantly enhanced employees' ability to perform various complex tasks from anywhere inside and outside the office with real-time communications (Vos and Dewulf, 1999; Koetsveld and Kamperman, 2011; Tagliaro and Ciaramella, 2016a). Future research into the integration of technology in building services and technological devices is required to reveal how innovative office workplaces are keeping up with the advancement of technology and how they are integrated. Workplaces that lag in technological advancement may affect employees' experience of the workplace and be a source of discontent. Additionally, future research into how organisations are supporting employees' technological needs during the urgent transition to working from home due to the COVID-19 lockdown and in the long-term will reveal how organisations are adapting to incorporate working from home as part of their office workplace solutions.

Organisational changes

Many aspects of organisations have changed over the years, resulting in a change in the demand for workplaces, aspects such as organisational structure (size of organisations, status, and hierarchy), management style, employee demands, and the type of work that employees conduct.

In terms of organisational size, there is a large variation, indicating that a one-size-fits-all solution may not be applicable to all organisations as they may have differing needs.

As discussed earlier, management styles and type of work conducted can be a key influence in the design of workplaces and how they are used. There is an increasing shift towards a flatter hierarchy, changing teams and cross-team collaboration, with managers managing based on output and what employees want (Laing, 1997; Vos and Dewulf, 1999). Therefore, future research to understand the direction of management styles is critical in designing future innovative workplaces to avoid misalignment between management style and the workplace.

Current research on Activity Based Working offices

As discussed earlier, the adoption of innovative offices such as Activity Based Working (ABW) offices is forecast to continue increasing owing to significant shifts towards more collaborative spaces, and increasing productivity through a larger variety of worksettings suited to employees' activity and offering employees more flexibility. This section provides an overview of the existing research on ABW offices to establish the future research areas on innovative offices. This section covers the performance of ABW offices relative to Second-generation offices, space pressure, employees' productivity, employees' sense of community and belonging, employees' satisfaction with the physical work environment, employees' health and wellbeing, technology, ABW implementation process and ABW workplace guidelines.

Comparing ABW with Second-generation offices

When comparing ABW against Second-generation offices, the results indicate that there is potential for ABW to outperform Second-generation offices in several aspects (Kim et al., 2016). In terms of distraction, one study found that both types of office performed similarly (Keeling et al., 2015) but another reported that Open-plan offices were found to have the highest level of distraction, followed by ABW offices then private offices (Seddigh et al., 2014). A few other studies found that from 47% (Rolfö et al., 2018) to 82% (Rolfö, 2018) of employees preferred the ABW offices post-relocation due to worksetting choice, aesthetics, ease of communications and superior lighting. Employees also reported being in better health in an ABW compared with Combi-offices as they were more physically active (Candido et al., 2019). ABW offices were also found to be superior to Second-generation offices in several aspects including Space for breaks, Interaction with colleagues, Personalisation of work area (ability to adjust worksetting to meet preferences), Space to collaborate, Comfort of furnishing, Indoor environmental quality, Unwanted interruption, Noise, Degree of freedom to adapt, Building overall, Productivity and Health (Kim et al., 2016). Higher productivity levels in ABWs, compared with employees in Second-generation offices, were found in cross-sectional studies (Appel-Meulenbroek et al, 2016; Candido et al., 2016, 2019). However, ABWs were inferior compared with Fixed desk offices with regard to storage space (Kim et al., 2016).

Future research investigating ABWs in more depth, to identify which architectural and functional features contribute to superior performance, may facilitate the transition of more Second-generation offices to ABWs and provide greater insight into the varied performance of ABW offices relative to Second-generation offices. The majority of existing research on ABW offices attempts to form generalisations using large-scale surveys that exclude details on the architectural and functional features. However, the architectural and functional features can vary greatly between ABW offices. Furthermore, existing research, as discussed below, has identified that specific architectural and functional features influence how ABW offices perform.

Space pressure

Space pressure is greater in ABWs compared with territorial offices (Rolfö et al., 2018) and may increase over time due to employment resulting in overcrowding (Skogland, 2017). Overcrowding is attributable to a decrease in the employee–workstation ratio as the workforce increases, a lack of guidelines on expected behaviours and a lack of guideline compliance (Appel-Meulenbroek et al., 2011; Rolfö et al., 2018). The occupancy rates in ABWs appear to be high, with one study finding an average occupancy rate of 76% and a maximum occupancy rate of 97% (Mosselman et al., 2009), and employees reporting underprovision of popular workspaces (Brunia et al., 2016; Kim et al., 2016; Tagliaro and Ciaramella, 2016a, 2016b).

The impacts of overcrowding result in unsuitable worksettings for employees, and additional mental and physical demands affecting their performance, satisfaction, health, wellbeing and more time being wasted looking for a suitable worksetting (Voordt, 2004; Mosselman et al., 2009; Kim et al., 2016; Rolfö et al., 2018). Some employees reported not being able to find a desk if they arrived at work after 8:30am and so had to work all day in the kitchen area (which is non-ergonomically set up) resulting in adverse health and wellbeing effects (Kim et al., 2016).

Space pressure is a new issue that was unreported in Second-generation offices and may have detrimental consequences if not dealt with and monitored on an ongoing basis. Future research on how to manage space pressure in the design phase of the ABW Implementation Process, and when the issue arises after employees have moved in, is required to avoid the effects of overcrowding discussed above.

Productivity

Existing studies on productivity levels are inconsistent, and vary post-relocation into an ABW, with some finding no significant changes (Blok et al., 2012; Rolfö, 2018; Rolfö et al., 2018; Haapakangas et al., 2019), a variation within the organisation (Kim et al., 2016), a decrease (Voordt, 2004; Arundell et al., 2018; Rolfö, 2018) and an increase (Voordt, 2004; Mosselman et al., 2009; Rolfö, 2018). One study found that productivity levels had the strongest positive associations with physical environment satisfaction, privacy and communications (Haapakangas et al., 2018). Inconsistent results were found on the factors affecting productivity levels indicating that ABWs have the potential to achieve higher productivity contingent to their ability to address some underlying issues. The five factors affecting productivity levels will be discussed subsequently.

Opportunities to concentrate, collaborate and interact

Inconsistent results were found for employees' opportunities to concentrate, collaborate and interact as they were dependent on the type of activity. These were dependent on several factors such as crowdedness (Rolfö, 2018), poor acoustics causing noise transmission from interaction areas into the semi-quiet areas (Rolfö, 2018), non-compliance with the speech guidelines (Rolfö et al., 2018), locating colleagues (Kim et al., 2016), sitting with those they had to collaborate with (Kim et al., 2016), space pressure (Kim et al., 2016), finding a suitable worksetting for their activity (Arundell et al., 2018) and neighbourhood zone allocation (Arundell et al., 2018; Rolfö et al., 2018; Haapakangas et al., 2019). Additionally, the right type of interactions should be encouraged as random interactions may increase but energy levels and team communications may fall, affecting the revenues and productivity of employees (Waber et al., 2014).

Switching behaviour in an ABW

There are inconsistent results on the effect of employees' switching behaviour (switching worksettings based on their activities) on productivity levels in the ABW (Blok et al., 2009). Even though one study recorded up to 14 worksetting switches daily (Gorgievski et al., 2010), another study indicated that the optimal number of switches is one to three times, as any fewer or more decreases productivity and wellbeing due to more time being spent looking for a worksetting (Haapakangas et al., 2018). Thus, there is a threshold to the benefits of switching, with more switches having more disbenefits than benefits, potentially due to the time and effort spent on practical arrangement (Haapakangas et al., 2018).

Other studies found that employees do not switch worksettings on a regular day or week (Appel-Meulenbroek et al., 2011; Hoendervanger et al., 2016; Tagliaro and Ciaramella, 2016a, 2016b; Babapour, 2019), with 70% of employees not switching worksettings more than twice a week (Hoendervanger et al., 2016). The majority of employees reported only working at the open desks (Blok et al., 2012; Tagliaro and Ciaramella, 2016a) with a minority using the meeting rooms (Blok et al., 2012). Of those employees that often use the open desks, a few studies reported consistent usage of the same desk daily (Berthelsen et al., 2018; Rolfö et al., 2018; Babapour, 2019), up to 86% in one study (Berthelsen et al., 2018). The popularity of desks and meeting rooms indicates that employees may be struggling to accept worksetting unavailability in Second-generation offices.

Some factors causing low switching behaviour are:

- Collaboration needs (Kim et al., 2016; Rolfö et al., 2018);
- Difficulty in moving files and personal belongings (Been et al., 2015; Babapour, 2019) owing, for example, to old age (Gorgievski et al., 2010);
- Guidelines ambiguity, with employees unsure how long they're allowed to occupy worksettings (Rolfö et al., 2018);
- Lack of variety in acoustics across worksettings (Rolfö et al., 2018);
- Loss of productivity owing to time-consuming tasks such as packing, unpacking, searching for a worksetting and adjusting it (Kim et al., 2016; Haapakangas et al., 2018; Rolfö et al., 2018; Babapour, 2019), which was exacerbated for employees that had to install ergonomic aids (Rolfö et al., 2018);
- Misfit between activities and worksettings (Gorgievski et al., 2010) such as low mobility profile;
- Non-compliance with speech guidelines at preferred worksettings (Babapour, 2019);
- Paper and book dependency (Gorgievski et al., 2010);
- Requirements to have materials close by (Babapour, 2019); and
- Social ties, norms and place attachments (Hoendervanger et al., 2016; Rolfö et al., 2018) and not wanting to feel 'homeless' and socially isolated (Becker and Steele, 1995).

Future research focusing on how employees experience the workplace and their involvement in the relocation process is required to ensure that the workplace is designed to suit their needs. This may involve more qualitative research to understand employees' experience rather than quantitative research that may limit their responses. Additionally, further research into whether a one-size-fits-all (employees of varying mobility profile) concept is appropriate is required. Even though a large variety of worksettings to suit various activities are provided, employees with little variation in their activity profiles and high paper-reliance are struggling to cope in ABWs.

Sense of community and belonging

Inconsistent results were found for social community and social support, with conflicting results between intra- and inter-team connections (Brummelhuis et al., 2012; Ekstrand and Hansen, 2016; Arundell et al., 2018; Berthelsen et al., 2018; Haapakangas et al., 2019). Whilst some studies found that non-face-to-face communications were responded to more promptly, preventing feelings of isolation (Brummelhuis et al., 2012), another ABW study in an academic setting reported that face-to-face socialising was rare, resulting in a deterioration of a sense of social community, and a deterioration in social support from colleagues and supervisors (Berthelsen et al., 2018).

Further research is required to investigate employees' sense of community and belonging and how this may vary across intra- and inter- team connections, and across industries. This points towards questioning whether a one-size fits all concept is appropriate across industries and various teams or exploring appropriate adjustments to create or improve the sense of community and belonging.

Satisfaction with the physical work environment

Inconsistent results on the satisfaction with regards to the physical work environment were found (Hoendervanger et al., 2016; Arundell et al., 2018; Berthelsen et al., 2018; Babapour Chafi and Rolfö, 2019). The physical environmental features influence employees' affective reactions as dissatisfaction with the physical features, resulting in employees reporting 'feelings of resignation towards the ABW' (Babapour, 2019).

This provides further support for future research on studying architectural features of ABW offices in-depth, as discussed earlier.

Health and wellbeing

The results on health and wellbeing were inconsistent (Been et al., 2015; Candido et al., 2016; Nijp et al., 2016; Tagliaro and Ciaramella, 2016b; Wohlers and Hertel, 2017; Arundell et al., 2018) with hygiene from sharing worksettings being a concern (Kim et al., 2016; Mesthrige and Chiang, 2019). Cleanliness was also found to be a dissatisfaction, but had limited impacts on productivity and wellbeing at work (Haapakangas et al., 2018). Employees' wellbeing was also found to have the strongest positive associations with satisfaction with the physical environment, privacy and communications (Haapakangas et al., 2018).

In a high space pressure environment, employees' health and wellbeing are at risk. Wellbeing levels declined when more than six minutes were spent looking for a workspace (Haapakangas et al., 2018) and when employees had to work on their laptop all day in a non-ergonomic worksetting (such as a kitchen) due to desks being unavailable, resulting in upper-body pain (Kim et al., 2016). This may result in more territorial behaviour, with employees arriving earlier to occupy their preferred worksetting, which also adversely impacts their work–life balance and wellbeing (Kim et al., 2016).

These results provide further support for more experience-based research to understand how employees' experience of the ABW affects their health and wellbeing and for more research to manage space pressure and cleanliness in the design phase and after moving into the ABW.

Technology

The few studies that evaluated technology found that it was a source of dissatisfaction (Haapakangas et al., 2018) and a challenging one to get right even when satisfaction levels were high (Brunia et al., 2016). Sources of technology dissatisfaction included the time consumed due to laptop cable connections and IT software updates (Brunia et al., 2016), complicated and inflexible IT systems (Been et al., 2015) and outdated technology limiting internet accessibility (Mosselman et al., 2009). To deal with the challenges of locating employees, an integration of technology to locate/find colleagues within the ABW office is proposed (Wohlers and Hertel, 2017).

Future research on seamless and functional technology to support the functioning of ABW offices is required, with a focus on both the design phase, when the technology to roll out is selected, and after moving into the ABW.

Implementation process

The ABW implementation process was quoted by interviewees as being in the top five positive and negative aspects of ABWs (Been et al., 2015). Several studies attributed undesirable outcomes to the implementation process:

- Lack of business objectives improvement (Blok et al., 2012);
- Lack of behavioural changes (Blok et al., 2012; Beltman, 2016);
- Lack of guidelines (Appel-Meulenbroek et al., 2011; Rolfö et al., 2018);
- Lack of compliance with guidelines (Appel-Meulenbroek et al., 2011; Rolfö et al., 2018); and
- Misfit between ABW and activities the employees conduct (Gorgievski et al., 2010).

Insufficient support and communications, such as employees having to proactively ask, resulted in a lack of knowledge, and inadequate ABW introduction negatively affected employees' experience of the ABW (Weerdenburg and Brunia, 2016).

However, employees' involvement and the communications from the implementation process could also positively impact employees' workplace acceptance (Brunia and Hartjes-Gosselink, 2009), ownership (Brunia and Hartjes-Gosselink, 2009) and guidelines acceptance (Babapour Chafi and Rolfö, 2019). Good communication or employees' involvement do not guarantee positive outcomes and may be limited if employees' feedback is not incorporated or addressed (Gorgievski et al., 2010; Berthelsen et al., 2018). For example, one study involved employees by gathering feedback and revealed that the preference for ABW amongst the academics was only 25%. Nevertheless, the university still proceeded with the ABW implementation (Berthelsen et al., 2018). On the contrary, when all employees were involved in both the decision-making process of adopting the ABW and the implementation process, very positive outcomes were achieved, such as increased perceived performance, satisfaction with the workplace environment, decreased distraction levels and positive affective reactions (inspiring, pleasant, calm) (Rolfö et al., 2017).

Two groups of employees that have to be focused upon pre- and post-implementation process are newly employed managers (Brunia and Hartjes-Gosselink, 2009) and employees moving from a private office (Haapakangas et al., 2019). Newly employed managers have struggled to accept the ABW as they have sought to find a position for themselves, resulting in an unsuitable management style and inability to lead by example (Brunia and Hartjes-Gosselink, 2009). Additionally, employees from private offices may experience the social support, quantitative demand and emotional demands more negatively than others from non-private offices (Haapakangas et al., 2019).

This provides further support for future research on the ABW implementation process and employees' involvement in it, as these aspects affect the physical ABW designed, the functional workplace guidelines and how employees experience the workplace change management process. It is critical to extend the research on the ABW implementation process to a few years post-moving in to study how the ABW can be continuously improved, how new employees are educated about the expected behaviours, how to maintain the ABW and how to monitor the space pressure within the workplace.

Workplace guidelines

The existing research indicates that employees are struggling to accept workplace guidelines and that the implementation process is crucial to address this. There is limited research specifically investigating the workplace guidelines in ABWs except for Rolfö and Babapour Chafi (2017) and Babapour Chafi and Rolfö (2019) who investigated the ABW workplace guidelines in four

Swedish organisations. Employees struggling to comply with the intended workplace guidelines led to the ABW malfunctioning (Babapour, 2019) and non-compliance introduced weaknesses into the ABW that reduced employees' mobility and autonomy (Babapour, 2019). The guidelines affected five working conditions: Autonomy, Physical resources, Mental resources, Intra-team resources and Inter-team resources (Babapour, 2019).

The primary issue with the workplace guidelines was their ambiguity due to implicit guidelines, lack of guidelines and lack of clarity in the communication of guidelines. This resulted in employees having different knowledge and interpretations of acceptable behaviour and negative affective reactions such as dissatisfaction, annoyance and confrontation (Weerdenburg and Brunia, 2016; Rolfö and Babapour Chafi, 2017; Arundell et al., 2018; Babapour Chafi and Rolfö, 2019). In some cases, the management intentionally had ambiguous, implicit guidelines to prevent employees from 'breaking rules'. However, employees preferred explicit rules to feel secure in their actions (Babapour Chafi and Rolfö, 2019). Guidelines that were explicitly and clearly communicated resulted in more positive work conditions and less physical and mental demands (Babapour, 2019).

Employees also used the lack of restrictions to justify their negligence and some implicit rules emerged that have the potential for workplace conflict (Babapour Chafi and Rolfö, 2019). The lack of a process to educate new employees on the workplace guidelines resulted in varying perceptions, as new employees were unaware of the guidelines (Mosselman, Gosselink and Beijer, 2009). Guidelines acceptance is even more crucial amongst newly employed managers as their management style will influence those under them (Brunia and Hartjes-Gosselink, 2009).

Confusion amongst employees also arose when the workplace guidelines dictating the activities accommodated conflicted with the design. In some instances, these confusions were due to implementation process errors (different colour of worksetting designed and implemented, when colours were a visual cue for activity type) (Skogland, 2017). In other instances, employees and the architects had conflicting perceptions of which activities were more suitable, and employees explained that some activities were naturally suited to the workplace design and their needs but contradicted the architects' intentions (Skogland, 2017). These two instances could have been avoided through the implementation process by avoiding errors and engaging employees in the workplace design process.

These points provide further support for more in-depth research on the functional workplace guidelines within ABW offices, the ABW implementation process pre- and post-moving in regarding how the functional workplace guidelines are designed and managed, and whether one-size-fits-all workplace guidelines are suitable for the various mobility teams within the organisation.

Summary

Several areas for future research have been identified throughout this chapter from reviewing the history of office workplaces, the historic drivers of workplace change and the current research on Activity Based Working offices, which are a form of innovative workplace whose adoption is forecast to increase in the future. Overall, the future direction of research on innovative workplaces is leaning towards transdisciplinary research to design an innovative workplace that can adapt to various changes, such as economic, social, technological and organisational drivers. Drivers of change should be integrated with the following disciplines in designing the physical and functional features of the future innovative workplace: Architecture, Corporate real estate, Facilities management, Workplace change management, Human resources management, Technology and Psychology.

References

Allen, T. J. and Gerstberger, P. G. (1973) 'A field experiment to improve communication in product engineering department: The nonterritorial office', *Human Factors*, 15(5), pp. 487–498. doi: 10.1177/001872087301500505.

Appel-Meulenbroek, R., Groenen, P. and Janssen, I. (2011) 'An end-user's perspective on activity-based office concepts', *Journal of Corporate Real Estate*, 13(2), pp. 122–135.

Appel-Meulenbroek, R., Oldman, T. and Susante, P. van (2016) 'How employees value the support of activity based and traditional work environments', in *Proceedings of the CIB World Building Congress*, pp. 296–304.

Aronoff, S. and Kaplan, A. G. (1995) *Total Workplace Performance: Rethinking the Office Environment*. Ottawa: WDL Publications, 1995. Available at: https://ezp.lib .unimelb.edu.au/login?url=https://search.ebscohost.com/login.aspx?direct=true& db=cat00006a&AN=melb.b2099092&site=eds-live&scope=site.

Arundell, L., Sudholz, B., Teychenne, M., Salmon, J., Hayward, B., Healy, G. N. and Timperio, A. (2018) 'The impact of activity based working (ABW) on workplace activity, eating behaviours, productivity, and satisfaction', *International Journal of Environmental Research and Public Health*, 15(5). doi: 10.3390/ijerph15051005.

Babapour, M. (2019) 'From fading novelty effects to emergent appreciation of activity-based flexible offices: Comparing the individual, organisational and spatial adaptations in two case organisations', *Applied Ergonomics*, 81(May), p. 102877. doi: 10.1016/j.apergo.2019.102877.

Babapour Chafi, M. and Rolfö, L. (2019) 'Policies in activity-based flexible offices – "I am sloppy with clean-desking. We don't really know the rules."', *Ergonomics*, 62(1), pp. 1–20. doi: 10.1080/00140139.2018.1516805.

Becker, F. D. and Steele, F. (1995) *Workplace by Design: Mapping the High-performance Workscape*. Jossey-Bass.

Becker, F., Quinn, K. L., Rappaport, A. J. and Sims, W. R. (1994) *The Ecology of New Ways of Working Implementing Innovative Workplaces: Organizational Implications of Different Strategies*. International Workplace Studies Program. New York.

Bedford, M. and Tong, D. (1997) 'Planning for diversity: New structures that reflect the past', *Reinventing the workplace*, Architectural Press, Oxford, pp. 64–75.

Been, I. De, Beijer, M. and Hollander, D. den (2015) 'How to cope with dilemmas in activity based work environments: Results from user-centred research', *EuroFM Research Papers 2015*, pp. 1–10.

Beltman, S. H. and van Diermen, O. G. (2016) 'Managing working behaviour towards new ways of working: A case study', *Journal of Corporate Real Estate*, 18(4), p. doi: 10.1108/JCRE-11-2015-0039.

Berthelsen, H., Muhonen, T. and Toivanen, S. (2018) 'What happens to the physical and psychosocial work environment when activity-based offices are introduced into academia?', *Journal of Corporate Real Estate*, 20(4), pp. 230–243. doi: 10.1108/JCRE-06-2017-0017.

Blok, M., De Korte, E. M., Groenesteijn, L., Formanoy, M. and Vink, P. (2009) 'The effects of a task facilitating work environment on office space use, communication, concentration, collaboration, privacy and distraction', in *Proceedings of the 17th World Congress on Ergonomics (IEA 2009)*. Beijing, China: International Ergonomics Association.

Blok, M. M., Groenesteijn, L., Schelvis, R. and Vink, P. (2012) 'New ways of working: Does flexibility in time and location of work change work behavior and affect business outcomes?', *Work*, 41(Suppl.1), pp. 2605–2610. doi: 10.3233/WOR-2012-1028-2605.

Brummelhuis, L. L. ten, Bakker, A. B., Hetland, J. and Keulemans, L. (2012) 'Do new ways of working foster work engagement?', *Psicothema*, 24(1), pp. 113–120. doi: 10.1108/PR-02-2017-0050.

Brunia, S., Been, I. De and Voordt, T. J. M. van der (2016) 'Accommodating new ways of working: Lessons from best practices and worst cases', *Journal of Corporate Real Estate*, 18(1), pp. 30–47.

Brunia, S. and Hartjes-Gosselink, A. (2009) 'Personalization in non-territorial offices: A study of a human need', *Journal of Corporate Real Estate*, 11(3), pp. 169–182. doi: 10.1108/14630010910985922.

Budd, C. (2001) 'The Office: 1950 to the Present', *Workspheres: Design and Contemporary Work Styles*, pp. 26–35.

Candido, C., Thomas, L., Haddad, S., Zhang, F., Mackey, M. and Ye, W. (2019) 'Designing activity-based workspaces: Satisfaction, productivity and physical activity', *Building Research and Information*, 47(3), pp. 275–289. doi: 10.1080/09613218.2018.1476372.

Candido, C., Zhang, J., Kim, J., deDear, R., Thomas, L. E., Strapasson, P. and Joko, C. (2016) 'Impact of workspace layout on occupant satisfaction, perceived health and productivity', *Windsor 2016*, (April), pp. 7–10.

Duerksen, G. J. (2012) 'Winning the war for talent', *International Food and Agribusiness Management Review*, 15(Special Issue A), pp. 13–17.

Duffy, F. (1992) *The Changing Workplace*. London: Phaidon, 1992. Available at: https:// ezp.lib.unimelb.edu.au/login?url=https://search.ebscohost.com/login.aspx?direct= true&db=cat00006a&AN=melb.b1691640&site=eds-live&scope=site.

Duffy, F., Cave, C. and Worthington, J. (2013) *Planning Office Space*. [Electronic resource]. Burlington: Elsevier Science. Available at: https://ezp.lib.unimelb.edu .au/login?url=https://search.ebscohost.com/login.aspx?direct=true&db=cat00006a &AN=melb.b5948126&site=eds-live&scope=site.

Duffy, F. and Powell, K. (1997) *The New Office*. London: Conrad Octopus.

Duffy, F. and Wankum, A. (1969) *Office Landscaping: A New Approach to Office Planning: Layout Planning in the Landscaped Office*. Anbar.

Ekstrand, M. (2016) 'Walk the talk: Creating a collaborative culture in an activity-based workplace', in *CIB Facilities Management Conference 2*, pp. 283–295.

Ekstrand, M. and Hansen, G. K. (2016) 'Make it work! Creating an integrated work-place concept', *Journal of Corporate Real Estate*, 18(1), pp. 17–29.

Forty, A. A. (1986) 'Taylorism and modern architecture', *Transactions*, 9(1), pp. 73–81.

Gatter, L. S. (1982) *The Office: An Analysis of the Evolution of a Workplace*. Massachusetts Institute of Technology.

Gorgievski, M. J., van der Voordt, T. J. M., van Herpen, S. G. A. and van Akkeren, S. (2010) 'After the fire', *Facilities*, 28(3/4), pp. 206–224. doi: 10.1108/02632771011023159.

Haapakangas, A., Hallman, D. M., Mathiassen, S. E. and Jahncke, H. (2018) 'Self-rated productivity and employee well-being in activity-based offices: The role of envi-ronmental perceptions and workspace use', *Building and Environment*, 145(June), pp. 115–124. doi: 10.1016/j.buildenv.2018.09.017.

Haapakangas, A., Hallman, D. M., Mathiassen, S. E. and Jahncke, H. (2019) 'The effects of moving into an activity-based office on communication, social relations and work demands – a controlled intervention with repeated follow-up', *Journal of Environmental Psychology*, 66(January), p. 101341. doi: 10.1016/j.jenvp.2019.101341.

Henry, D., Hunt, S. and Marasco, J. (2020). *The Future of the Office Space*. Colliers Insights (Vol. Office). Available at: https://doi.org/10.1177/0013916582145006.

Hoendervanger, J. G. et al. (2016) 'Flexibility in use', *Journal of Corporate Real Estate*, 18(1), pp. 48–62.

Keeling, T., Clements-Croome, D. and Roesch, E. (2015) 'The effect of agile workspace and remote working on experiences of privacy, crowding and satisfaction', *Buildings*, 5(3), pp. 880–898. doi: 10.3390/buildings5030880.

Kim, J., Candido, C., Thomas, L. and de Dear, R. (2016) 'Desk ownership in the work-place: The effect of non-territorial working on employee workplace satisfaction, per-ceived productivity and health', *Building and Environment*, 103(April), pp. 203–214.

Koetsveld, R. Van and Kamperman, L. (2011) 'How flexible workplace strategies can be made successful at the operational level', *Corporate Real Estate Journal*, 1(4), pp. 303–319.

Kuang, C. (2009) 'Evolution of office spaces reflects changing work attitudes towards work'. *Wired*. Available at: https://www.wired.com/2009/03/pl-design-5/.

Laing, A. (1997) 'New patterns of work: The design of the office', *Reinventing the Workplace*, Architectural Press, Oxford, pp. 23–38.

Lang, S., Smith, Y. R., Wightman, N. and Gardner, D. (2020) *Office FiT Survey Results: The Office is Vital, but Needs to Change*. Available at: https://pdf.savills.com/ documents/Savills-Office-FiT-Survey-Results_.pdf.

Mawson, A. (2002) *The Workplace and its Impact on Productivity, 4.* Publication No. 8, Advanced Workplace Associates, London. Available at: www.occupier.org.

Mesthrige, J. W. and Chiang, Y. H. (2019) 'The impact of new working practices on employee productivity: The first exploratory study in Asia', *Journal of Facilities Management,* 17(2), pp. 122–141. doi: 10.1108/JFM-03-2018-0020.

Mosselman, N., Gosselink, A. and Beijer, M. (2009) *Long-term Effects of Activity-based Working.* Holland Education, pp. 9–10.

Nenonen, I. K. S. (2016) 'Typologies for co-working places in Finland – what and how?', *Facilities,* 34(5/6).

Nijp, H. H., Beckers, D. G. J., van de Voorde, K., Geurts, S. A. E. and Kompier, M. A. J. (2016) 'Effects of new ways of working on work hours and work location, health and job-related outcomes', *Chronobiology International,* 33(6), pp. 604–618. doi: 10.3109/07420528.2016.1167731.

Ortony, A., Clore, G. L. and Foss, M. A. (1987) 'The referential structure of the affective lexicon', *Cognitive Science,* 11, pp. 341–364.

Petrulaitiene, V. and Tuuli, J. (2015) 'The perceived value of workplace concepts for organisations', *Journal of Corporate Real Estate,* 17(4), pp. 260–281. doi: 10.1108/ JCRE-06-2015-0014.

Rolfö, L. V. (2018) 'Relocation to an activity-based flexible office – design processes and outcomes', *Applied Ergonomics,* 73(June), pp. 141–150. doi: 10.1016/j. apergo.2018.05.017.

Rolfö, L. and Babapour Chafi, M. (2017) 'Policies for sharing workspaces in activity-based flex offices', pp. 339–344. Available at: http://www.diva-portal.org/ smash/record.jsf?pid=diva2%3A1136592&dswid=4056.

Rolfö, L., Eklund, J. and Jahncke, H. (2018) 'Perceptions of performance and satisfaction after relocation to an activity-based office', *Ergonomics,* 61(5), pp. 644–657. doi: 10.1080/00140139.2017.1398844.

Rolfö, L., Eliasson, K. and Eklund, J. (2017) 'An activity-based flex office: Planning processes and outcomes', *48th Annual Conference of the Association of Canadian Ergonomists: 12th International Symposium on Human Factors in Organizational Design and Management,* pp. 330–338.

Savills Real Estate Advisory. (2020). *Adapt: Easing Back to the Office.* Available at: https://www.savills.com.au/publications-pdf/office-fit-easingbackin-v2.pdf.

Seddigh, A., Berntson, E., Bodin Danielson, C. and Westerlund, H. (2014) 'Concentration requirements modify the effect of office type on indicators of health and performance', *Journal of Environmental Psychology,* 38, pp. 167–174. doi: 10.1016/j. jenvp.2014.01.009.

Skogland, M. A. C. (2017) 'The mindset of activity-based working', *Journal of Facilities Management,* 15(1), pp. 62–75. doi: 10.1108/JFM-05-2016-0016.

Stone, P. J. and Luchetti, R. (1985) 'Your office is where you are', *Harvard Business Review,* 63(2), pp. 102–117.

Sundstrom, E. D. and Sundstrom, M. G. (1986) *Work Places: The Psychology of the Physical Environment in Offices and Factories.* Cambridge, UK; New York: Cambridge University Press. Available at: https://ezp.lib.unimelb.edu.au/login?url =https://search.ebscohost.com/login.aspx?direct=true&db=cat00006a&AN=melb .b1392227&site=eds-live&scope=site.

Tagliaro, C. and Ciaramella, A. (2016a) 'Experiencing smart working: A case study on workplace change management in Italy', *Journal of Corporate Real Estate,* 18(3), pp. 194–208.

Tagliaro, C. and Ciaramella, A. (2016b) 'How to manage corporate real estate and end-users engagement into smart workplace change strategies: A case study', in *Proceedings of the CIB World Building Congress*, pp. 750–766.

Telsyte (2015) *Australian Digital Workplace Study 2015*. Available at: http://www.samsung.com/au/business/resources/activity-based-working-whitepaper.pdf.

Veldhoen + Company (no date) *What is Hot Desking?* Available at: http://www.veldhoencompany.com/en/publications/publication/1841/what-is-hot-desking/ (accessed 14 June 2016).

Voordt, T. J. M. Van Der (2004) 'Productivity and employee satisfaction in flexible workplaces', *Journal of Corporate Real Estate*, 6(2), pp. 133–148.

Vos, P. G. J. C. and Dewulf, G. P. R. M. (1999) *Searching for Data: A Method to Evaluate the Effects of Working in an Innovative Office*. Delft University Press.

Waber, B., Magnolfi, J. and Lindsay, G. (2014) 'Workspaces that move people', *Harvard Business Review*, 92(10), pp. 121–177.

Warner, L. (2013) *Activity Based Working: Impact on the Sydney CBD Office Market*. Jones Lang LaSalle and Property Council of Australia.

Weerdenburg, M. van and Brunia, S. (2016) *New Ways of Working: Sense Making Processes of Non-managerial Employees – A Case Study*. Center for People and Buildings, Delft, Netherlands, pp. 11–28.

Wohlers, C. and Hertel, G. (2017) 'Choosing where to work at work – towards a theoretical model of benefits and risks of activity-based flexible offices', *Ergonomics*, 60(4), pp. 467–486. doi: 10.1080/00140139.2016.1188220.

Wyllie, T., Green, M., Nagrath, R. and Town, A. (2012) *Activity Based Working*. Jones Lang LaSalle. Available at: http://www.jll.com.au/australia/en-au/Documents/jll-au-activity-based-working-2012.pdf.

5 Housing share: opportunities and challenges for interdisciplinary research

Djordje Stojanovic

Introduction

Housing share is an elusive term because it involves different aspects of housing, it thrives in varied forms of tenure, it assumes various ways of provision and includes diverse property ownership. The objective of this chapter is to establish a backdrop against which procurement of specific housing projects could be investigated further, and against which beneficial aspects of housing share could be studied and upscaled to become a more viable alternative in housing provision.

Housing share is not a scholarly term and has no exact and agreed-upon meaning. However, the concept of shared living is increasingly receiving attention from researchers across several disciplines such as architecture, property, planning, sociology and urban geography. While researchers have recognized an increase of shared housing in developed countries and have made attempts to contextualize this trend within the broader field of housing policy research, housing share remains understudied from an interdisciplinary perspective capable of encompassing its multifaceted nature.

Shared living is defined as housing shared with non-kin (Heath et al. 2018). It implies the joint use of living space in many forms of communal living, varying in tenure, ownership, development, and management, while many different housing forms may be associated with the emergence of this elusive housing trend.

Communal living is associated with financial necessities and practical reasons or deliberate intentions to live in a community (Vestbro 1992). Demographic changes, such as the growing population along with income stagnation and inflation of housing prices, have resulted in a lack of affordable housing solutions in many cities. They have contributed to the rising of the rental sector (Kemp 2015) and the surge of home-sharing in short-term and long-term rentals (Maalsen 2020). An increase of non-nuclear family households, such as single-person households and single-parent families, resulting from diversified lifestyles may have contributed to the growing demand for alternative housing solutions, including housing share. As a result, commercially driven providers of co-living rental solutions have appeared in London, New York and some other cities adding another dimension to the spectrum of housing share options. In addition to the rental sector, there is also a growing number of homeownership schemes based on different ways of space sharing. Balancing between private dwellings and communal areas and rooms, developed on co-housing principles (McCamant and Durrett 1994) and often through a cooperative model and a form of social economy, such schemes have proved to be viable options for residents. They could be examined closely for their housing provision potential at a larger scale (Tummers 2015a, 2015b).

Space sharing is becoming a defining characteristic of many different housing forms. To that end there is a need to improve the understanding of ownership, development, management and investment potentials enabling housing share options. This chapter aims to establish a platform for further research leading to a better understanding of housing share and its potential implications on planning policies and trends in the property market. An introduction to different housing models, which are detailed later in the chapter, may help the reader understand different aspects of shared housing.

This chapter will proceed as follows. The literature review and the clarification of critical terms will be provided in the first part. With references to recent research efforts, the focus on housing share will be established through an overview of the following topics: sharing economy and short-term rentals, private rented sector, knowledge economy and co-living, co-housing and user participation, cooperatives and social economy, and self-development housing groups. The discussion concentrates on establishing the grounding for deeper research into housing share through qualitative and quantitative methods. In conclusion, the case for further cross-disciplinary research and intersectoral collaboration involving multiple stakeholders is presented.

Short-term rentals

How are innovative economic models impacting housing provision? The sharing economy refers to an "economic model that involves creating access to underutilized resources" (Ferrell et al. 2017, p. 3) and provides an "alternative to ownership" (Belk 2007; Ferrell et al. 2017, p. 4; Weber 2014). The short-term rentals exemplify this model by providing access to the underutilized property. However, despite the common denominator in their names, shared economy and shared living are not necessarily the same. In fact, quantitative studies have shown that a vast majority of bookings made through Airbnb are made for the entire place and not for a room within an existing household, resulting in temporary cohabitation (Alizadeh et al. 2018).

What is the broader impact of short-term rentals on residential neighbour-hoods? The emergence of Airbnb that is "practically synonymous with the sharing economy" (Schor 2014; Crommelin et al. 2018, p. 430), has trans-formed the market of short-term and vacation rentals (Guttentag 2015). It is recognized that short-term rental business conducted via an online platform is "delivering advantages and new forms of opportunities for local and national economies" (Crommelin et al. 2018, p. 430), but that the scale and impacts of the phenomenon are not being fully assessed by urban researchers (Gurran 2018). The influence of sharing economies on residential neighbourhoods has both positive and negative sides (Ioannides et al. 2019). Amongst the negative effects is the "removing properties from the market for long-term rental or purchase" (Crommelin et al. 2018, p. 429). Airbnb is "absorbing permanent housing stock" (Gurran 2018, p. 300). In response, some local governments are trying to regulate short-term rentals by imposing limits such as "the number of guests, nights and times a property can be rented, demands certain safety precautions and information provision, or requires primary residency" (Nieuwland and van Melik 2020, p. 811).

Private rented sector

Is diversification of housing share options related to the growth of the private rented sector? Much like short-term rentals discussed in the previous section, the entire private rented sector is on the rise and now stands for a signifi-cant portion of overall housing tenures. Evidence-based studies show that owner-occupation tenure has been falling since the early 2000s in developed countries: "In recent years, the private rented sector in Britain, for example, has grown in size after many years of decline" (Kemp 2015, p. 601). And "After peaking at around 70% between 2003 and 2005 in the UK, the USA and Australia, rates of owner-occupation in all three countries began to fall, driven by diminishing entry among the young" (Ronald 2018, p. 17). Other research points out the changing nature of this sector: "Once a transitional tenure in the

UK, the private rented sector is now housing more and more young people, and for longer periods of their lives" (McKee et al. 2019, p. 1). It is also true that there are more nuclear families along with low-income groups such as students, migrants and young professionals relying on the evolving private rental market (Rugg and Rhodes 2018).

Who is renting and sharing their home? "The inability of young people to realise the 'normalised' goal of homeownership is hugely significant" (McKee 2012, p. 844). Researchers are now using the term "Generation Rent" to define a cohort of young people who are dependent on private rent, as homeownership is not something they can afford (Crawford and McKee 2018; Hoolachan et al. 2017; McKee 2012; McKee et al. 2019; Ronald 2018). The spike in rental housing tenure is identified as an intergenerational problem (Willets 2011), and a consequence of a divide between the older home-owning generation of Baby Boomers and the ownership-deprived younger population of Millennials (Hoolachan and McKee 2019; Willets 2011). Moreover, the gap extends into further housing inequalities within the younger generation (Searle 2018; McKee et al. 2019) as mechanisms of intra-family and intergenerational support facilitate easier access to homeownership (Druta and Ronald 2017).

The formal rules and informal practices that characterize the private rented sector have changed (Kemp 2015). "Long-term renting has been increasingly bound, especially since the Financial Crisis, with sharing and co-living as well as more chaotic housing pathways, which has significant implications for long-term household formation and adult life-course transitions" (Ronald 2018, p 21). Researchers who gathered information from an online flatmate-finding platform (flatmates.com.au) show that the share housing market grew by more than 36 per cent in 2015 in Australia (Maalsen 2019). "One of the leading UK shared housing websites, SpareRoom, has seen the number of adverts placed on its site rise from 140,000 in 2010 to 700,000 in 2016, a five-fold increase" (Heath et al. 2018). The primary reasons for sharing a home with unrelated occupants remain of a financial and social nature around the world. In China, where housing share is a relatively stable residential choice, the results of a study based on a questionnaire survey and case studies found that economic considerations are the most important motivation for entering housing share (Wang and Otsuki 2016). In Japan, the rise of housing share "both enables the pursuit of new experiences of 'home' and further entrenches traditionalist views of the needs and wants of solo dwellers" (Druta and Ronald 2020, p. 1).

In addition to different forms of rental living arrangements which stipulate sharing of only certain facilities between tenants, "room sharing with strangers has become an important form of housing in many global cities" (Nasreen and Ruming 2019, p. 151). The same study points out "how room sharing practices simultaneously provide an affordable housing option for tenants and maximize rental returns for landlords" (Nasreen and Ruming 2019, p. 152). At the same time, other researchers identify the increase of intentional community living arrangements in Australia (Hilder et al. 2018) and suggest that a "growing public awareness of the benefits of communal living is likely to place pressure upon planners" (Hilder et al. 2018, p. 12). However, housing share still stands for "informal and unregulated subsection of the rental market" (Maalsen 2019). "A survey conducted by the Tenants' Union of NSW (2017) found that more than three-quarters of respondents in shared housing live without written sub-tenancy agreements and legal protection against unfair eviction" (Nasreen and Ruming 2019, p.152).

The increase of housing share in private rentals is sustained with the development of information and communication technologies (Maalsen 2020). Digitally mediated peer-to-peer platforms have supported the escalation of the rental market and housing share options, as an opportunity for living with strangers has expanded (Parkinson et al. 2020). The impact of online platforms on longer-term rentals is as equally transformative as the emergence of businesses based on sharing economy principles discussed in the previous chapter.

> This juxtaposition of exploitation, trust and reciprocity reveal three types of exchange where the trust cultures within the informal shared rental household adapt and become more easily facilitated through peer-to-peer platforms, which we term as – the live-in host, the affordable rental hoarder, and the room rental entrepreneur. (Parkinson et al. 2020, p. 8)

Such forms of housing facilitation demonstrate the proliferation of the private rental sector by simultaneously including elements of provision, tenure, and property management. Platforms such as Flatmate finders, which currently gains 2700 members weekly in Australia, uses personal information and algorithms, similar to online dating techniques, to match flatmates (www .flatmatefinders.com.au). Research into such flatmate matching and other platforms facilitating financial transactions for home rental leads researchers to suggest that "thinking of home as shared, rented and digitalized forces us to rethink classic housing career trajectories" (Maalsen 2020, p. 107).

Co-living

Different from self-organized housing share in the private rented sector, co-living is a "for-profit, intentional, purpose-driven, privately managed and delivered shared housing, emerging as a commercial [response] to the specific needs of young professionals sharing in large cities" (Heath et al. 2018, p. 129). Co-living is becoming a profitable real estate industry. For example, in London alone, companies have invested more than one billion pounds into co-living spaces (www.space10.com). Commercially driven providers such as Node, Common, and Roam in the US, Medici Living in Germany, the Collective Old Oak in the UK, and Tokyo Share House in Japan offer housing solutions located in central zones of big cities, carefully tailored according to the needs of young professionals, often combining informal workspaces and recreational facilities with dwelling spaces. Moreover, the industry is expanding to include other social groups. For example, the recently established company 'Kin', an offshoot of 'Common', is an inner New York provider of co-living solutions for families and their offer is focused on "kid-friendly spaces and on-site childcare solutions" (www.kinfamilies.com). Similar to the hotel industry, they offer all-inclusive housing packages, easing the procedural burden associated with property rentals.

The Association of Coliving Professionals states that motives for the co-living industry include rapid urbanisation and increasing population, increasing property values, rising rents, new working patterns, and social values (www .co-liv.org 2020). While co-living includes aspects of short and longer-term rentals, it is a concept that could be brought into relation with boarding homes that originated in Northern Europe at the turn of the century and workers' settlements that predated modern living. A renewed interest in this form of housing is in its appeal to a large group of residents whose income is tied to the knowledge economy. The group is characterized by their ability to work remotely, from home or elsewhere. Their employment is usually sessional and often requiring relocation from one city to another. All of this, coupled with the barriers to homeownership faced by the younger generation as well as deterring complexities of the framework regulating the private rented sector discussed in the previous section, make co-living an attractive and viable option. Perceived benefits are not only practical and financial but also social. Co-living also offers an instant way into a community and a possibility of establishing social contacts.

Co-housing

In owner-occupied tenure, as in the rental sector, housing share appears in a variety of forms. In co-housing, private dwellings are combined with communal facilities. Communal use of housing space has both practical and social benefits, and the creation of a community is made part of the housing solution. Co-housing is understood as a long-term housing solution. Vestbro (1992), places co-housing amongst five collective housing models that have originated in Northern Europe at the turn of the twentieth century. The defining characteristic of collective housing is a provision of communal spaces or collectively organized facilities, which may not be found in conventional housing (Vestbro 2000). There is a distinction between the Danish version of collective housing, which is oriented toward creating a sense of community between residents, and the Swedish version, which is more pragmatic and primarily focused on reducing housework (Vestbro 1992). In Denmark, 'bofællesskab' living communities were formed to replace living within the nuclear family, while in Sweden, 'kollektivhuse' provided a way to rationalize everyday life and, in particular, to help women access the labour market (Gutzon Larsen 2019). The co-housing model was popularized in the US in the early 1990s by McCamant and Durrett, acknowledging the housing solution which originated in Denmark. The concept was inspired by values of traditional living and vernacular architecture, namely a strong sense of the community between residents.

> In Denmark, people frustrated by the available housing options have developed a new housing type that redefines the concept of neighbourhood to fit contemporary lifestyles. Tired of the isolation and impracticalities of single-family house and apartment units, they have built housing that combines the autonomy of the private dwelling with the advantages of community living. Each household has a private residence, but also shares extensive common facilities with the larger group, such as a kitchen and dining hall, children playroom, workshops, guest rooms, and laundry facilities. (McCamant and Durrett 1994, p. 12)

More "recent literature has described the re-emergence of cohousing as pragmatic, rather than utopian" (Tummers 2016, p. 2333). "It is argued the cohousing formula produces a cooperative and communitarian organization rationally constituted in order to ensure not only a livelihood but also a higher quality of life and a higher degree of socialization inside and outside the community" (Ruiu 2016, p. 168). Over the past few decades, many co-housing projects have been delivered in the US and other countries, such as Germany, Switzerland and, most recently, in Spain and Australia. While there is a significant difference between them, arising from the specifics of legal frameworks and economic circumstances in each of these countries, "it is important to recognize that the underlying concept is essentially socio-spatial rather than specifying a particular legal and financial model of land purchase or construction" (Jarvis 2015, p. 95).

The impact of co-housing on urban planning and socio-spatial development is a worthy research topic. Some researchers point out the adverse effects. For example, "Danish cohousing was almost exclusively based on that hallmark of bourgeois society: individual property rights in the form of owner-occupation" (Gutzon Larsen 2019, p. 1356). Furthermore, doubts are also raised "about a completely positive interpretation of the phenomenon and about policies for promoting it" (Chiodelli and Baglione 2014, p. 20). The debate on the similarities between co-housing and gated communities suggests that "both types of the community tend to exclude the poor because of the costs of accessing housing units" (Chiodelli 2015, p. 2568).

Some of the key aspects of co-housing are user participation in the design process, management of the communal spaces and "consensus-based collective self-governance" (Jarvis 2011). It is described as a set of "micro-social practices that self-organising resident groups engage in over the years that it takes to build a cohousing community" (Jarvis 2015, p. 93). Both procurement and management of co-housing solutions "requires a great effort of inhabitants in terms of intentionality, time, financial resources, and willingness to collaborate and negotiate private stakes" (Ruiu 2016 p. 168). "There are a variety of inter-related terms used both in practice and in the literature, often interchangeably, to refer to collective self-organised housing, such as collaborative housing, community-led, resident-led, participative housing or cohousing" (Czischke 2018, p. 57). What unifies them is that "through collective self-organisation, households can benefit from the power of collective action and capital" (Palmer 2020, p. 3).

Self-development housing groups

Co-housing schemes are commonly based on private investment, and owner occupation. The achievements of cooperative self-development housing groups (*Baugruppen*) in Germany are widely reported. In Berlin, "in the '90s, the city government even gave financial and institutional support to self-organized housing projects under a self-build housing programme" (Droste, 2015 p. 85). By 2003, the Berlin Senate had ceased funding housing construction (Ring 2013) and the Federal government's withdrawal of housing subsidies in 2006 completed the shift from state-led to market-led provision (Palmer 2020).

Together, a tradition of progressive housing provision and a pressing need led to increased activity of collective and cooperative self-development housing. The expansion was also enabled with the existence of the legal framework, which recognizes self-development and housing groups. Researchers report that, as a result, in Germany, "over half of all new homes are produced independently from volume-build developers" (Hamiduddin and Gallent 2016, p. 365). However, not all of it is delivered with the financial backing from local municipalities, nor it is enabled through a co-production economy, as discussed in the previous section.

Self-development groups receive a critique for their "exclusionary path to housing delivery" (Hamiduddin and Gallent 2016) "largely because of the wealth required to participate" (Sharam 2020, p. 107). However, self-development achieves two important goals in developing housing solutions according to users' needs and in financial saving, which comes from removing the cost of developers' fees. Researchers, therefore, make the distinction between developer-led speculative development and resident-led collaborative self-organized housing provision or "deliberative development" (Sharam 2020, p. 107). In Australia, collective self-development is exemplified in the Nightingale Model, which inherits some of the Baugruppen ideas and applies some of the co-housing principles, including the participation of residents during the design and construction process, and distinguishes itself from speculative development. This development approach is architect-led, maintaining the transparency of the process and enabling residents' engagement (Nighingalehousing.org 2020). The first housing project delivered via this model has been highly recognized and awarded both in Australia and internationally. This niche model offers itself to upscaling into the housing industry (Doyon and Moore 2019). Currently, there are several completed and a few more ongoing projects, while demand is exceeding production to the extent that the purchase of Nightingale housing is subject to the balloting process (Nighingalehousing.org 2020).

> What is required now is to develop a better understanding of the processes and opportunities that such housing models offer policymakers, housing researchers, and building industry stakeholders to achieve a broader scale uptake of sustainable housing both in Australia and globally. (Moore and Doyon 2018, p. 1)

Cooperatives

Co-housing solutions are also delivered by cooperatives through means of social economy. In some countries, such as the Swiss Confederation, community-led provision of housing is rooted in traditions and "housing cooperatives are not only supported by public authorities but have also recently been promoted through new political interventions at the local level" (Balmer and Gerber 2018, p. 362). Researchers have identified core benefits such as social capital, housing quality and stability, health and wellbeing, skills acquisition, lower operating costs, and broader economic or development outcomes (Crabtree et al. 2019). In Spain, the establishment of housing tenures such as surface rights, shared and temporary homeownership, and cessation of use has enabled the application of social economy in the provision of innovative housing solutions, such as a recently completed project in the Can Batllo neighbourhood of Barcelona (Cabré and Andrés 2018). The project is developed by a La Borda cooperative and based on the Andel model, first developed in Denmark, allowing for a long-term or indefinite use rather than ownership of the property. In this way, cooperatives enable "housing options that sit between the historically dual tenure poles of renting and owning" (Crabtree et al. 2019, p. 1). One of the defining elements of the recently completed project in Barcelona is the agreement between the cooperative and the City Council to transfer surface rights for the affordable levy for 75 years (Cabré and Andrés 2018). The project is delivered through the social economy framework, with participation of professionals and businesses belonging to the network of cooperatives (Cabré and Andrés 2018).

Discussion and conclusions

After referencing recent research efforts focusing on different forms of housing share, this section will discuss potential topics for future studies. The aim is to set grounding for more in-depth research into housing share through both qualitative and quantitative methods. An overview of well-known housing models featuring shared housing aspects is provided in Table 5.1. The summary is carried according to four main categories named: spatial configuration, tenure type, household type and size, and provider type.

The short-term rentals category based on sharing economy principles and the use of underutilized housing resources may have more significance in future as the solution appeals to tourists but also workers who travel for work between cities. Further research into short term rentals may help develop a better understanding of provision mechanisms as well as patterns of occupation and use. Acquiring accurate data may be of use to predict its impact on the property market, while its implications on the local communities could be taken into account with planning and development policies. Likewise, the success of sharing economies achieved in the short term rental sector may potentially

Table 5.1 Overview of housing systems incorporating shared housing aspects

		Short-term Rentals	Private-rented	Co-living	Co-housing	Self-development	Co-operatives
Spatial Con-figuration (shared use of space)	Bedroom	Y	Y	N	N	N	N
	Living Area	Y	Y	Y	Y	N	Y
	Kitchen	Y	Y	Y	Y	N	Y/N
	Laundry	Y	Y	Y	Y	Y/N	Y
	Outdoor Area	Y	Y	Y	Y	Y	Y
Tenure Type	Informal Rental Agreement	Y	Y	N	N	N	N
	Formal Short-Term Rental Agreement	Y	Y	Y	N	N	N
	Formal Mid-Term Rental Agreement	N	Y	Y	N	N	N
	Formal Long-Term Rental Agreement	N	Y	N	N	N	Y
	Ownership	N	N	N	Y	N/Y	N
Household Size and Type	Single Person Household	Y	Y	Y	Y	Y	Y
	Couples	Y	Y	Y	Y	Y	Y
	Families with Children	N	Y	Y/N	Y	Y	Y
	Multi-generation Families	N	N	Y	N	Y	N
Provider	Public: Government	N	N	N	N	N	N
	Private: Speculative	N	Y	Y	N	N/Y	N
	Private: Non-speculative	N	N	N	Y	Y	Y
	Inter-sectoral	N	N	N	Y	Y	Y

hold significance for other forms of tenure. Researchers suggest that "one critical area for housing policy research in the coming years is exploring whether there are lessons to be gleaned from the sharing economy, exemplified by companies like Uber and Airbnb" (Gould Ellen 2015, p. 783). From the perspective focused on low-income households, more research is needed toward innovative forms of tenure, which may include "time-limited subsidies" and "market-rate rental buildings in many urban areas that allow for new forms of shared living" (Gould Ellen 2015, p. 784).

The private rented category could benefit from studies that would help create better tenancy regulations. Since homeownership is proving to be more difficult for younger generations, in particular, a better understanding of the rental sector is required. There is a need for deeper research into the provision of affordable and accessible rental stock. The impact of planning policies and development strategies on the provision of rental housing solutions offers itself as a topic for further research. In addition to the examination of the planning framework, further research should be conducted to inform the regulatory context. An important research question is how communal living can be regularized to grant tenure security yet allowing easy entry and exit for tenants.

The recent emergence of the co-living model has not received enough research attention. Its defining features include aspects of both short and longer-term rentals, and further studies may inquire into the dual nature of this new form of housing tenure, which sits halfway between vacation rentals and the private rented sector. The transitory nature of this housing solution is an intriguing topic for more in-depth research. Equally important would be to look at the impact of the co-living industry on other housing systems and the property market.

The continuing research interest in the co-housing model is sustained for its potential for innovative housing provision (Tummers 2015b). Co-housing benefits are already captured in a series of qualitative studies, while quantitative research could help develop further insights. The role of local authorities for the development of co-housing initiatives has been highlighted (Lang and Stoeger 2018), and further research could help formulate specific investment and development frameworks relevant to local conditions. While "some municipalities have adopted this model as a key element in housing and neighbourhood policies" (Droste 2015, p. 79), further research is needed to investigate how to upscale co-housing projects into the mainstream housing provision. While it is understood that user participation and community building play an important role in the co-housing model, the relationship between resident communities and institutional stakeholders including housing providers and local authorities is less well understood (Czischke 2018).

In the context of this chapter, a model delivered by self-development housing groups is posited separately from the co-housing model as its defining characteristics are related to the provision of housing, and not to its social or spatial nature. In contrast to a developer-led speculative approach, a self-development model is a deliberative housing development, and it is based on users' ability to take on the risk of development to pursue their housing needs (Sharam 2020). Further research into finance and land procurement solutions for self-development housing would be significant to provide users access to this model.

The lack of housing options demands continued studies and a better understanding of new economic approaches. Further research is needed to understand and to develop housing tenures that go beyond the duality of home ownership and rental (Feather 2018). More in-depth research into the potential of an upscaling cooperative model could help the provision of affordable housing. "The diversity in cooperative forms can make comparison difficult and also make it hard to identify appropriate policies and incentives to enable cooperatives to grow and diversify" (Crabtree et al. 2019, p. 2). In addition to economic innovations, improvement of housing systems is dependent on the adequate regulatory framework. The legal form is crucial for a co-housing project because it links the conceptual level with the very important financial level (Ache and Fedrowitz 2012).

This chapter presents the need for further studies into the housing share and a sustained inquiry into the housing models focusing on the communal use of space. It builds the case for further interdisciplinary research and intersectoral collaboration to improve financial, legal, and planning mechanisms enabling innovative housing solutions. The provided overview of recent research aims to establish a platform for further studies leading to a better understanding of housing share and its implications on planning policies and trends in the property market. To that end, the opportunities and challenges for advanced studies are observed through the involvement of multiple stakeholders and innovative partnerships in housing provision.

References

Ache, C. and Fedrowitz, M. (2012). The development of co-housing initiatives in Germany. Co-housing in the making. *Built Environment*, 38(3), 406.

Alizadeh, T., Farid, R., and Sarkar S. (2018). Towards understanding the socio-economic patterns of sharing economy in Australia: An investigation of Airbnb listings in Sydney and Melbourne metropolitan regions. *Urban Policy and Research*, 36(4), 445–463.

Balmer, B. and Gerber, J.D. (2018). Why are housing cooperatives successful? Insights from Swiss affordable housing policy. *Housing Studies*, 33(3), 361–385.

Belk, R.W. (2007). Why not share rather than own? *Annals of the American Academy of Political and Social Science*, 611(1), 126–140.

Cabré, E. and Andrés A. (2018). La Borda: A case study on the implementation of cooperative housing in Catalonia. *International Journal of Housing Policy*, 18(3).

Chiodelli, F. (2015). What is really different between cohousing and gated communities? *European Planning Studies*, 23(12), 2566–2581.

Chiodelli, F. and Baglione, V. (2014). Living together privately: For a cautious reading of cohousing. *Urban Research & Practice*, 7(1), 20–34.

Crabtree, L., Perry N., Grimstad, S., and McNeill. J. (2019). Impediments and opportunities for growing the cooperative housing sector: An Australian case study. *International Journal of Housing Policy*, 21, 138–152.

Crawford, J. and McKee, K. (2018). Hysteresis: Understanding the housing aspirations gap. *Sociology*, 52(1), 182–197.

Crommelin, L., Troy, L., Martin, C., and Pettit, C. (2018). Is Airbnb a sharing economy superstar? Evidence from five global cities. *Urban Policy and Research*, 36(4), 429–444.

Czischke, D. (2018). Collaborative housing and housing providers: Towards an analytical framework of multi-stakeholder collaboration in housing co-production. *International Journal of Housing Policy*, 18(1), 55–81.

Doyon, A. and Moore, T. (2019). The acceleration of an unprotected niche: The case of Nightingale housing, Australia. *Cities*, 92, 18–26.

Droste, C. (2015). German co-housing: An opportunity for municipalities to foster socially inclusive urban development? *Urban Research & Practice*, 8(1), 79–92.

Druta, O. and Ronald, R. (2017). 'Young adults' pathways into homeownership and the negotiation of intra-family support: A home, the ideal gift. *Sociology*, 51, 783–799.

Druta, O. and Ronald, R. (2020). Living alone together in Tokyo share houses. *Social & Cultural Geography*, 22(9), 1223–1240.

Feather, C. (2018). Between homeownership and rental housing: Exploring the potential for hybrid tenure solutions. *International Journal of Housing Policy*, 18(4), 595–606.

Ferrell, C., Ferrell, L., and Huggins, K. (2017). Seismic shifts in the sharing economy: Shaking up marketing channels and supply chains. *Journal of Marketing Channels*, 24(1-2), 3–12.

Gould Ellen, I. (2015). Housing low-income households: Lessons from the sharing economy? *Housing Policy Debate*, 25(4), 783–784.

Gurran, N. (2018). Global home-sharing, local communities and the Airbnb debate: A planning research agenda. *Planning Theory & Practice*, 19(2), 298–304.

Guttentag, D. (2015). Airbnb: Disruptive innovation and the rise of an informal tourism accommodation sector. *Current Issues in Tourism*, 18(12), 1192–1217.

Gutzon Larsen, H. (2019). Three phases of Danish cohousing: Tenure and the development of an alternative housing form. *Housing Studies*, 34(8), 1349–1371.

Hamiduddin, I. and Gallent, N. (2016). Self-build communities: The rationale and experiences of group-build (Baugruppen) housing development in Germany. *Housing Studies*, 31(4), 365–383.

Heath, S., Davies, K., Edwards, G., and Scicluna, R.M. (2018). *Shared Housing, Shared Lives: Everyday Experiences across the Lifecourse*. Oxon: Routledge.

Hilder, J., Charles-Edwards, E., Sigler T., and Metcalf B. (2018). Housemates, inmates and living mates: Communal living in Australia. *Australian Planner*, 55(1), 12–27.

Hoolachan, J. and McKee, K. (2019). Inter-generational housing inequalities: 'Baby Boomers' versus the 'Millennials'. *Urban Studies*, 56, 210–225.

Hoolachan, J., McKee, K., Moore, T., and Soaita, A.M. (2017). 'Generation rent' and the ability to settle down: Economic and geographical variation in young people's housing transitions. *Journal of Youth Studies*, 20, 63–78.

Ioannides, D., Röslmaier, M., and van der Zee, E. (2019). Airbnb as an instigator of 'tourism bubble' expansion in Utrecht's Lombok neighbourhood. *Tourism Geographies*, 21(5), 822–840.

Jarvis, H. (2011). Saving space, sharing time: Integrated infrastructures of daily life in cohousing. *Environment and Planning A: Economy and Space*, 43(3), 560–577.

Jarvis, H. (2015). Towards a deeper understanding of the social architecture of co-housing: Evidence from the UK, USA and Australia. *Urban Research & Practice*, 8(1), 93–105.

Kemp, P. (2015). Private renting after the global financial crisis. *Housing Studies*, 30(4), 601–620.

Lang, R. and Stoeger, H. (2018). The role of the local institutional context in understanding collaborative housing models: Empirical evidence from Austria. *International Journal of Housing Policy*, 18(1), 35–54.

Maalsen, S. (2019). I cannot afford to live alone in this city and I enjoy the company of others: Why people are share housing in Sydney. *Australian Geographer*, 50(3), 315–332.

Maalsen, S. (2020). 'Generation Share': Digitalized geographies of shared housing. *Social & Cultural Geography*, 21(1), 105–113.

McCamant, K. and Durrett, C. (1994). *Cohousing: A Contemporary Approach to Housing Ourselves*. Berkeley, CA: Ten Speed Press.

McKee, K. (2012). Young people, homeownership and future welfare. *Housing Studies*, 27(6), 853–862.

McKee, K., Soaita, A.M., and Hoolachan J. (2019). 'Generation rent' and the emotions of private renting: Self-worth, status and insecurity amongst low-income renters. *Housing Studies*, 35(8), 1468–1487.

Moore, T. and Doyon, A. (2018). The uncommon nightingale: Sustainable housing innovation in Australia. *Sustainability*, 10, 3468–3485.

Nasreen, Z. and Ruming K. (2019). Room sharing in Sydney: A complex mix of affordability, overcrowding and profit maximisation. *Urban Policy and Research*, 37(2), 151–169.

Nieuwland, S. and van Melik, R. (2020). Regulating Airbnb: How cities deal with perceived negative externalities of short-term rentals. *Current Issues in Tourism*, 23(7), 811–825.

Nightingale Housing (2020). Available from: www.nightingalehousing.org (accessed 14 November 2021).

Palmer, J.S. (2020). Realising collective self-organised housing: A network agency perspective. *Urban Policy and Research*, 38(2), 1–17.

Parkinson, S., James, A., and Liu, E. (2020). Luck and leaps of faith: How the digital informal economy transforms the geographies of shared renting in Australia. *Social & Cultural Geography*, 22(9), 1274–1290.

Ring, K. (2013). *Self-made City*. Berlin: Jovis.

Ronald, R. (2018). 'Generation rent' and intergenerational relations in the era of housing financialisation. *Critical Housing Analysis*, 5(2), 14–26.

Rugg, J. and Rhodes, D. (2018). *The Evolving Private Rented Sector: Its Contribution and Potential*. Research Report. York: Centre for Housing Policy.

Ruiu, M.L. (2016). Participatory processes in designing cohousing communities: The case of the community project. *Housing and Society*, 43(3), 168–181.

Schor, J. (2014). Debating the sharing economy. A great transition initiative essay. Available from: http://www.greattransition.org/publication/debating-the-sharing-economy (accessed 14 November 2021).

Searle, B.A. (2018). *Generational Interdependencies: The Social Implications for Welfare*. Delaware, USA: Vernon Press.

Sharam A. (2020). Deliberative development: Australia's Baugruppen movement and the challenge of greater social inclusion. *Housing Studies*, 35(1), 107–122.

Tummers, L. (2015a). Understanding co-housing from a planning perspective: Why and how? *Urban Research & Practice*, 8(1), 64–78.

Tummers, L. (2015b). Introduction to the special issue: Towards a long-term perspective of self-managed collaborative housing initiatives. *Urban Research & Practice*, 8(1), 1–4.

Tummers, L. (2016). The re-emergence of self-managed co-housing in Europe: A critical review of co-housing research. *Urban Studies*, 53(10), 2023–2040.

Vestbro, D.U. (1992). *From Central Kitchen to Community Co-Operation – Development of Collective Housing in Sweden*. Stockholm: Royal Institute of Technology.

Vestbro, D.U. (2000). From collective housing to cohousing – a summary of research. *Journal of Architectural and Planning Research*, 17(2), 164–178.

Wang, Y. and Otsuki, T. (2016). A study on house sharing in China's young generation – based on a questionnaire survey and case studies in Beijing. *Journal of Asian Architecture and Building Engineering*, 15(1), 17–24.

Weber, T.A. (2014). Intermediation in a sharing economy: Insurance, moral hazard, and rent extraction. *Journal of Management Information Systems*, 31(3), 35–71.

Willetts, D. (2011). *The Pinch: How the Baby Boomers Took Their Children's Future – and Why They Should Give it Back*. New York: Atlantic Books.

PART II

Values: investment and risks

6 Market value in a sea of values: re-examining the 'theory of value' of land and property through the lens of 'capability theory'

Jyoti Shukla and Mike McDermott

Introduction

Real estate appraisal practices are underpinned by the mathematically exact abstraction of inexact understanding of the 'theory of value' (Canonne & Macdonald, 2003), and thus fail to explain property value beyond market price, as observed in multiple cases, for example in the appraisal of unregistered land, community-owned land, and compulsorily acquired land (McDermott et al., 2018; Rao, 2018b, 2019). Canonne and Macdonald (2003) attribute this problem to the weak theoretical foundation of the real estate profession in the haste to advance the field from art to science, and from trade to a profession. Through an examination of a wide range of literature,[1] Canonne and Macdonald (2003) find that the theory of economic value, which underpins the real estate appraisal profession, has found little importance in the real estate literature, thus resulting in systematic errors in the valuation profession.

> Has the theory been explained well, only to have practitioners' water down or set aside essential concepts to simplify the practice? Has evaluation practice been broken down to the lowest common denominator? Or could it be that the researchers and writers in this field have neglected the fundamentals? Could it be the classroom that is to blame and not the students? Do practitioners 'simplify' things because that is what they have been taught, or because they have been given no reason to do otherwise? (Canonne & Macdonald, 2003, p. 113)

Canonne and Macdonald (2003) raise the above questions and examine the writings and teachings of economics in the twentieth century, as well as in the field of the evaluation, and find that the theory of value and its history has, by and large, been neglected by property theorists and practitioners. In the wave of 'scientific positivism' and 'mathematization' of economics, economists in the twentieth century concentrated on the econometrical analysis of prices rather than on the political economy study of value (Canonne & Macdonald, 2003). As a consequence,

> practitioners short circuit the practice of evaluation; the fundamental notion of value did not enter the classroom because it finds little or no foundation in the literature, with blatant errors in the theory of value and the history of value thought. (Canonne & Macdonald, 2003, p. 114)

There are continuing efforts being made towards achieving social fairness in societies across the globe. Equitable distribution of resources across different members of society has been one of the central concerns of economists, and land (and property) are among the most crucial resources. A slight disturbance to the arrangements of the distribution of land and property has, from time to time, caused significant disturbance to developmental objectives concerning physical infrastructure, political stability, social and economic development of countries. Governments across many countries (at differential stages of social, economic, and political development) have adopted, from time to time, difficult (to execute) land policies that aimed at the equal redistribution of land, and at times at its compulsory acquisition for public purposes. Such policies are society's acknowledgement of plural stakes on land (of multiple stakeholders although with varying levels of rights and duties) and the multidimensional role of land for each stakeholder. To explain more, 'plural' is used because any parcel of land may have multiple stakeholders with varying levels of rights and duties; for example, landowner, land user, community, society, and the government; and 'multidimensional' because of the role of property across multiple dimensions of life for each stakeholder, such as social, economic, political, personal and familial, spiritual, environmental, and any other dimension.

Even though policymakers have been acknowledging the multidimensionality and plurality of land and property in achieving social welfare objectives, as discussed above, it has been challenging to build this multidimensionality and plurality into real estate appraisal practices. This is primarily because of the lack of a comprehensive theory to rationalise and measure multidimensional roles of land across plural stakeholders with varying levels of claims, such as private owners, users, community, and the government. To give an example, it has been difficult to rationalise and measure the spiritual and religious value of land using the theoretical framework of traditional neoclassical economics (Rao, 2018b). After a thorough examination of a wide range of literature on the economic value of land and property, Canonne and Macdonald (2003, p. 132) write that from the pre-historic debut of this discussion via the Greeks

– Xenophon (427–355 BC), Plato (427–347 BC) and Aristotle (384–324 BC) – continuing up to the present "no one has been unable to close the confrontation of work-value vs. utility-value, nor the debate between objective value and subjective value, nor has any hidden passage been found from value-in-use to value-in-exchange."

This chapter moves away from traditional neoclassical economics and uses Amartya Sen's 'capability theory' as the theoretical framework to explain the value of land and property beyond money, in terms of 'functionings'[2] and 'capabilities'.[3] To some extent 'capability theory' has provided a rational explanation to the value of land beyond money, as discussed in this chapter, and the bigger task of theorising the plural value of land in completeness is still pending. Considering the comprehensiveness of 'capability theory' it may be possible to knit together multiple strands of the value of land in a single rational framework, and the topic is open for discussion. As the first attempt towards this discussion, this chapter presents answers to two complicated questions: "Why is the value of land different for an individual, community, and the market?", and "Why is land always more valuable than its market value?"

The theory of value

Departing from classical economists such as Adam Smith and David Ricardo, Carl Menger (1840–1921) proposed a 'subjective theory of value' to say that

> value is thus nothing inherent in goods, no property of them, nor an independent thing existing by itself. It is a judgment economizing men make about the importance of the goods at their disposal for the maintenance of their lives and well-being. Hence value does not exist outside the consciousness of men. It is, therefore, also quite erroneous to call a good that has value to economizing individuals a 'value', or for economists to speak of 'values' as of independent real things, and to objectify value in this way. For the entities that exist objectively are always only particular things or quantities of things, and their value is something fundamentally different from the things themselves; it is a judgment made by economizing individuals about the importance their command of the things has for the maintenance of their lives and well-being. (Menger, 2007 [1976])

Comegna (2021) acknowledges that, so far, Menger has revised the theory of value and an economic revolution is underway once subjective and marginal utility enter the mainstream economic discussions.

Four hundred years ago, William Shakespeare observed that valuation depends not only on the quantities and qualities of what was being valued, but also the desires of those doing the valuing.[4] Three hundred years later Commons, in endorsing Thorstein Veblen's observation that "value must be constructed out of the habits and customs of social life" (Commons, 1924, p. vii), further developed Shakespeare's observation as follows:

> This process has three attributes which give us three meanings of value, each of which was separately emphasized by different schools of economists. Value has that subjective or volitional meaning of anticipation which may be named psychological value, and which is the moving force. It has next that objective meaning of commodities produced, exchanged and consumed, which may be named real value. It has lastly that behaviouristic meaning of prices which emerge in the transactions of buying, borrowing and hiring, in terms of standards of weights and measures prescribed by the working rules, which may be named nominal value. ... Every transaction has these three aspects of valuing. It is a meeting of wills, a transfer of commodities, a determination of their prices. A transaction is thus a compendium of psychological value, real value and nominal value. (Commons, 1924, pp. 8–9)

A year later, Whitehead wrote:

> There is something between the gross specialised values of the mere practical man, and the thin specialised values of the mere scholar. Both types have missed something; and if you add together the two sets of values, you do not obtain the missing elements. What is wanted is an appreciation of the infinite variety of vivid values achieved by an organism in its proper environment. (Whitehead 2011, p. 250)

An appreciation of all three such value categories – psychological, real, and nominal – is required of those embarking upon professional-level market valuations.

For market valuers, then, the authorities are not abstractions. They are the persons who have transacted comparable property rights who meet the definition of the value concerned in the relevant market, Whitehead's "organisms in their proper environment" who have arrived at an agreement relevant to the property right being valued. That proper environment may not be confined to that of the society within that geographical area; the market value may involve societies from far away (for example, mining companies entering a society from elsewhere).

Market values swim in a sea of values, and they have capabilities and functionings at differing levels and scales. In the context of land rights, Whitehead's "infinite varieties of vivid values" include values that would not be traded at any price as they are essential to the identities of those holding them. Yet sometimes they must be taken from them for socially legitimate reasons by the relevant government. These identity-core values can occur at all levels of identity construction – individual, social, religious, national and others (Scannell, 2013).

Last century, it was considered that such values were "sentimental" and:

> Sentimental value[s] which cannot be measured in terms of money are beyond the scope of the valuation of real estate. The loss of a property with family associations may be a very real one to the dispossessed owner, but he cannot find a market for his dispossessed feelings. (Murray, 1954, p. 52)

However, researchers have now confirmed that to classify psychological values, Commons' moving force, as being necessarily merely "sentimental" was grossly negligent reductionism. The infinite variety of vivid values that can be attached to land, but which are not measurable in terms of money, are prime motivators for both the payment and receipt of money. And while some of that variety remains beyond the scope of a market valuer, they are recognised in both science and law, and they can be more real to the value-holder than either money or the social recognition of the relevant right. Furthermore, as Murray implies, even some sentimental values can be measured in terms of money: a market valuer's task is to identify the plurality of values that are marketable in the market for the highest and best legal use of the property rights involved. Psychological and sentimental values are therefore not beyond the scope of the valuation of real estate; quite the contrary, they are the motive force of markets, and hence the market values.

Despite such reductionism, it was still recognised that "Value in the economic sense means the benefit conferred by ownership, which includes not only the possibility of exchange for other commodities, but all the satisfaction that may arise from possession" (Murray, 1954, p. 52). Even back then, therefore, the valuer was obliged to discern which vivid values in that sea of values were relevant in that market, and to what degree. Life is painting a picture, not just doing a sum (Holmes, 1913, p. 96).[5] Because markets are part of life, you cannot professionally conduct a market valuation, let alone any other kind, without understanding the roles of both in the market concerned. Our values decide what pictures we paint, and our sums how much we make from them.

In order to do that, as part of due diligence in the compulsory acquisition of land rights it is relevant to know which values are present in the environment, but which are not reflected in the market value, and the loss of which can still be destructive to one's personal, socio-cultural identity and other aspects of wellbeing (as discussed by Rao, 2018a, 2018b, 2019). To distinguish market-relevant values from market-irrelevant values, and their degrees of influences, one must be aware of the plurality of values potentially involved. Only with that understanding can the authorities adequately address the compensation, if any, legally required for the loss of property with such values attached by the owner of the land rights.

The essential principle in this process is the Principle of Equivalence:

> The first general matter is the principle which is said to underlie the whole of the law of compensation, and to provide guidance for the interpretation of the statutory provisions and a touchstone by reference to which all claims for compensation can be tested, that is the principle of equivalence. The principle of equivalence is the general, and perhaps obvious, principle that the compensation payable to a person who is deprived of his land in the public interest should be equal to the true and actual loss suffered by that person by reason of that deprivation and should be no more and no less than that amount. So viewed the law of compensation is a series of rules designed to give detailed effect to the principle of equivalence by identifying the loss suffered by a landowner and stating how that loss is to be converted into a monetary sum which becomes payable by the acquiring authority to the land-owner. (Barnes QC, M. 2014)

The heads of compensation developed to fulfil that principle are (i) market value, (ii) disturbance (covering the monetary costs the landowner suffers through the expropriation, for example those of moving somewhere else), (iii) injurious affection (loss of value of any remaining land due to works on acquired land), (iv) severance (loss of value of any remaining land resulting from reductions in its functionality by dint of losing the land taken), and (v) *solatium* (a payment to communicate solace for losses of those non-marketable values). Solatium has been described as something of a dark art: this chapter's intention is to shed some light on that darkness and explain why land is always more valuable than its market value.

This chapter uses Sen's capability theory to rationalise the plural/multidimensional value of land and property constituted by a wide range of functionings offered to multiple stakeholders with different levels of claims.

Value of land in terms of 'wellbeing'

Sen (1987a) identifies three different approaches to interpreting 'wellbeing': (1) utility; (2) opulence; and (3) functionings (which Sen defends). Also, there are three different types of data for the assessment of wellbeing: (i) market purchase data which reveals the monetary value of tradable commodities; (ii) response to the questionnaire; and (iii) non-market observations of the personal states of individuals. Traditional welfare economics relies on a utilitarian interpretation of wellbeing and uses market purchase data as an estimate of utility, which is a combination of (1) and (i). First, Sen (1987a) criticises the utilitarian interpretation of wellbeing (on grounds of 'welfarism', 'consequentialism', and 'sum-ranking' discussed in Sen, 1987a); and second, he criticises market purchase data for being an inadequate reflection of both wellbeing and utility derived from a commodity. It is the latter issue which we discuss in this chapter, that is, the market value of land or property is an inadequate measure of wellbeing and utility for its owner.

The above discussions raise two important questions in the context of wellbeing associated with property:

1. In what ways does property contribute to an individual's wellbeing, both monetary and non-monetary?
2. Is there a way to measure the non-monetary contribution of property to an individual's wellbeing?

This chapter uses Sen's 'capability theory' to find answers to both questions. Through a series of publications, Rao (2018a, 2018b, 2019) and Rao et al. (2017) try to answer the first problem of the identification of the functionings of land. Rao (2018a) derived a list of ten fundamental functionings of land which are generally valuable to landowners/users across the globe: (i) secure means to basic ends; (ii) having social equity; (iii) self-respect and self-identity; (iv) financial security; (v) familial wellbeing; (vi) political empowerment; (vii) power to take decisions on land matters; (viii) having social capital; (ix) personal comfort and convenience; and (x) having psychological wellbeing. In a later work, Rao (2019) also attempts to order functionings using the theoretical framework of Maslow's hierarchy of needs. However, Maslow's framework is less useful in determining the order of sub-functionings within the same category of 'need'. Also, the question of estimating the value of these functionings is open for discussion. The unanswered questions are (i) whether it is possible to derive a deterministic order or ranking of functionings as per their contribution to landowners'/users' wellbeing; and (ii) how to measure the value of these functionings?

To answer the above questions, we apply Sen's (1987a) argument of ordering functionings (derived from utilising commodities) to the context of land and property. Also, we explain why market value is an inadequate measure of the losses associated with land arising out of compulsory acquisition or other forms of man-made and natural disasters. First, we will discuss the ordering problem followed by the measurement of value. Referring to the ten fundamental functionings identified by Rao (2018a), and many sub-functionings within each, as identified in the context of India and Scotland by Rao (2019) and Rao et al. (2017) respectively, it is understandable that several orders or rankings are possible based on the subjective assessment of functionings by individual landowners/users. Suppose P is the universal set of the ordered list of ten 'fundamental' functionings, where each order reflects the subjective assessment of landowners/users i. Taking the example of a small society of three people ($i = 1, 2, 3$) it is possible to explicitly state P^1 as the chosen order of functionings by landowner i. Put simply, P represents the full set of ordered lists of the ten fundamental functionings of which landowners 1, 2 and 3 chose P^1, P^2, and P^3, For simplicity, it is assumed that landowners 1, 2, and 3 have a complete and unique order of all ten functionings (F1 to F10) as stated in Figure 6.1.

As Sen (1987a) emphasises, the conversion of a commodity (like land and property in this case) into functionings would depend on the characteristics of the commodity, the personal characteristics of the landowner/user and the social and political institutions in which they operate. In the above example, we assume that the three landowners possess different personal and social attributes that are stated in Figure 6.1. To explain more, it is assumed that the society is fragmented (as is often the case) and landowner 1 is lower in the social hierarchy, which may be due to the landowner's lower-income as a small farmer; gender; or even a lower caste. In addition, landowner 1 is a small farmer and land is the means to basic ends such as shelter and food. These differences in personal and social characteristics across the three landowners explain the difference in their assessment of fundamental functionings (F1 to F10). In the example above, we observe that functioning F2, that is social equity arising out of land ownership, has been valued the second most important by landowner 1, who is lower in the social hierarchy. On the contrary, landowners 2 and 3 do not derive social equity from land ownership given their higher social position, which might be due to higher financial status, gender, or caste. For similar reasons functionings F1, F3, F8, F9, and F10 are also ordered differently by the three landowners. On the contrary, functionings F4 to F7 are sequentially and similarly ordered by all three landowners, even though their ranking is different for each landowner.

The intersection of functionings, highlighted as a grey box in Figure 6.1, represents a partial ordering[6] of fundamental functionings F4 to F7, in descending order of importance where F4 is most important among the four objectively ordered functionings. However, the landowners attach a different level of

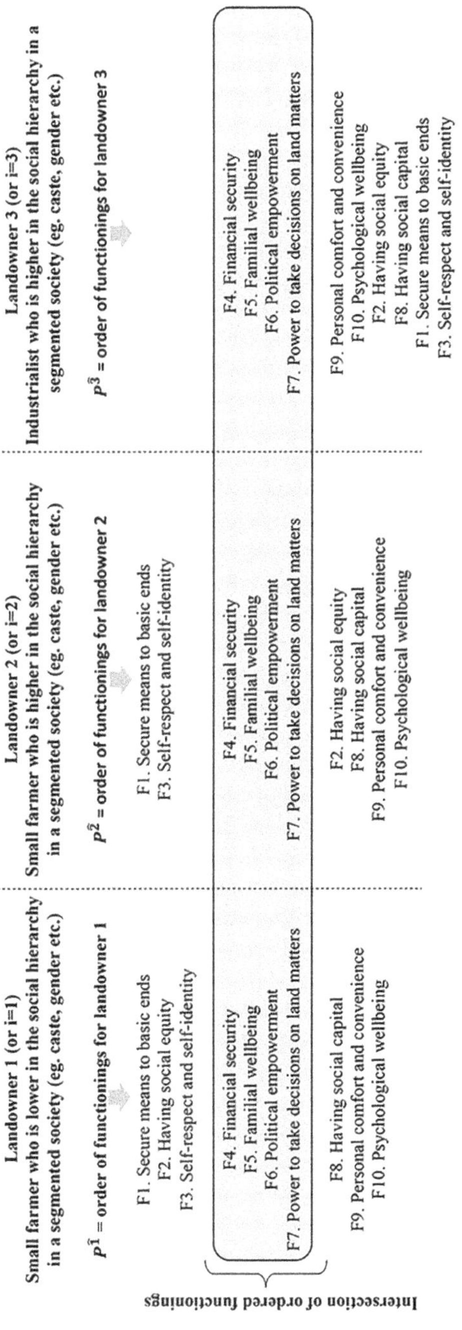

Landowner 1 (or i=1)
Small farmer who is lower in the social hierarchy
in a segmented society (eg. caste, gender etc.)

P^1 = order of functionings for landowner 1

F1. Secure means to basic ends
F2. Having social equity
F3. Self-respect and self-identity

F4. Financial security
F5. Familial wellbeing
F6. Political empowerment
F7. Power to take decisions on land matters

F8. Having social capital
F9. Personal comfort and convenience
F10. Psychological wellbeing

Landowner 2 (or i=2)
Small farmer who is higher in the social hierarchy
in a segmented society (eg. caste, gender etc.)

P^2 = order of functionings for landowner 2

F1. Secure means to basic ends
F3. Self-respect and self-identity

F4. Financial security
F5. Familial wellbeing
F6. Political empowerment
F7. Power to take decisions on land matters

F2. Having social equity
F8. Having social capital
F9. Personal comfort and convenience
F10. Psychological wellbeing

Landowner 3 (or i=3)
Industrialist who is higher in the social hierarchy in a
segmented society (eg. caste, gender etc.)

P^3 = order of functionings for landowner 3

F4. Financial security
F5. Familial wellbeing
F6. Political empowerment
F7. Power to take decisions on land matters

F9. Personal comfort and convenience
F10. Psychological wellbeing
F2. Having social equity
F8. Having social capital
F1. Secure means to basic ends
F3. Self-respect and self-identity

Intersection of ordered functionings

Figure 6.1   Subjective and objective functionings of landowners

importance to all other functionings. Taking inspiration from Sen (1987a) we assume that the value[7] attached to functionings F4 to F7 is the same across all landowners. In the above example, the partial order of functionings F4 to F7 defines the lower limit[8] of objectively valuable functionings.

These are 'objectively' valuable functionings (as opposed to subjectively valuable), which firstly means they are valuable across all landowners/users of land and therefore tradable or exchangeable between buyers and sellers; and secondly the value of each tradable functioning, howsoever it may be measured, is the same for landowners/users. Put another way, objective functionings lie at the intersection of a subjectively ordered list of functionings across many landowners/users, and their order and value are the same for all.

Redefining 'market value' of land using 'capability theory'

Based on the above explanation, market value of land can be redefined as the cumulative value of objective functionings which are exchangeable/tradable and are objectively valued by the market players. That is:

$$MV = \sum v_{\text{objective functionings}}$$

where,

MV is market value of a land parcel; and

$v_{\text{objective functionings}}$ is the 'value' of objective functionings. An interested reader

may refer to Shukla (2020a) for a detailed discussion on the conversion of commodities to functionings, and the definition of 'value' of functionings of land.

In the above example, market value of land is the cumulative value of functionings F4 to F7:

$$MV = \sum_{i=4}^{i=7} v_{Fi}$$

Understanding monetary and non-monetary value of land through 'functionings'

In the above example, each landowner derives functionings F1 to F10 from land and orders them as per the level of importance the landowner subjectively attaches to it. Functionings F4 to F7 lie at the intersection of these subjectively ordered lists of functionings and have the same value for each landowner (as explained earlier). In reference to functionings, the value of land for any owner will be the total value of all the functionings they derive from land (Shukla, 2020a). Put simply, the value of land for its owner/user will be the cumulative value of all subjective and objective functionings, that is:

$$v_{land} = v_{land,\ subjective\ functionings} + v_{land,\ objective\ functionings}$$

The above equation can be rewritten in terms of the market value, MV:

$$v_{land} = v_{land,\ subjective\ functionings} + MV$$

A landowner will dispose of land only when the monetary value offered to the owner creates a higher or more valuable set of functionings. Thus, the condition for wilful sale in terms of 'functionings' is:

$$v_{land} \le v_{MV}$$

where:

v_{MV} is the cumulative value of all subjective and objective functionings

derived from using the money MV received from selling land. That is:

$$v_{MV} = v_{MV,\ subjective\ functionings} + v_{MV,\ objective\ functionings}$$

This is to say, a landowner would sell their land when the cumulative value of all functionings, both subjective and objective, created by money (as a commodity or means to procuring other commodities) is equal to or greater than the value of functionings of land:

$$v_{land,\ subjective\ functionings} + v_{land,\ objective\ functionings} \le v_{MV,\ subjective\ functionings}$$
$$+ v_{MV,\ objective\ functionings}$$

For simplicity we may assume that the value of the objective set of functionings created by land can be either fully recreated or replaced with a more valuable set of functionings from using money so that the overall wellbeing of the landowner improves from selling land. That is:

$$v_{\text{land, objective functionings}} \leq v_{MV, \text{ objective functionings}}$$

In saying this, we are also assuming that the ability of landowners to convert money into functionings is at least equal to or greater than their ability to convert land into functionings. In the worst-case scenario, we would expect that the landowner's functionings from using land equate (in terms of value) with functionings from using the monetary value of land. In which case, we can simplify the condition for sale as follows:

$$v_{\text{land, subjective functionings}} \leq v_{MV, \text{ subjective functionings}}$$

In summary, even when the value of objective functionings of land is fully compensated by the monetary value of land, a landowner may be reluctant to sell the land if the value of subjective functionings for him/her is any less than the value of subjective functionings created by money. For example, referring to the earlier example of landowner 1, subjective functionings from land include a means to basic ends, social equity, self-identity, social capital, personal comfort and convenience, and psychological wellbeing. Subjective functionings, like self-identity in territorial identity (as explained by Rao 2018a), which are linked with the location of land, cannot be recreated from using money or buying alternative land parcels at any other location. Therefore, for a wilful sale to happen, the landowner must be prepared to replace a few subjective functionings of land with those arising out of money or purchasable commodities so that the overall wellbeing of the landowner improves or remains unchanged.

Is 'market value' an inadequate measure of the loss of land?

The above discussion uses Sen's (1987a) 'capability theory' and creates the theoretical foundation to answering the question of why monetary compensation, equal to the market value of land, is an inadequate measure of losses associated with the loss of land and property that may be as a consequence of either a man-made or natural disaster, such as the compulsory acquisition of land, inundation, earthquake, bushfire or any other reason. While money may recreate or replace the objective functionings of land and property, it is not always possible to rebuild subjective functionings. A 'comprehensive restitution and compensation mechanism' for overcoming the loss of land and property would mean rebuilding or substituting the original set of valuable subjective and objective functionings of the affected landowners so as to put them back in the original state of 'capability', if not a better state. A comprehensive mechanism may well be a combination of monetary and non-monetary strategies of compensation and restitution that may be designed and executed together with the affected landowners. This is an emerging area of research (for example Gardoni & Murphy, 2008) and further work on the application of the capability approach to the design of policies and strategies for disaster restitution, particularly concerning losses associated with land and property, may inform policies and strategies of disaster restitution.

Can capability theory be used to understand the value of community owned land?

Property institution theorists, including Kivell and McKay (1988), Ellickson (1993), Alexander (1997), Heller (2000), have long argued in favour of the plural role of property that stretches across individuals, community, and the state. These scholars acknowledge the problem of strict categorical separation of realms of property into private versus public ownership, individual versus social interests, and market versus state-led realms. Paradigm compartmentalisation makes it difficult to explain the plural roles of property that actually intersect across individuals, community, and the state (Shukla, 2020b).

In the earlier works of Rao (2018a, 2018b, 2019), the focus has been on identifying functionings of land (and property under private ownership) which are valuable to its owner due to their contribution to an individual's wellbeing. Most of Rao's works aim at informing the design of a comprehensive restitution and compensation model for individuals who lose land and associated wellbeing (defined in terms of functionings and capabilities) such that they can be put back to their original condition, if not better. The context of person-specific loss of functionings is underpinned by the private property paradigm.

Given the plural role of land, and the ability to contribute to the wellbeing of the community and society at large, it is important to inquire about the 'social' functionings of private land which contribute to the wellbeing of the larger community. The answer as to whether 'social' functionings can also contribute to the wellbeing of the original landowner may be found in Adam Smith's concept of 'thumos'. To explain in the clear words of Lisa Hill (2012, p. 2), Smith interpreted the classical provenance of this term as the "desire for status, social recognition and approval", such that to Smith thumos is the most important force in economics, that it is "far more layered and subtle than is commonly understood", and that "thumos-driven agents (unwittingly) sacrifice individual utility to system utility".[9] So, while the questions of community and individual functionings are separate, they are interrelated via the community-membership aspects of the individual members' thumos-constructed identities.

In the construction of 'capability' theory, Amartya Sen (1987b) draws intensively from Adam Smith's rich analysis of human behaviour in 'The Theory of Moral Sentiments' and 'The Wealth of Nations'. Referring to Smith throughout his work, Sen (1977, 1987b) strongly criticises the mainstream welfare economics account of a self-interested utility maximising human behaviour, or the so-called 'mechanistic rational model' (Eiffe, 2010) and writes "between the claims of oneself and the claims of all lie the claims of a variety of groups – for example, families, friends, local communities, peer groups, and economic and social classes" (Sen, 1977, p. 318). This argument is particularly useful in explaining the plural role of private property (including land).

Jeremy Waldron argues that "private property[10] is a concept of which many different conceptions are possible, and that in each society the detailed incidents of ownership amount to a particular concrete conception of this abstract concept" (Waldron, 1988). To explain the above, Waldron (1988) describes how private property is not merely a relationship between the owner and physical property but rather a complex legal relationship between people, that is the owner and other members of society. Liberties and duties are the basic stuff of ownership which can be combined differently to create multiple bundles of rights (Waldron, 1988). Given that these liberties and duties are separable and can be combined differently, each combination gives rise to a new bundle of property rights, as observed across geographies. Thus, variations are possible in the bundle of rights across jurisdictions and the terms 'ownership' and 'private property' do not convey any determinate idea of legal relations.

Other scholars, such as Di Robilant (Holden and Pagel, 2013) implicitly suggest moving beyond the bundle of sticks metaphor altogether. Di Robilant noted that comparative property law is still a largely unexplored field and claimed that a model was required that could better balance the social and individual elements of property more than the static bundle of sticks metaphor does (Holden and Pagel, 2013, p. 907). Such a metaphor should also better account for the complicated structure of property rights, and that property rights share a duty to perform social functions and duties concerning basic resources, such as land (ibid, p. 931). Finally, she adds that a weakness of the analogy is that it does not give proper weight to the fact that property entails coercion (ibid,

p. 931). Rather than a bundle, McDermott (2018, p. 142) recommends a return to another description of Maine's for property rights: a "legal clothing" (Maine, 2013, p. 60). He sees Maine's clothing metaphor as a more information-rich metaphor for property rights. That is because clothing varies in its fitness for purpose in different places, and functions in different environments for different purposes including, importantly, cultural signifier purposes.

Although Waldron's (1988) reference was to a private property right, the same argument is useful in defining the communal property rights of a land user. That is, communal property rights are the clothing or costume of the liberties and duties for the land user, and, when compared with private property rights, communal rights are likely to have a relatively lower level of liberties and a higher level of duties. In addition, different communities would combine these liberties and duties differently to give rise to a new type of communal right as observed across jurisdictions and communities. Understandably, certain decisions concerning community-owned land are jointly formed by the community, and the opinion of each member is important but not conclusive. Broadly speaking, any reduction or improvement in landowners'/users' liberties and duties will have a direct impact on the functionings they can derive from the land. Nevertheless, the value of land can still be expressed as the sum of the subjective and objective functionings of the land user, irrespective of the nature of functionings.

In the case of community ownership of land, 'objective functionings' would mean (i) an ordered set of functionings, which is valuable across all land users and thus the community as a whole; (ii) depending on the system of exchange/trade in the community, objective functionings will be exchangeable/tradable across the members of the community (e.g. as use rights); and (iii) the value of land for the community would mean the cumulative value of these objective functionings.

It is important to mention here that the market value of land will be different from the value observed by the community when market players are from outside the community. This is because the set of objectively valuable functionings for the community may not overlap with that of the market if it is constituted by an external group of individuals operating under different property rights regimes and laws, which create a very different set of functionings of land. To understand these differences more clearly it would be important to identify the functionings of land users in a community as well as for the market. This could be interesting for future researchers. Other questions related to the plural role of property that are of relevance to contemporary society include: (i) "can capability theory provide a comprehensive theoretical

framework that can comprehend the plural role of property in completeness?";
(ii) "can 'capability theory' be useful in the identification and measurement
of a social role (or functionings) of privately owned property?"; and (ii) "can
'capability theory' be useful in the identification and measurement of the social
benefits of public projects?".

Conclusion

This chapter takes its motivation from an inadequate discussion on the 'theory
of value' of land/property and the lack of a theoretical framework that can
fully rationalise the 'value' of land in its plural and multidimensional form
beyond the transaction value. While the 'theory of value' has been extensively
debated by economists, Canonne and Macdonald (2003) find that the real
estate profession, both theorists and practitioners, have paid little attention
to these theories. The problem has deeper roots given that mainstream neoclassical economics, in the first place, oversimplifies the concept of 'value' by
equating it to the transaction value of commodities. As a consequence, the real
estate profession has been struggling to find satisfactory answers to questions
on the determination of 'value' beyond transaction value, particularly in
non-standard settings or when standard assumptions underpinning appraisal
practices are not met in the real world. McDermott et al. (2018) identify some
of the standard assumptions which commonly fail:

1. Standard appraisal practices assume 'private property right' to be a typical
    bundle of right to use, exclude, and dispose of land/property. However,
    there are many ways to combine property rights and duties to include
    customary, environmental, religious, and other socio-cultural rights. The
    application of standard valuation methods fails to account for these varia-
    tions and may therefore result in undervaluation of land/property.
2. Standard valuation methods do not take account of the risks associated
    with unregistered land, or land on which rights are claimed through
    informal institutions using socio-cultural, religious, and environmental
    evidence. For example, in many parts of Africa, graves are significant evi-
    dence of land rights.
3. Standard valuation methods are difficult to apply for valuing land that is
    compulsorily acquired by public agencies for public purposes, that is when
    the standard assumption of wilful exchange by the buyer and seller fails.
4. Standard appraisal practices do not take account of the plural stake of
    multiple stakeholders, including an individual landowner, the user of land,
    community, and also the government as a representative of the society

at large. The level of claims of each stakeholder may vary, thus creating different systems of property rights, the most common ones being private property rights and communal property rights. Real estate appraisal practices fail to respond to these variations.

Theorists such as Menger (2007 [1976]), Commons (1924), and Whitehead (2011) have presented rational arguments in favour of the multidimensional value of land/property including individual, social, religious, and psychological value. However, Canonne and Macdonald (2003) find, after a thorough examination of a wide range of literature on the economic value of land and property, that gaps in the theory of value continue to exist, and from the pre-historic debut of this discussion through to the Greeks – Xenophon (427–355 BC), Plato (427–347 BC) and Aristotle (384–324 BC) – and continuing to the present, "no one has been able to close the confrontation of work-value vs. utility-value, nor the debate between objective value and subjective value, nor has any hidden passage been found from value-in-use to value-in-exchange" (ibid, p. 132).

This chapter initiates the discussion on using Sen's 'capability theory' as a comprehensive framework that can fully explain the plural and multidimensional value of land. Rao (2018a, 2018b, 2019) and Rao et al. (2017) contribute to this discussion through a series of publications looking at the 'value' of land in terms of 'functionings' or states of wellness. Rao (2018a) deduced a list of ten fundamental functionings of land which, as per Rao, are valuable to many landowners/users across the globe: (i) secure means to basic ends; (ii) having social equity; (iii) self-respect and self-identity; (iv) financial security; (v) familial wellbeing; (vi) political empowerment; (vii) power to take decisions on land matters; (viii) having social capital; (ix) personal comfort and convenience; (x) having psychological wellbeing.

Using the lens of 'capability theory', this chapter redefines the market value of land in terms of 'functionings'. In theory, the cumulative value of all 'functionings' which contribute to the wellbeing of the landowner/user is defined as the subjective value of land to its owner/user. Among these subjective functionings, a few lie at the intersection of a subjectively ordered list of functionings across many landowners/users (Figure 6.1). These are called 'objective' functionings (a subset of subjective functionings) for which the order and value are the same across all landowners/users. Therefore, these are tradable or exchangeable between buyers and sellers. The market value of land is redefined as the cumulative value of 'objective' functionings, for which the value, howsoever it may be measured, is the same across all buyers and sellers. In other words, market value is defined as the cumulative value of objective functionings that lie at the intersection of a subjectively ordered list of functionings across many landowners/users. Nevertheless, the problem of measuring the value of land in terms of functionings is still open for discussion and has similar challenges to measuring 'functionings' (refer to Alkire, 2015 for more details on measuring functionings and capabilities).

Sen's 'capability theory' provides the rational framework to answer questions such as "why is land necessarily more valuable than its market value?"; "why is monetary compensation, equal to the market value of land, an inadequate measure of losses associated with the loss of land and property that may be as a consequence of either man-made or natural disasters, such as the compulsory acquisition of land, inundation, earthquake, bushfire or any other reason?"; and "why is land valued differently by an individual, community and the market?". The above discussions pave the way for future works on similar other challenging aspects of the plural and multidimensional value of land, for example: (i) how to incorporate variations in rights and duties under different systems of property rights (such as private versus communal property rights); (ii) can 'capability theory' be used to identify and measure the social benefits (or functionings) of privately owned property; and (iii) can 'capability theory' be used to identify and measure the social benefits of public projects?

Notes

1. Literature included "one hundred major North American real estate handbooks and real estate appraisal manuals, treatises and anthologies, starting with Hurd (1903) and covering one hundred years" (Canonne & Macdonald, 2003, p. 113).
2. *Functioning* may be defined in simple terms as the usefulness derived from any resource or commodity such that it contributes to the wellbeing of the individual and thus gives them the reason to value it (Rao, 2018b). Sen (1987a) defines functioning as the state of being or doing, such as being well-nourished and doing bicycling.
3. Capability, as defined by Sen (1987a), is the chosen set of functioning from the range of functionings accessible to a person. The wider the set of accessible functioning, the more freedom a person has to choose and thus greater is the "wellbeing". In other words, wellbeing, as per 'capability theory' is the level of freedom to choose valuable 'functionings'.
4. Troilus and Cressida, Act II, Scene II.
5. Oliver Wendell Holmes, in his "Address to the Harvard Alumni Association to the Class of '61", in *Speeches* (1913), p. 96.
6. Traditional welfare economics adopts a purely subjective approach to ranking wellbeing where interpersonal variations are permitted (refer to Binder, 2013 for details on a Subjective Well Being approach to measuring wellbeing). Sen (1987a) rejects a purely subjectivist approach to measuring wellbeing and rather claims

the possibility of an objectivist approach, while clarifying that objectivity does not imply a complete and unique ranking of wellbeing. For example, if state A and B imply higher wellbeing than state C, then person 1's belief that A is higher than B can coexist with person 2's belief that B is higher than A (Sen, 1987a). Both views are consistent with the objective partial ordering of C being lower than A and B (Sen, 1987a). Sen (1987a) clarifies that an objectivist approach, characterised by partial and non-unique ordering, as seen in the example earlier, would make room for interpersonal variations while also allowing assessment of wellbeing.

7. The problem of valuing functionings is open for discussion and useful reference includes Alkire (2015).

8. Sen (1987a, p. 25) writes: "It reflects the minimum that can safely be said, i.e., without contradicting any of the non-eliminated orderings (partial or complete) in *P*. We may well want to say more. In fact, for a person who believes, after reasoned reflection, that a particular ranking *Pj* is exactly right, the possibility of saying a good deal more than *P*, up to the full extent of *Pj* is obviously open."

9. "System utility is a term first used by John Gray to describe F.A. Hayek's work on spontaneous order (Gray, 1989). It denotes efficiency and adaptivity within social systems and is usually contrasted with individual utility." (Hill, 2012, p. 2).

10. "In a system of private property (as opposed to the socialist system of common property), the rules governing access to and control of material resources are organized around the idea that resources are on the whole separate objects each assigned and therefore belonging to some particular individual... The owner of a resource is simply the individual whose determination as to the use of the resource is taken as final in a system of this kind" (Waldron, 1988).

References

Alexander, G. S. (1997). *Commodity and Propriety: Competing Visions of Property in American Legal Thought 1776-1970* (1st ed.). Chicago; London: The University of Chicago Press.

Alkire, S. (2015). The Capability Approach and Well-Being Measurement for Public Policy. *Oxford Poverty & Human Development Initiative (OPHI) Working Paper no 94*, 1–34.

Barnes QC, M. (2014). *The Law of Compulsory Purchase and Compensation.* Kindle Location 4781–4789: Bloomsbury Publishing (Kindle Edition).

Binder, M. (2013). Subjective Well-Being Capabilities: Bridging the Gap Between the Capability Approach and Subjective Well-Being Research. *Journal of Happiness Studies, 15*, 1197–1217.

Canonne, J., & Macdonald, R. J. (2003). Valuation without Value Theory: A North American 'Appraisal'. *Journal of Real Estate Practice and Education, 6*(1), 113–162.

Comegna, A. (2021, April 23). *Menger's Principles of Economics: What Makes Something Valuable?* Retrieved from Libertarianism.org: https://www.libertarianism.org/essays/mengers-principles-economics-what-makes-something-valuable.

Commons, J. (1924). *Legal Foundations of Capitalism.* New York: The Macmillan Company.

Eiffe, F. F. (2010). Amartya Sen Reading Adam Smith. *History of Economics Review, 51*(1), 1–23.

Ellickson, R. C. (1993). Property in Land. *The Yale Law Journal, 102*(1315), 1315–1400.
Gardoni, P., & Murphy, C. (2008). Recovery from Natural and Man-made Disasters as Capabilities Restoration and Enhancement. *International Journal of Sustainable Development and Planning, 3*(4), 317–333.
Gray, J. (1989). *Liberalisms: Essays in Political Philosophy.* London: Routledge and Kegan Paul.
Heller, M. A. (2000). Critical Approaches to Property Institutions. *Columbia Law School: Scholarship Archive*, pp. 417–434.
Hill, L. (2012). Adam Smith on Thumos and Irrational Economic 'Man'. *The European Journal of the History of Economic Thought, 19*(1), 1–22.
Holden, J., & Pagel, M. (2013, January). *Transnational Land Acquisitions: What are the Drivers, Levels, and Destinations, of Recent Transnational Land Acquisitions?* Retrieved from Economic and Private Sector PEAKS: https://assets.publishing.service .gov.uk/media/57a08a48ed915d3cfd0006ac/Transnational_land_acquisitions_10 .pdf.
Holmes, O. W. (1913). *Address to the Harvard Alumni Association to the Class of 1961.* Cambridge: Speeches.
Kivell, P. T., & McKay, I. (1988). Public Ownership of Urban Land. *Transactions of the Institute of British Geographers, 13*(2), 165–178.
Maine, H. (2013). *Ancient Law. Its Connection with the Early History of Society and its Relation to Modern Ideas.* London: Taylor & Francis (online).
McDermott, M. (2018). *Wicked Valuations: People and Landed Property.* London: Routledge.
McDermott, M., Myers, M., & Augustinus, C. (2018). *Valuation of Unregistered Land: A Policy Guide.* Nairobi: United Nations Human Settlements Programme UN-Habitat.
Menger, C. (2007 [1976]). *Principles of Economics* (James Dingwall and Bert F. Hoselitz Trans.). Auburn, Alabama: Ludwig von Mises Institute, https://mises.org/library/ principles-economics (Original work published 1976).
Murray, J. F. N. (1954). *Principles and Practice of Valuation.* Reprint, Sydney: John Andrew and Company, 1968.
Rao, J. (2018a). Fundamental Functionings of Landowners: Understanding the Relationship between Land Ownership and Wellbeing through the Lens of 'Capability'. *Land Use Policy, 72*, 74–84.
Rao, J. (2018b). *Functionings of Land: Analysing Compulsory Acquisition Cases from Scotland* (1st edn). Singapore: Palgrave Macmillan.
Rao, J. (2019). A 'Capability Approach' to Understanding Loses Arising out of the Compulsory Acquisition of Land in India. *Land Use Policy, 82*, 70–84.
Rao, J., Tiwari, P., & Hutchison, N. E. (2017). Capability Approach to Compulsory Purchase Compensation: Evidence of the Functionings of Land Identified by Affected Landowners in Scotland. *Journal of Property Research, 34*(4), 305–324.
Scannell, L. (2013). Retrieved from *The Bases of Bonding: The Psychological Functions of Place Attachment in Comparison to Interpersonal Attachment*: https://dspace.library .uvic.ca/bitstream/handle/1828/5074/Scannell_Leila_PhD_2013.pdf?sequence=3.
Sen, A. (1977). Rational Fools: A Critique of the Behavioral Foundations of Economic Theory. *Philosophy & Public Affairs, 6*(4), 317–344.
Sen, A. (1987a). *Commodities and Capabilities* (1st edn). Oxford: Oxford University Press.
Sen, A. (1987b). *On Ethics and Economics.* Malden, Oxford: Blackwell Publishing.

Shukla, J. (2020a). Designing Fair Compensation for the Compulsory Acquisition of Land: Case of Bengaluru, India. In P. Tiwari, G. B. Stillman, & N. Yoshino, *Equitable Land Use for Asian Infrastructure* (pp. 199–239). Tokyo: Asian Development Bank Institute.

Shukla, J. (2020b). Property Institutions and Their Impact on Land Assembling Strategies. In P. Tiwari, G. B. Stillman, & N. Yoshino, *Equitable Land Use for Asian Infrastructure* (pp. 53–75). Tokyo: Asian Development Bank Institute.

Waldron, J. (1988). *The Right to Private Property* (1st edn). Oxford: Oxford University Press.

Whitehead, A. N. (2011). *Science and the Modern World.* Cambridge: Cambridge University Press.

7 Circular economy in the real estate sector

Ashish Gupta and Piyush Tiwari

Introduction

As per a United Nations report, the global urban population has increased from 30% in 1950 to 55% in 2018 and is expected to increase to 68% by 2050. Between 1950 and 2018, the urban population has increased by 5.6 times (United Nations, 2018). Cities have become engines of growth for global economies contributing 75% to their GDP and consuming 75% of the global primary energy (UN-Habitat, 2012). In the last century, industrialization and urbanization increased global GDP, with improvements in living standards and reduction in poverty putting pressure on natural resources and resulting in environmental degradation. UNEP (2012) estimated this has increased the extraction of construction minerals 34 times during the 20th century. Business as usual will result in the extraction of natural resources increasing from 60 billion tonnes in 2012 to 140 billion tonnes annually by 2050. This raises concern for governments, industries and all stakeholders about the future of our planet in case we continue in this business-as-usual scenario.

Moving from a linear to a circular economy?

The traditional linear approach to take–make–use–dispose, also called cradle-to-grave, has led to the excessive extraction of natural resources, environmental degradation leading to global warming and waste ending up in landfills. The present system assumes an endless supply of material for human consumption and leads to the creation of waste across the entire lifecycle. This is a consequence of the historical availability of plentiful and cheap resources such as land, labor and material. Continuous exploitation of these resources for economic growth is leading to their fast depletion. To reduce this waste, embedding the concept of circularity in the DNA of the business generates new opportunities for wealth creation. This would require fresh thinking and a different approach to businesses.

Circular economy (CE) has emerged as a new paradigm that focuses on the decoupling of economic growth from sustainable resource management to minimize negative externalities to the environment as a result of this growth. UNEP (2012) has recommended that this decoupling will require resource efficiency through finance, innovation, capacity building, using green technology, policy intervention and revisiting existing subsidies. The focus of CE is on re-utilization of the resources and material, it relies on green energy, strives to extend the productive life, minimizes all kinds of waste and believes in recycle–reuse of residual products at end of life. Businesses focusing on CE look at the judicious resource management at each stage of the product lifecycle, then just resource optimization during the production. Nothing is waste in CE; as in nature, one organism's feces (waste) is another's food. See Table 7.1 for more details on the linear vs circular economy.

The advantages of a transition to a circular economy

- Estimated benefits for the global economy
  - Estimated CE opportunity to be $4.5 trillion by 2030 by targeting to eliminate waste in the linear economy (Accenture, 2015).
  - Adopting the CE will provide Europe net economic benefits of €1.8 trillion by 2030 (McKinsey, 2015).
  - Adopting CE, the emission footprint of housing can be reduced by 13.5 billion tonnes and construction and demolition waste from housing could be reduced by 9.5 billion tonnes, i.e. diverted from landfills (PACE, 2021).
  - Green building offers a $24.7 trillion investment opportunity in emerging market cities in the next decade (IFC, 2019).
- Benefits for businesses
  - This acts as a risk mitigation strategy by decoupling economic growth from the availability or scarcity of resources.
  - Opens up the opportunity for newer business models in repair–reuse–recycle and across the operative life of the product.
  - Supports sustainable and eco-friendly business models that are preferred by investors and supports their ESG obligations.
  - In buildings, research has shown that green buildings provide savings across the life of an asset due to a reduction in operating expenses (OpEx).

Table 7.1   Linear economy and circular economy

Linear economy	Circular economy
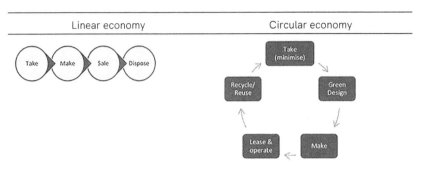	
• Focus on the take, make, sale and dispose.	• Focus on the take, design, make, lease and operate, re-design, recycle and reuse.
• Maximizes product value through the exploitation of resources, and efficiencies are considered during production.	• Maximizes the value of the product through waste reduction across the various stages of the product life; not just production.
• Limited regard to sustainability and environmental impact.	• Sustainability and environmental impact are the focal points.
• Limited focus on repair, recycle and reuse.	• Focuses on repair, recycle and reuse.
• While manufacturing focus is on CapEx.	• While manufacturing focus is on CapEx and OpEx and a trade-off is considered.
• End-of-life product is disposed and ends up in a landfill.	• End-of-life product is recycled and reused.

Source: The authors

Significance of circular economy to real estate

Construction is one of the key sectors of the global economy with about $10 trillion annual expenditure, contributing about 13% to the global GDP and employing 7%[1] of the working-age population (McKinsey Global Institute, 2017). Building and building construction consumes 35% of the global energy and contributes 38% CO_2 emissions.[2] Buildings operations alone are responsible for 55% of the total global electricity consumption (UNEP, 2020). Two-thirds of countries do not have mandatory building energy codes for new construction and refurbishing, and most of these countries will see the majority of the new incremental buildings (UNEP, 2021). Adoption of CE using innovative technology in sustainable buildings is expected to reduce the energy requirement of a building by 30% by 2050, although during this period the floor space is also expected to double (IEA, 2019).

The productivity of the construction sector has been below par when compared with other sectors. If it catches up with the global economy using CE principles, it could add $1.6 trillion additional productivity that would add 2% to the global GDP. Global construction productivity can be increased by 50–60% through improvements in regulations, contracts, design, procurement and supply chains, onsite execution, technology and innovation, and by reskilling the labor force (McKinsey Global Institute, 2017).

There is increasing obsolescence of existing built stock globally. Adopting CE principles, the operative life of these buildings can be increased and energy requirements decreased by refurbishing and retrofitting them. UNEP (2021) estimated there would be a need for the refurbishment of existing buildings by 1.5 and 2% in developing countries and 2 and 3% in developed countries by 2025 and 2040 respectively. In Europe, the EU Commission aims to double renovation rates to increase the operational efficiency of 35 million buildings by 2030. This would provide 0.16 million green jobs in construction (UNEP, 2020).

Green building offers a $24.7 trillion investment opportunity in emerging market cities in the next decade (IFC, 2019). In another estimate, globally sustainable buildings require, over the next decade, an additional annual investment of $27 billion, in addition to $4.9 trillion already invested annually on building construction and renovation. This clean energy investment will lead to a 50% reduction in household spending in energy by 2050 from 5% to 2.5% (IEA, 2019).

Principles of circular economy in real estate

There is a strong case of transition to CE, but businesses inherently operate by the take–make– sale–dispose mindset of the linear economy. Making the transition to CE is not easy: businesses will need a strong vision, and societal, regulatory and economic initiatives to embark on this journey. This will require a strong alignment to circular thinking and that would require freedom from the linear business-as-usual mindset. This will require the formulation of new business models based on the principles of CE (see Table 7.2).

Resilient supply chains of green material: To maintain competitive advantage requires the creation of resilient supply chains of renewable, recyclable, reusable and biodegradable materials. Green energy sources, such as wind and

Table 7.2   Circular economy business models and principles

Author	CE business model and principles
(Accenture, 2015) (OECD, 2018)	• Circular supply-chain • Recovery and recycling/Resource recovery models • Product life extension • Sharing platform/models • Product as service
(Ellen MacArthur Foundation, 2013)	• Design out waste • Build resilience through diversity • Rely on energy from renewable sources • Think in systems • Waste is food
(Ellen MacArthur Foundation, 2019) (ARUP & Foundation, 2018)	• Design out waste and pollution • Keep products and material in use • Regenerate natural systems
(ARUP & Ellen MacArthur Foundation, 2020)	Circular business models for real estate • Flexible spaces • Adaptable assets • Relocatable buildings • Residual value • Performance procurement
(ARUP, 2016)	The six elements of CE are regenerate, share, optimize, loop, virtualize and exchange.
(Arup et al., 2017)	• Circular design model • Circular use model • Circular recovery model

solar energy, are being explored and promoted by the governments. Green buildings[3] provide significant business opportunities for resource conservation in the built environment.

Systems and processes for waste reduction: Systems and processes should be designed and used to increase productivity and waste reduction in terms of material, cost, labor and time. The use of technologies such as BIM, 3-D printing, drones, artificial intelligence, virtual reality and digital platforms help in bringing efficiencies in real estate and construction.

Sharing and service economy: Moving from product ownership to service opens up opportunities in the sharing economy, such as co-working, co-living and Airbnb type models. It also brings in operating efficiencies in the entire ecosystem.

Flexible spaces: Many spaces in buildings are underutilized, for example a playground in a school; auditorium and lecture rooms in a college; an atrium in an office building; and a terrace. These spaces can be designed to be utilized for multiple purposes and in different shifts across the day.

Life extension strategies: Products can be designed so that at the end of economic life, they can be re-designed and re-positioned. Certain types of structural designs in buildings, such as modular and steel frame structures, make repurposing, retrofitting, and refitting easier.

Recovery of material: Buildings should be designed and constructed of a material that can be easily recycled, reclaimed and reused.

Adoption of circular economy in real estate

As pointed by ARUP & Ellen MacArthur Foundation (2020), to implement circular principles in buildings it is important to understand the project lifecycle. This would mean evaluating various phases of value addition across the lifecycle stages of a project, such as land stage, market research and feasibility, design and planning, financing, construction and project management, lease, operations and maintenance (O&M), extended life (refitting–retrofitting–repurposing) and end-of-life salvage value extraction (recycle–reuse–redevelopment). This will require innovative adaption of technology, circular design thinking, newer ownership and financing structures, improvement in construction productivity by using technology, improved O&M systems, capital expenditure (CapEx) in sustainable and durable plant and machinery, development in recycling and reuse technology, and modification in regulatory and legal systems to support sustainable development. Various stages across the lifecycle of a project are shown in Figure 7.1. Discussed below are sources of waste, opportunities and challenges faced across these stages.

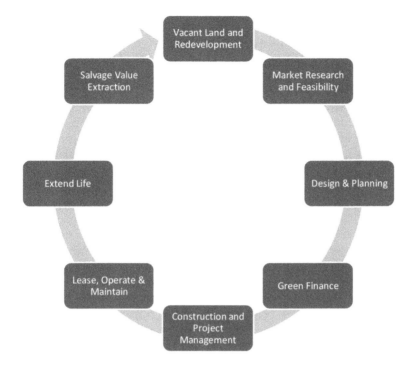

Figure 7.1   Adoption of circularity across the lifecycle of a real estate project

Table 7.3   Optimum utilization of vacant lands and redevelopment

Waste	Opportunity	Challenge
• Vacant land: Sub-optimal utilization of city infrastructure. • Old buildings: Operate at sub-optimal efficiencies.	• Creation of temporary housing on vacant land parcels (concrete pipe houses, container houses). • Redevelopment and re-densification of old properties.	• The legal framework discourages/does not allow the creation of temporary and move-able houses. • Enact regulations to discourage vacant land and houses. • Draconian legis-lation discourages redevelopment.

Vacant land and redevelopment

Vacant land parcels with development potential result in the sub-optimal utilization of city infrastructure. Providing urban infrastructure is challenging, expensive and uses resources extensively. Its sub-optimal utilization adds to material and environmental degradation and should be avoided. Vacant land can be utilized for the creation of temporary housing using prefab and modular structures. These land parcels could be leased to the operators to provide temporary and moveable housing solutions such as concrete pipe and container houses. These operators may provide short leases with options to move between a portfolio of properties managed by them, providing mobility and options at different locations to city residents and travelers. Many legal structures do not allow the creation of temporary and moveable houses in cities. Regulations such as rent control and tenancy acts need to take cognizance of the need for short leases for these kinds of business models. Regulations and urban taxation should discourage keeping land and built-up space vacant through vacant land and vacant property taxes.

Many old buildings, due to physical and economic obsolescence, operate at sub-optimal efficiencies. For example, there are many residential colonies[4] used primarily by government employees as staff quarters that were built decades ago and are near the end of their physical/economic lives and have the potential for densification. These properties have high redevelopment potential due to the increased Floor Area Ratio (FAR) and their location. Laws and regulations on one hand should support redevelopment and repositioning of old properties; and, on the other, should ensure that these new developments are based on the principle of CE, having the least negative externalities on the existing environment and local communities.

Market research and feasibility

Project feasibility is conducted considering the build–exit model. Owing to this in the long-term, product positioning as an Op-Asset is compromised and, in the short-term, salability of the project is the key objective of the feasibility exercise. The focus of this model is buyers/investors, which often leads to speculative construction activities that lead to unoccupied stock with a high vacancy in certain micro-markets. Considering the CE paradigm of operating assets with long life, long-term product positioning would be focused, which would result in projects that have long-term value and utility to users and return to investors. This would lead to the development of projects with long-term utility and value.

Table 7.4   A new approach to market research

Waste	Opportunity	Challenge
• Project feasibility is conducted considering the build-exit model. This results in speculative construction activities, subsequently high vacancy and no consideration for extended life.	• In the build-operate-exit model long-term product positioning to be evaluated. • This will also align the interest of the owner to increase the product life.	• This will require a new mindset of build, operate and exiting once an asset is stabilized.

The key question in developing a long-term perspective in property development is: are real estate advisory firms, investors and developers ready for this new mindset of build, operate and exiting once an asset is stabilized? Once this mindset is achieved, there seems little challenge to incorporating these changes in the project feasibility.

Design and planning

The traditional design follows the approach of take–make–use–dispose. This results in wastage at each stage of the project from land, construction, operating life to end of life (physical obsolescence). There is significant scope for extensive improvements in designing buildings with green materials, for longer life, lower OpEx and higher residual value. Design helps to weed out waste at each stage by adopting green design using recyclable materials, design for durability (long life) and operational efficiency, having flexible design[5] features, designed for deconstruction and ease of segregation of reusable material at end of life (reuse and recycle). Akanbi et al. (2018) found that buildings designed using steel structures and prefabricated components have high reusable and recyclable components at the end of the useful life of the building. Other design features, such as open offices and agile planning,[6] can improve

Table 7.5   Implementing CE principals through design and planning

Waste	Opportunity	Challenge
• The traditional linear approach results in wastage at each stage of the project from land, construction, operating life to end of life.	• Green product design. • Design for long life. • Flexible design. • Design for deconstruction i.e. recycling and reuse.	• Uncertainty due to higher CapEx and longer recovery. Making it risky and unattractive to adopt.

the usability and density of offices. British Council for Offices (2018) estimated that over the core part of the day, office desks are unoccupied 40% of the time. In an agile work environment, there is 10% more space utilization as compared with the traditional office. In the ABN Amro Pavilion in Amsterdam, Arup et al. (2017) found that circular design and collaboration results in an end-of-life residual value of 60%.

There are limited data points justifying risks related to additional CapEx and long recovery, technological efficiency and market response to adopting CE in real estate, making it risky and unattractive to be adopted by developers and investors. This will require a change in the mindset of various stakeholders and close coordination for creating sustainable buildings. The regulatory regime would need to adapt, support and incentivize this new paradigm.

Green finance

Traditional financing does not consider sustainability issues whereas green financing rewards firms for the adoption of sustainability. With the mandatory reporting of Environmental, Social and Governance (ESG) parameters, the last few years have seen a phenomenal increase in green finance. The benefits of green financing include improved long-term performance, positive brand image and risk reduction. Giese et al. (2019) demonstrated that the ESG performance gets translated to the company's performance, higher valuation and lower systematic risk. Survey results show that the real estate firms have shown commitment to 13 of the 17 United Nations Sustainable Development Goals.[7] However, still existing financing mechanisms in real estate focus on the build and exit models. New long-term financing models are required that have a robust real-estate specific framework. Long-term investors, such as pension funds and insurance companies, will play an important role in CE financing in real estate.

Table 7.6   Adopting green finance

Waste	Opportunity	Challenge
• Traditional financing does not reward sustainability issues. This creates waste across the product lifecycle.	• Benefits for green financing include improved long-term performance, positive brand image and risk reduction.	• Long-term financing models customized to operating real estate assets are required. • Mechanisms to value and finance the green component are evolving.

Table 7.7   Implementing CE principals in building construction

Waste	Opportunity	Challenge
• Waste results due to sub-optimal use of labor, rework, material waste and poor processes.	• To use recycled materials. • Reduction of material wastage, labor and reworks through technologies such as BIM.	• Implementing CE increases cost. • There is limited acceptance of CE in construction. • The regulatory impetus is required (incentive and punitive actions).

Construction and project management

Construction processes generate waste in the form of material waste, sub-optimal use of labor, reworks, poor systems and processes and other productivity issues. This results in extensive wastage of natural resources, project delays, legal disputes and litigations. McKinsey Global Institute (2017) estimated an increase in construction productivity can add $1.6 trillion to the global GDP and boost it by 2%. Reduction of various types of wastes, such as material, labor and reworks, can be achieved through better planning and project management tools and technologies, such as Building Information Modeling (BIM). The use of technology and green materials will reduce the carbon footprint. Green construction technologies and green buildings have been estimated as a $24.7 trillion investment opportunity by 2030 (IFC, 2019). In cement production, innovative technology improvements can bring an 80% reduction in resources and emissions (UNEP, 2012).

Implementing CE in construction increases CapEx; this will require justification, rethinking and repositioning the business models. Currently there is a lot of interest in sustainable construction but its implementation on the ground would need regulatory impetus by governments both in incentive and punitive actions.

Lease, operate and maintain

In the take–make–sale–dispose model, developers maximize return on investment (ROI) by minimizing upfront CapEx, resulting in sub-optimal OpEx efficiency of buildings. They use non-green virgin material and average quality plant and machinery that results in high energy consumption in building operations. Developers have limited interest in durability (long life) and operational efficiencies as they don't have a long-term operating commitment to buildings. The primary focus is investor demand, with low regard for end-user demand.

Table 7.8 Adopting lease, operate and maintain model

Waste	Opportunity	Challenge
• Developers minimize upfront CapEx resulting in lower OpEx efficiency. • The sale model results in the creation of speculative supply.	• The service model opens up many new opportunities in the sharing economy (co-working, co-living, Airbnb). • New opportunities in Operations and Maintenance (O&M). • Improved lifecycle occupancy cost.	• Developers don't have the means and incentive to retain operating assets. • Many legal systems don't provide finance for land procurement, forcing developers to exit. • Legal uncertainty in terms of the taxes related to operating leases.

This results in the creation of speculative supply giving rise to underutilized and vacant buildings.

Moving from ownership to service model through leasing opens up many new business opportunities in the sharing economy. Popular and emerging shared economy models are co-working, co-living, student housing, time-share and Airbnb. The focus on services results in opportunities in the O&M of various asset classes. The focus of CE is on improving the lifecycle occupancy cost to justify this additional CapEx in green construction.

The critical question is: do developers have any incentive to retain these Op-Assets for recurring income or exit for capital value? The answer lies in the fact that, in many countries, laws do not allow institutional finance for land procurement, which is between 30 and 70%[8] of the project cost. This forces developers to sell their completed buildings for the purchase of land for future projects; often leading to speculative investment in land and the creation of land banks. This defeats one of the paradigms of CE that supports suppliers to retain the ownership of the services and products. In many legal systems, elements of buildings are considered as fixtures, essentially an integral part of the building. This gives rise to legal ambiguity, which does not support circular business models and operating leases (Ploeger et al., 2019).

There needs to be a change in the mindset of various stakeholders from considering buildings as pure-play Cap-Assets to Op-Assets. ARUP & Ellen MacArthur Foundation (2020) reported a potential saving of 18% of net present rent cost over 12 years by analyzing a tenanted office in Milan through operating efficiencies. Gupta and Tiwari (2016) found, in the context of developing economies, that exit from commercial properties is considered the key risk for investors in the absence of exit vehicles such as Real Estate Investment Trusts (REITs). Developing CE in real estate would require new financing models with long-term capital and exit options for developers, such as REITs (in emerging economies). Developers should be incentivized to retain at least a part ownership in these leased or operational assets through regulatory, monetary and taxation frameworks.

Extend life

McKinsey Global Institute (2017) estimated 13% of global GDP is spent on construction-related goods and services. Currently, with limited focus to extend the life of buildings, the resources spent on buildings are not optimally utilized. These resources can be made more productive by extending the life of the building by designing for long life.

The buildings are designed using steel prefabricated and modular material which can be easily renovated and refabricated. And the structural components can also be replaced. These buildings can be repositioned and their life can be extended through innovative and flexible design. This creates business opportunities around extended life strategies such as renovation, refurbishment and retrofitting.

This will require investment in the technology and building systems. Many of these assets may be Op-Assets with tenants, thus their renovation, refurbishment and retrofitting could be challenging. Planning guidelines, regulations and financing mechanisms should support repair, renovation, refurbishment and retrofit.

Table 7.9   Extending the life of buildings

Waste	Opportunity	Challenge
• The resources used in building construction are not optimally utilized, as buildings are not designed for extended life.	• This creates business opportunities around extended life strategies such as renovation, refurbishment and retrofitting.	• Investment is required in the technology and building systems. • Many of these assets have tenants, making renovation, refurbishment and retrofitting challenging. • Planning guidelines, regulations, financing mechanisms and health and safety guidelines do not support repair, renovate, refurbish and retrofitting.

Table 7.10   Implementing salvage value extraction

Waste	Opportunity	Challenge
• Take, make, sale and dispose results in the creation of waste at the end of life that ends up in a landfill.	• Extracting the salvage value in buildings can be a big business opportunity. • To develop an ecosystem enabling technology, equipment and reverse logistics to reuse and recycle demolition waste.	• Requires investment in the development of suitable reuse and recycling technologies and equipment. • This will become financially viable with achieving the economics of scale. • Regulatory support, incentives and enabling policies are required.

Salvage value extraction

Take, make, sale and dispose results in the creation of waste at the end of life of a building that ends mostly in a landfill. Sometimes, due to economic obsolescence, the life of the building is further reduced, aggravating the problem. In developing countries there is a large unorganized industry (for example, called *kabariwala* in India) recycling and reusing end-of-life products. Reusing and transforming the salvage value in buildings could be a big business opportunity. The extraction of material should be cost, time and resource efficient.

Moving the demolition waste offsite many times may be expensive, for which we need to develop a reverse logistic infrastructure. Apart from this, it would require the development of suitable technology and equipment for the transformation of material for reuse and recycle. Akanbi et al. (2018) recommended BIM could be used to audit the end-of-life removable, reusable and recyclable structural material. They found BIM to be a helpful tool for surveyors and demolition teams to conduct an audit before demolition at the end of the life of a building.

Heavy construction equipment manufacturer Caterpillar in 2020 collected 131 million pounds of end-of-life material for remanufacturing and has achieved a 51% greenhouse gas reduction compared with 2006. Between 2018–2030, the company intends to achieve a 25% increase in sales and revenue from remanufacturing, and to reduce landfill intensity by 50%.[9] These waste recycle and reuse strategies would result in the reduction of input cost for new construction and wastage at end-of-life. PACE (2021) in the Circularity Gap Report 2021 estimated CE strategies could reduce construction and demolition waste by 9.5 billion tonnes annually.

Business models around end-of-life strategy will become economically viable once the economics of scale is achieved. This would need regulatory support, incentives and enabling policies to promote and incentivize the industry to recycle waste and reuse in new construction. Along with this, there should be considerations of the health and safety of the suitability of the recycled material.

Conclusion

The circular economy has emerged as a new reality for governments and businesses. Successful business models demonstrated by Caterpillar and Airbnb show that CE is not just a theoretical construct but is the emerging reality of the current times and the future of business. It increases resource productivity, opens up new business opportunities, creates sustainable business practices, and reduces risk and uncertainty. Within real estate companies, there is a lot of interest in sustainable development, but there are gaps between the intended and on-ground implementation. They need a cultural change in thinking and a strategy supported by tools to implement CE in property development (Ionaşcu et al., 2020). The green shoots of acceptance and implementation of the CE and ESG investment are evident. The research has shown a positive correlation between high ESG scores and valuation and the performance of the businesses.

Developing 'circular building' requires an ambitious vision, a new process integrating various processes in the supply chain, collaborative response within stakeholders, and developing innovative business and ownership partnerships. The government as a key stakeholder has to create an enabling environment with supportive policies and laws for punitive action against the defaulters. This is an emerging area with scope for technological advancement in systems, processes and equipment to achieve a circular economy in real estate. In the absence of hard data in this field, future research should focus on the perspective of key stakeholders for policy formulation to achieve a holistic circular economy in the real estate and construction sector.

We have only one earth to live on and it is an inheritance that needs to be passed to future generations.

Notes

1. UNEP (2021) provides an estimate of 12% for many countries.
2. In 2019, CO_2 emissions from the building sector were the highest ever recorded.
3. IFC (2019) discussed the advantages of green buildings, such as a decrease in operational expenses, higher capital value, faster sales, higher rentals and higher occupancy rates, thus making a strong case for adoption of these principles in the form of Green Buildings.
4. https://www.news18.com/news/india/high-court-may-permit-redevelopment-in-6-delhi-colonies-if-approvals-granted-1897477.html
5. Real estate markets are dynamic and take a long time between product design and completion. During this time demand may change for the product. Thus, flexible designs have the potential for adapting to these changes.
6. "A term describing a range of work styles that are technology-enabled, not dependent on a single place of work, characterized by a high level of choice and mobility, and usually involving some desk-sharing" (British Council for Offices, 2018).
7. ESG in real estate finance, part 2: Considering societal impact | Real Estate Capital (recapitalnews.com).
8. As per industry sources.
9. https://reports.caterpillar.com/sr/2020_Caterpillar_Sustainability_Report.pdf?_ga=2.108497282.1264515907.1625266634-2071107307.1625266634

References

Accenture. (2015). *Waste to Wealth: The Circular Economy Advantage* (1st edn). Palgrave Macmillan.

Akanbi, L. A., Oyedele, L. O., Akinade, O. O., Ajayi, A. O., Davila Delgado, M., Bilal, M., & Bello, S. A. (2018). Salvaging building materials in a circular economy: A BIM-based whole-life performance estimator. *Resources, Conservation and Recycling, 129*, 175–186. https://doi.org/10.1016/j.resconrec.2017.10.026

ARUP. (2016). *The Circular Economy in the Built Environment*. https://www.arup.com/perspectives/publications/research/section/circular-economy-in-the-built-environment

Arup, BAM, & CE100. (2017). *Circular Business Models for the Built Environment*. http://www.duurzaam-ondernemen.nl/circular-business-models-for-the-built-environment-research-report-by-arup-bam/

ARUP, & Ellen MacArthur Foundation. (2020). *From Principles to Practices: Realising the Value of Circular Economy in Real Estate*. https://www.ellenmacarthurfoundation.org/assets/downloads/Realising-the-value-of-circular-economy-in-real-estate.pdf

ARUP, & Foundation, E. M. (2018). *From Principles to Practices: First Steps Towards a Circular Built Environment*. https://www.arup.com/perspectives/publications/research/section/first-steps-towards-a-circular-built-environment

British Council for Offices. (2018). *Office Occupancy: Density and Utilisation*. http://www.bco.org.uk/Research/Publications/Office_Occupancy_Density_and_Utilisation.aspx

Ellen MacArthur Foundation. (2013). Towards the circular economy: Economic and business rationale for an accelerated transition. In *Ellen MacArthur Foundation*. https://www.ellenmacarthurfoundation.org/assets/downloads/publications/Ellen -MacArthur-Foundation-Towards-the-Circular-Economy-vol.1.pdf

Ellen MacArthur Foundation. (2019). Complete the picture: How the circular economy tackles climate change. In *Ellen MacArthur Foundation*. www.ellenmacarthur foundation.org/publications

Giese, G., Lee, L.-E., Melas, D., Nagy, Z., & Nishikawa, L. (2019). Foundations of ESG investing: How ESG affects equity valuation, risk, and performance. *Journal of Portfolio Management, 45*(5), 69–83.

Gupta, A., & Tiwari, P. (2016). Investment risk scoring model for commercial properties in India. *Journal of Property Investment & Finance, 34*(2), 156–171.

IEA. (2019). *Perspectives for a Clean Energy Transition. The Critical Role of Buildings.* IEA.

IFC. (2019). *Green Buildings: A Finance and Policy Blueprint for Emerging Markets.* https://www.ifc.org/wps/wcm/connect/a6e06449-0819-4814-8e75-903d4f564731/ 59988-IFC-GreenBuildings-report_FINAL_1-30-20.pdf?MOD=AJPERES&CVID= m.TZbMU

Ionașcu, E., Mironiuc, M., Anghel, I., & Huian, M. C. (2020). The involvement of real estate companies in sustainable development – An analysis from the SDGs reporting perspective. *Sustainability, 12*(3). https://doi.org/10.3390/su12030798

McKinsey. (2015). *Europe's Circular-economy Opportunity.* https://www.mckinsey .com/business-functions/sustainability/our-insights/europes-circular-economy -opportunity

McKinsey Global Institute. (2017). *Reinventing Construction: A Route to Higher Productivity* (February issue). http://www.mckinsey.com/industries/capital-projects -and-infrastructure/our-insights/reinventing-construction-through-a-productivity -revolution

OECD. (2018). *Business Models for the Circular Economy: Opportunities and Challenges from a Policy Perspective.* https://www.oecd.org/environment/waste/policy -highlights-business-models-for-the-circular-economy.pdf

PACE. (2021). *The Circularity Gap Report 2021.* https://www.circularity-gap.world/ 2021

Ploeger, H., Prins, M., Straub, A., & Van den Brink, R. (2019). Circular economy and real estate: The legal (im)possibilities of operational lease. *Facilities, 37*(9–10), 653–668. https://doi.org/10.1108/F-01-2018-0006

UN-Habitat. (2012). *Energy.* https://unhabitat.org/topic/energy

UNEP. (2012). *Responsible Resource Management for a Sustainable World: Findings from the International Resource Panel.* https://wedocs.unep.org/bitstream/handle/ 20.500.11822/10580/responsible_resource_management.pdf?sequence=1&amp %3BisAllowed=

UNEP. (2020). *2020 Global Status Report for Buildings and Construction: Towards a Zero-emissions, Efficient and Resilient Buildings and Construction Sector.* https:// globalabc.org/sites/default/files/inline-files/2020BuildingsGSR_FULLREPORT.pdf

UNEP. (2021). *Why Buildings? Our Key Messages.* http://globalabc.org/media-global -advocacy/why-buildings-our-key-messages#building-7

United Nations. (2018). *World Urbanization Prospects 2018.* https://population.un.org/ wup/

8   Climate change and risk to real estate

Georgia Warren-Myers and Anna Hurlimann

Introduction

The progression of climate change will have a resounding effect on real estate (property) and real estate (property) markets.[1] Whilst initial effects are starting to be felt, the limited action to address climate change risks across the sector suggests a lack of foresight of the implications that will evolve over time. The challenge to address climate change is twofold, first society must concurrently mitigate greenhouse gas (GHG) emissions, which contribute to the escalation of climate change. Second, to ensure adaptation is implemented to minimise the effects that changes in climate have, some of which are already occurring and cannot be avoided. Whilst mitigation and adaptation actions have been addressed in recent years, actions largely fall short of what is required to curtail the impact of climate change.

Over 50% of the world's population live in urban areas, with built environments contributing in the order of 40–70% of GHG emissions through activities such as those involving the burning of fossil fuels, for example, electricity generation and transport, according to UN-HABITAT (2011). Hence, the role that the real estate sector plays in urban areas could make it a key contributor to driving down GHG emissions that are the source of climate change, and thus influence risk reduction. Further, there are significant risks to the real estate sector from climate change impacts. For example, conservative estimates of an anticipated global mean sea level rise of 56 cm by the end of the century is expected to directly impact more than 48 million people (Rasmussen et al. 2018). Others calculate 4°C of warming by the end of the century with 8.9 m of sea level rise and 627 million people living below that level based on 2010 figures (Strauss et al. 2015). Given the land and property affected by climate change, real estate has an important role in adapting to climate change impacts, whilst minimising loss and damage to existing assets of public and private benefit.

This chapter begins with an overview of key aspects of climate science and demonstrates the need to rapidly reduce GHG emissions over the next decade. The chapter then moves to examine key climate change impacts on real estate, and considers the implications these have. Throughout the chapter we identify five key challenges that climate change poses to the real estate sector. We then address these in the conclusion, presenting a crucial future research agenda to understand the challenges of climate change risk, to assist in decision-making now and in the long term, across the real estate sector and beyond.

Climate change – the need for substantial and immediate action

Over the past three decades the Intergovernmental Panel on Climate Change (IPCC) has become the authoritative source for the analysis and synthesis of research related to climate change and its impacts across the globe. Their research collates a body of evidence that human activities have contributed to increased GHG emissions responsible for a 1.0°C warming to date (IPCC 2018). Future expectations of climate change and its implications are not promising, with the consequences of inaction severe. The direct and indirect effects of climate change will be significant and catastrophic for human societies, and for the built and natural environments. Whilst locational variations exist, it is anticipated there will be increased extreme weather events, longer periods of drought, increased frequency of temperature extremes, increased bushfire and wildfire risk, and sea level rises. In turn, these impacts will significantly impact human health, wellbeing and economies. Current international agreements, such as the Paris Agreement (United Nations 2015) seek to limit global warming to 1.5°C above preindustrial levels by 2100, in order to limit risk, and avoid catastrophic climate change (IPCC 2018). However, the current trajectory of global GHG emissions is set to result in between 3.2 and 5.4°C of warming by 2100 (IPCC 2015). Additionally, even if the commitments that countries have pledged under the Paris Agreement are achieved, it is projected we will still have 3.2°C of warming as detailed by the UN Environment Program (UNEP 2019). Hence the scale and speed in which society must cut GHG emissions is significant, requiring substantial and immediate action.

Without significant action to reduce GHG emissions across all sectors of the economy, the inability to limit warming will leave built and natural environments exposed to the risks associated with rising seas and coastal erosion, and increases in extreme weather event intensity and frequency. This in turn has a range of implications on resources, ecosystems, and cities, across cultural, social, environmental and economic perspectives (IPCC 2018). Already the effects of 1°C of warming have resulted in coral reef bleaching, changing weather patterns – increasing periods of heatwaves and droughts, increasing severity and frequency of extreme weather events, and melting glaciers, ice sheets and permafrost (IPCC 2018). The implications for built environments, and specifically real estate, have seen increases in damage costs, insurance premiums (or having assets that are uninsurable), losses in values and revenue as occupiers and investors seek better located or more robust properties or bear the damages to property, infrastructure and agricultural production (Steffen et al. 2019). These impacts are all expected to increase, as warming increases. Even if warming is limited to 1.5°C, there will be significant effects on natural and built environments that will result in ever increasing social, environmental and economic costs.

A summary of the anticipated impacts of climate change is detailed in Table 8.1. Note, much of the literature focuses on identifying the physical impacts of 1.5 and 2°C warming, and in general notes the significant negative impacts of warming beyond that – the trajectory on which we are headed. Without significant mitigation efforts, it is very likely that by 2100 between 3.2–5.4°C of warming will be realised, with severe and widespread impacts, for example to unique and threatened systems; substantial species extinction; risks to food security; constraints to human activities; and increased likelihood of triggering critical thresholds (tipping points) (IPCC 2015, p. 86). These metrics do not convey the social and cultural impacts of these changes, which will be significant and should be considered (Graham et al. 2013).

In examining mitigation and adaptation, it is important to consider that these are separate entities, but which also need to be integrated to reduce the overall impacts of climate change (Grafakos et al. 2018). In order to minimise the amount of adaptive investment required, the impacts of climate change need to be minimised (through mitigation). There is already a level of locked-in implications of our GHG emissions to date; but there is opportunity to minimise further emissions and further associated impacts. Thus, action is required to mitigate GHG emissions and adapt to future climate change risks in order to be ready for climate change impacts that can be no longer avoided, and to prepare for missed mitigation targets (e.g. limiting warming to 1.5°C) and its consequences.

Table 8.1   Impacts of climate change under 1.5°C and 2°C warming
scenarios

	Meet Paris Agreement goals*		Higher end emissions
Temperature change*	1.5°C	2°C	4°C +
Hot weather – global (Betts et al. 2018)	16% more hot days	24% more hot days	
Global population facing severe heatwave at least once every 5 years (Dosio et al. 2018)	13.8%	36.9%	
Area burned by wildfires – Mediterranean (Turco et al. 2018)	Up 41%	Up 62%	
Sea level rise			
Sea level rise – conservative (Rasmussen et al. 2018)	48 cm	56 cm	
Sea level rise – high-end projections (Strauss et al. 2015)	3.1 m	4.7 m	8.9 m
Population below sea level rise – conservative (based on 2010 population figures) (Rasmussen et al. 2018)	46.12 million	48.76 million	
Population below sea level rise – high-end projections (Kulp and Strauss 2019)	190 million		230 million
Annual flood damage losses from sea level rise (Jevrejeva et al. 2018) in trillions of dollars	US$10.2 trillion	US$11.7 trillion	US$14.3 trillion
Weather extremes			
Increased flood risk based on percentage increase in average annual losses for investment portfolios (AAL) by 2050 (UK, North America and Pacific Rim) (Cambridge Institute for Sustainability Leadership (CISL) 2019)		40–43%	70–80%
Percentage increase in AAL for residential mortgages in the UK (CISL 2019)		61%	130%

	Meet Paris Agreement goals*	Higher end emissions
Percentage increase in residential properties in the UK at significant risk of flooding (CISL 2019)	25%	40%
Frequency of extreme rainfall on land (Betts et al. 2018)	Up 6%	Up 3.5%

Note: *Our current trajectory of global warming will see in the order of 3.2°C of warming by 2100 if Paris Agreement targets are met (UNEP 2019)

Climate change and implications for real estate

Here we detail some implications of climate change for the real estate sector, and identify five key challenges. As detailed in the previous section, the impacts of inadequate action to curtail climate change are significant. Climate change impacts, and hence the adaptive actions required to address the impacts, including in the real estate sector, will not be uniform across the globe. Locations within countries, within states, and within cities will bear different effects and impacts from climate change. Yet, much of the data about climate change impacts is at the global scale, hence:

Challenge 1: There is a need for a detailed understanding of climate change implications on real estate at the local level to enable and facilitate more effective adaptation decision making for the sector.

Additionally, much of the information about climate change has not been translated into a form that can be directly applied to real estate sector needs and decision making. We discuss this further by addressing the diversity of climate change impacts across real estate sectors, before detailing actions in the sector that have occurred to date, by adaptation and mitigation potential.

Diverse climate change impacts across real estate sub-sectors

The real estate sector, and the actors within it are diverse, which is important to recognise when discussing climate change implications for the sector. Climate change presents a variety of risks applicable to real estate. The risks are broad and far-reaching and can affect different real estate types in different parts of the world to different degrees. Even the variability of sea level rise will affect different areas to different levels due to proximity to the equator, and differential heating and salinity changes in various ocean layers, with the subsequent effects on population dependent on a nation's stage of development and its current adaptation responses (Hinkel et al. 2018; Yin et al. 2010).

The various real estate sectors are often affected in the same way by climate change risks, however, some are more exposed than others. Sea level rises will affect all properties situated in low-lying areas, either through complete inundation and loss, or increased flooding risks resulting in more recurrent flooding and associated damages. In addition, as coastal low-lying areas are some of the most highly populated locations in the world, it will not just be economic costs felt, but substantial social costs including human loss and injury and depreciation of natural capital (Warren-Myers et al. 2018). Further, sea level rises will affect the productive capacity of agriculture and viability of agricultural activities, placing strain on the food supply. In addition, there will be loss of farming land and increased salt water intrusion into groundwater, creating increasing salinity issues and resulting in ruination of crops, and damage or loss to livestock, land and infrastructure (Steffen et al. 2019).

It is estimated that if greenhouse gas emissions continue to rise, AU$226 billion of commercial, industrial, road, rail and residential assets in Australia will be at risk of sea level rise by 2100 (Department of Climate Change and Energy Efficiency, 2011). Increased temperatures and more frequent heat-waves, droughts and bushfires will also affect agricultural land, and, for built environments, create greater stresses on building infrastructure across the spectrum through increased demands for cooling, thus placing additional load on energy grids. A heatwave across south-eastern Australia in 2009 saw direct financial losses estimated at AU$800 million, which were primarily a result of disruptions to electricity, transport and emergency services (Queensland University of Technology 2010). Yet real costs are well underestimated, as just the reduction in labour productivity due to heatwaves annually is estimated around AU$8.7 billion per year (Zander et al. 2015). The Victorian Bushfires Royal Commission (2010) reported that the 2009 Black Saturday bushfire is estimated to have cost AU$4.4 billion. Of this amount, property associated losses covered by insurance comprised AU$1.2 billion. Yet this is likely underestimated as 13% of homes were not insured. Extreme weather events comprising increases in wind speeds, storm severity and precipitation are esca-lating. This is causing increases in building, infrastructure and land damages and losses, with increasing insurance premiums and an increasing number of properties identified as uninsurable over the coming decade (Furnnell 2020).

Challenge 2: There is a diversity of sub-sectors within real estate, with heteroge-neous types of real estate, characteristics, actors and associated climate change impacts. Research is needed to understand the climate change impacts across the diversity of the real estate sector, to inform decision making.

Climate change risks will vary across the diversity of the real estate sector. There are three key types of losses that are considered to have a direct effect on a property's value and risk profile: direct, indirect, and consequential:

- Direct losses – losses associated with damage or total loss of tangible assets, for example loss or damage to dwellings, offices, buildings, infrastructure or public facilities, increased costs related to materials or resources, increased insurance premiums (Kron et al. 2012, p. 542);
- Indirect losses – losses associated with the operational aspects of the building, for example loss of rent, loss of revenue from business generation, loss of jobs and costs or losses associated with transport to the building (Kron et al. 2012, p. 543);
- Consequential losses – losses that are essentially considered "secondary costs", which occur as a result of repercussions of the event, for example lower direct investment, increased vacancy, loss of demand, loss of competitiveness in the market (Bienert 2014, p. 9).

Other losses that may affect property values and risk profiles, which provide a greater unknown, are the social costs and losses, including the loss of human life and injury costs. These have implications for occupational health and safety considerations and requirements for capital investment to prevent such losses, or they may affect the market demand and market competitiveness of the asset. Further losses are related to natural capital, where losses may relate to ecosystem damage or loss, and this could also include cultural heritage and heritage structures that are damaged or lost due to climate-related events (Bienert 2014; Warren-Myers et al. 2018).

Additionally, business and regulatory risks will be associated with each of the three identified loss aspects (direct, in direct and consequential) as these depend on actions by industry and/or government regulation across both mitigation and adaptation. For example, recent changes to have a minimum level of energy performance under the Energy Performance Certificate (EPC) has led to a stranding of assets – having a detrimental impact on value and utility (Muldoon-Smith and Greenhalgh 2019). There are two further types of losses. These relate to human loss and injury costs; and costs associated with the loss of natural capital. Whilst they are important considerations, and have broader implications for real estate owners, investors, occupiers and managers for reputational and business risk perspectives, they are outside the direct scope of this chapter. Table 8.2 details selected climate change risks, their implications for real estate, and the loss and value implications.

The preparedness and action of the real estate sector relies on examining and understanding the risks associated with climate change to enable suitable responses in the form of both mitigation and adaptation actions. Physical risk is likely the easiest to model and quantify; however, the other risks are often classed as 'unknown' because they are not usually insured, unlike the direct physical risks, and are often considerably larger than first thought. For example, evidence is beginning to emerge that private property owners are increasingly discounting properties exposed to sea level rise by up to 7% (Bernstein et al. 2019). However, the perceived discounting of property at risk of sea level rise is highly dependent on whether you believe in climate change. Baldauf et al. (2020) found that those who were 'believers' discounted properties at risk compared with those in denier neighbourhoods.

Sea level rise is, in effect, largely a 'future' event, yet even estimating current effects is challenging as amenities (like those associated with living close to the coast) outweigh perceived risk (Atreya and Czajkowski 2014). However, there is evidence that flood risk properties are often discounted (Beltrán et al. 2018), even if discounting for sea level rise is not yet evident (Murfin et al. 2020; Fuerst and Warren-Myers 2021). The growing emphasis on climate change and its role in current natural hazards such as hurricanes (cyclones), wildfires and blizzards, is generating strong sceptic behaviour in relation to climate change (Dixon et al. 2019). Yet evidence is also emerging that certain affected industries, or groups who are feeling the effects of events, are more adverse to climate change risks (Hamilton-Webb et al. 2017). Understanding climate change related risks can be easily expanded by understanding the potential losses associated with climate change. There is already emerging evidence that certain climate change related effects are impacting property through various means. Table 8.3 provides an overview of some recent events demonstrating vulnerability to these climate change risks and the implications of this now and into the future.

The need for better information about climate change impacts for the real estate sector

Since the publication of the IPCC's first assessment report in 1990, there has been increased awareness of climate change and its future impacts. Yet, at the same time, there has been an acknowledgement that the largely scientific information presented in these reports needs to be translated into a format that is suitable for the needs of decision makers working in government and industry.

Table 8.2 Climate change risks and how they are translated to loss and value implications for real estate

Climate change and related risks	Implications for real estate	Types of loss and value implications
Sea level rise [1]	• Inundation • Increased flooding and damage • Ongoing increased costs: damage and preventative • Uninsurable • Salt intrusion into ground water and coastal wetlands	**Direct:** Total loss of real estate/ property and value associated with land and buildings (permanent inundation); increased flood damage costs over time.[1,3] **Indirect:** Utility of asset periodically affected or lost entirely, loss of rent/income generated through ownership, lost revenue for businesses, costs associated with jobs or access, subsequent effect on value.[1] **Consequential:** Discounting of property value with reoccurrence of event, lower direct investment, increased vacancy, loss of demand, increased depreciation and obsolescence.[1] **Value:** Long-term complete loss of property/ significantly discounted value due to damage and prevention costs, increased depreciation and obsolescence, uninsurable status.[1]
Temp- erature changes	• Increased number of days with higher temperatures • Increased capacity require- ments of building cooling systems due to higher average temperatures[2] • Higher energy demand (peak), potential blackouts[3]	**Direct:** Costs of maintenance and replacement, reduced rents,[2] retrofitting assets with better thermal qualities (insulation, windows), lower heat generating and energy efficient equipment and greater capacity air conditioning systems.[3] **Indirect:** May result in periods of rental or income loss. **Consequential:** Reduced rentals, increased vacancy, increased obsolescence and lower market values. **Value:** Properties will need to adapt and improve energy efficiency and mechanical ventilation capacity in order to maintain value; failure will result in value discounting by occupiers and investors.

Climate change and related risks	Implications for real estate	Types of loss and value implications
Bushfires	• Increase in number of days with very high and extreme heat and fire danger[3] • Fire damage to property and assets – leading to damages or total loss of property • Increased insurance levies	**Direct:** Total loss of buildings and fire-related damage costs. [3] **Indirect:** Loss of rent/income generated through ownership, lost revenue for businesses, costs associated with jobs or access. [3] **Consequential:** Discounting of property as reoccurrence of event, lower direct investment, increased vacancy, loss of demand, increased obsolescence, insurance premiums increase or uninsurable status.[3,5] **Value:** Increased risk exposure could lead to property being uninsurable, and exposed to total loss or damage costs.
Extreme weather events	• Increased frequency and severity of storms • Increased intense rain events • Cyclone frequency may reduce but increased intensity resulting in more severe damage and loss[3] • Property damage costs from wind, hail, flood	**Direct:** Increased damage costs, from hail, wind, flooding.[2,3] **Indirect:** Loss of rent/income due to damages, lost revenue for businesses, costs associated with jobs or access. [2,3] **Consequential:** Discounting of property with reoccurrence of event, lower direct investment, increased vacancy, loss of demand, increased obsolescence, increased insurance costs.[3] **Value:** Increased risk exposure could lead to increased annual property damages (direct and indirect), potential for building to be uninsurable and exposed to long term value discounting.[2,5]

Climate change and related risks	Implications for real estate	Types of loss and value implications
Regulatory and Adaptation Costs Market Risks Resource Availability Reputation and Competition	• Increased costs associated with regulatory compliance and management[3] • Increased costs for resources, building materials, energy, water disposal of waste[3] • Higher adaptation costs to protect buildings and make them more efficient[2,3] • Increased taxes: e.g. GHG emissions; funding adaptation measures[2] • Stranding of assets: exposure to vulnerable areas/locations, or changes in legislation	**Direct:** Increased compliance and management costs; loss of market share and income; increased construction costs; increased costs associated with taxation, such as carbon taxation.[2,3] **Indirect:** Reduction or loss in rental income (rental demand); reputation and brand risk; exposure to declining markets.[3] **Consequential:** Increased obsolescence and reduction in property values if not compliant with regulations and adapting to resource efficiency to mitigate carbon cost implications.[3] **Value:** Increased risk exposure could lead to property being uninsurable, and exposed to total loss or damage costs. Declining market values due to exposure to market risks, reduction in demand, and/or regulatory requirements that result in stranded assets.

Notes: [1] Warren-Myers et al. (2018); [2] Bienert (2014); [3] Smith (2013); [4] Urban Land Institute and Heitman (2019); [5] CISL (2019).

Efforts have been made to publish 'summary reports' for policy makers. Subsequent reports by the IPCC, research and information produced by the Investor Group on Climate Change (2016), industry bodies and organisations such as the Urban Land Institute (ULI and Heitman 2019); Royal Institution of Chartered Surveyors (RICS), UN Environment Programme Finance Initiative, and academia, who have sought to examine the variability and uncertainty of climate change impacts and implications, gather and generate data and provide scenario analyses for the real estate industry and associated sectors. However, recent research by Hurlimann et al. (2018a) and Warren-Myers et al. (2020a; 2020b) have found that information and data are difficult to attain by many in the Australian construction and property sector, and that barriers are prevalent across information, cost and investment, organisational capacity, regulatory changes and ability to adapt (see Table 8.4).

Challenge 3: There is limited accessible information about the direct impacts of climate change for the real estate sector. There is a need for an increase in the quality, reliability and sharing of data on climate change and its implications.

Table 8.3 Examples of the realisation of real estate effects and implications

Climate change risk	Location/s	Current implications for real estate	Future implications	Reference
Sea level rise	Kiribati	• Increased flooding and storm damage – residents have to take refuge	• Complete loss of land and buildings	Hermann and Kempf (2017)
	Carteret Islands (Pacific)	• First location in the world to require population relocation due to sea level rise	• Climate refugees. Purchase of land in other countries for migration	Connell (2016) James (2018)
Extreme weather events	Fiji	• Cyclone Winston – strongest cyclone ever to hit landfall in southern hemisphere	• Increasing severity, generation of storm surges resulting in extreme sea levels	Walsh et al. (2012)
	Atlantic	• Cyclones have been increasing in severity by 25-30% per degree of warming • Current losses from hurricanes in the US have increased 100% since 1980	• Anticipated losses by 2100 will have increased 300%	Elsner (2020) Elsner et al. (2008)
Droughts	Cape Town, South Africa	• Without ample water supply, the viability of settlements is compromised • Suppressed economy, social and health impacts, potential for stranded assets	• Some locations may no longer be viable for human settlement due to changes in water availability	Wessel (2018) Hurlimann and Dolnicar (2011)

Climate change risk	Location/s	Current implications for real estate	Future implications	Reference
Bushfires	Australia (2019/2020) Russia (2020) California (2019)	• Increased frequency and intensity of bush-fire risk days; insurance and damage costs	• Potential for uninsurable property; increased costs of insurance/damages. Loss of prop-erty value • More fre-quent cycle of damages • Impacts for multiple life support systems	Morris (2020) Shvidenko and Schepaschenko (2013) Mueller et al. (2009)

Actions to address both climate change mitigation and climate change adaptation in the real estate sector

There is urgent need for more research from a property and property industry perspective in order to engage stakeholders and enact mitigation and adaptive action. There are important considerations that span local to global scales, and reach across the varied sectors within the real estate industry, that need to be identified, examined, and modelled with the aim of developing possible solutions and avenues for change. Increasing awareness is paramount across the sector. As identified by Warren-Myers et al. (2020a) knowledge and infor-mation in the Australian property industry is limited, with similar experiences noted elsewhere (Teicher 2018). Grasping the sector's responsibility and enact-ing the changes necessary to limit global warming is considerably more diffi-cult as the majority of the industry continues in a 'business as usual' approach. Further, the risks of climate change will vary across locations, and the effects and implications may also be localised. As a result, it may not necessarily be a case of one solution fits all, and more research, tailoring solutions to local environments, governance and policy arrangements and economic markets is needed. The timing is also uncertain and, whilst planning strategies exist for flood-prone properties, at present planning strategies for properties likely to be inundated by sea level rise is not widely practised and implemented.

Table 8.4   Barriers to climate change action in the property and construction sectors

Climate change risks and transition risks	Information barriers	Cost and investment barriers	Capacity barriers	Regulatory barriers
Sea level rise [1]	Lack of certainty and nuanced modelling for all locations. Lack of understanding of the implications of other measures affected by sea level rise, such as storm surge, high tides and waves. Ability to identify if your property is at risk and to what extent.	Damage cost estimates for your property. Understanding insurance information and the impact of premiums or un-insurance for at-risk properties. Loss in property values either completely or incrementally over time.	Identifying valid sources of information. Having the personnel who are knowledgeable and able to translate the information into operational practices and decision-making.	Lack of federal, state and local government action on a policy and implementation aspect. Local government attempts to apply through the planning process have been met with wide-scale criticism.
Temp-erature changes	Information providing detailed forecasting of future hot temperatures. Prediction and estimation of exposure to bushfire risks. Impact of future hot days, heat waves and impacts on building HVAC systems and energy power loads.	Retrofitting or constructing additional capacity for building to cope with changing environment. Damage costs associated with heat or fire events.	Identifying valid sources of information. Having the personnel who are knowledgeable and able to translate the information into operational practices and decision-making.	Changes to building codes – increases in costs to build (or rebuild). Understanding where are prohibited areas for development. Government buy back schemes of risky property.

Climate change risks and transition risks	Information barriers	Cost and investment barriers	Capacity barriers	Regulatory barriers
Extreme weather events	Prediction and estimates of severity and likelihood changes and varies by location. Insurance coverage unknown, and unknown what insurers consider for the property.	Damage cost estimates for property. Understanding insurance information and the impact of premiums or un-insurance for at-risk properties.	Identifying valid sources of information. Having the personnel who are knowledgeable and able to translate the information into operational practices and decision-making.	Changes to building codes – increases in costs to build (or rebuild).
Regulatory and adaptation costs	Lack of information about the costs and cost-benefits of new regulatory requirements, or adaptation costs for assets.	Increased costs associated with regulatory compliance and management.[3] Higher adaptation costs to protect buildings and to make them more resource efficient.[2,3] Stranding of assets, either through exposure to vulnerable areas or locations, or through changes in legislation.	Changing regulatory landscape and capacity in-house or for outsourcing of understanding the implications for the organisation and how to develop new strategies to align with climate action policies.[3]	Industry associations resistance and public opinion.

Climate change risks and transition risks	Information barriers	Cost and investment barriers	Capacity barriers	Regulatory barriers
Market risk, reputation and competition	Understanding the effect of inaction on reputation. Competitive risk and information required on cost-benefit of strategies and actions.	Increased taxes – in terms of carbon and also funding of adaptation infrastructure.[2] Value lost due to stranding of assets, either through exposure to vulnerable areas or locations, or through changes in legislation.	The need to have the right team for business strategy alignment of CSR strategies, rating systems and disclosure requirements. Competitive resilience (Teicher, 2018), identifying the potential to utilise CSR, mitigation and adaptation actions as competitive edge, but resources and costs will be associated.	Stranding of assets, either through exposure to vulnerable areas or locations, or through changes in legislation.
Resource availability	Information about resource costs and consistency of supply into the future, i.e. energy costs.	Increased costs for resources, building materials, energy, water, and disposal of waste.	Ability to identify new resources and technologies; this may also require different internal skillsets in procurement.	Lack of support for research and development in new technologies and resources. Threat of regulatory changes may cause further cost implications and security of access.

Notes: [1] Warren-Myers et al. (2020a); [2] Warren-Myers et al. (2020b, 2021); Hurlimann et al. (2018a, 2018b); [3] Hurlimann et al. (2019)

Mitigation action in the real estate sector

The Paris Agreement, along with its predecessors, sets GHG emission reduction targets for many of the developed and developing nations around the world. Whilst there is still uncertainty about the capacity to meet these targets, these and other global commitments have led to various approaches by governments and markets to regulate or enable GHG emission reductions. Given real estate could be considered a major contributor to GHG emissions, the sector has been seen as an area of great opportunity to reduce them. Many policies, regulations and voluntary market tools have been developed to engage and reduce GHG emissions in the real estate sector. Some notable policies and tools for commercial and residential property include: Energy Star (US), Energy Performance Certificates (EPC) (UK and Europe) and, in Australia, the residential Nationwide House Energy Rating Scheme (NatHERS) and the commercial National Australian Built Environment Rating Scheme (NABERS). The competitive market has seen significant uptake and engagement with rating tools and systems. This has been reflected, particularly where mandatory disclosure has been implemented, in improved ratings, and raised levels of efficiencies and sustainability in market values and rents across the world in both residential and commercial properties. A sample of such systems includes Fuerst and Warren-Myers (2018), Fuerst et al. (2015), Newell et al. (2014) and Fuerst and McAllister (2011). However, this competitive market has also meant that information sharing has been limited, and often the 'star' ratings, which are a useful marketing and communication tool, are simplified in order to hide or mask the requirements and actual strategies applied. This is often further complicated by whether the buildings are 'designed' to perform, or whether the reporting is based on actual operational performance information.

There is a broader range of sustainability-based tools which have a wider approach to sustainability consideration. These are often targeted at the design stage of new builds and major renovation, however, more tools are emerging that assess the sustainability performance of buildings across the spectrum. The next wave of targets, policy and regulation relates to the concept of 'Net Zero Emission' targets. In the built environment the adaptation of this concept is Net Zero Energy/Emission Buildings (NZEB), and according to the World Green Building Council (2020),

> buildings that are energy efficient, and supply energy needs from renewable sources (on-site and/or off-site) is a more appropriate target for the mass scale required to achieve Paris Agreement levels of global emission reductions.

This has led to commitments from governments and individual organisations to commit to net zero emission targets and tools. These include Green Building

Councils in France, Canada, Brazil, South Africa, the United States, Germany and the UK. In addition, governments have also created commitments to NZEB (or Nearly Zero Energy Buildings).

From an industry perspective, recent announcements from some of Australia's top Australian Stock Exchange (ASX) listed real estate organisations making commitments for their portfolios to achieve Net Zero *operating* emissions across their properties by 2030 included statements from AMP Capital Wholesale Office Fund, Cbus Property, Cundall, Commonwealth Bank, Dexus, Frasers Property Australia, GPT Group and Multiplex, Nightingale Housing and Stockland (Green Building Council Australia 2018). However, similar to the loopholes noted with the rating tools, the term 'operation' has different interpretations and often only refers to the operational (and in some cases only the base building operational) energy considerations; further, there is no consideration of the embodied energy consumed by buildings in their development, and across the whole life cycle of the building.

Whilst it is apparent that many of these tools and schemes are generating behavioural change in the real estate sector, reducing GHG emissions, broader and more ambitious action is needed in order to meet Paris Agreement targets to limit global warming to 1.5°C. A further challenge of these current schemes, objectives, policies and tools, is the lack of consideration of embodied GHG emissions in property. It is anticipated by Röck et al. (2020) that an estimated 20–25% of annual anthropogenic GHG emissions are embodied emissions. In buildings, they can account for between 10–97% of emissions across the life cycle (Chastas et al. 2016). In an analysis by Schmidt et al. (2020) on housing Australia's growing population over the next ten years (to 2030) and 40 years (to 2050), the total life cycle emissions of new housing will be responsible for 883 $MtCO_2e$ and 3654 $MtCO_2e$ respectively. This is considerably higher than Australia's total emissions optimum target of 441 $MtCO_2e$ by 2030. This demonstrates that the consideration of embodied and operational emissions emitted throughout the life cycle of built environments has greater impact on emissions than current calculations and estimations (current estimates do not consider initial and recurrent embodied calculations). Whilst operational energy as previously noted has had an increasing role in mandatory schemes driving change, there are still sectors of the built environment, including property, that have limited or very little drivers for change in the development or operation of buildings. In addition, all sectors are presently missing the broader implications of the hidden but still prominent embodied GHG emissions.

Challenge 4: For significant GHG emission targets to be met (to limit climate change impacts), further research is required on life cycle consideration of GHG emissions, and drivers and levers to generate mainstream change across the real estate industry.

Climate change adaptation actions in the real estate industry

At present, action on the adaptation side is focused on post-disaster recovery, where federal governments come to the aid of those affected who reside in disaster-prone areas. The figures in Australia alone have an average cost per year, including tangible and intangible costs, exceeding AU$9 billion (approximately 0.6% of GDP) and are anticipated to increase by 50% to reach AU$33 billion annually by 2050 (Deloitte Access Economics 2016). When examining the impact of natural disasters and extreme events, there was AU$7 billion attributable to the 2009 Black Saturday bushfires (AU$3.1 billion tangible and AU$3.9 billion intangible); and to the Queensland Floods in 2011–2012, AU$14.1 billion (AU$6.7 billion tangible and AU$7.4 billion intangible) (Deloitte Access Economics 2016). In the US in 2020, to 8 July, there had already been ten extreme weather and climate-related events, each totalling more than US$1 billion in losses (NOAA National Centers for Environmental Information 2020). In Europe, disasters associated with weather (floods and windstorms) that have exceeded 100 deaths or have a minimum US$5 billion in losses between 2006 and 2016, comprise seven key events, totalling US$55.3 billion (inflation adjusted to 2018, Kron et al. 2019).

As cumulative totals are realised, and the real costs of inaction are more apparent, the current 'Band-Aid' approach of post-disaster rescue is not a sustainable approach for government, businesses, communities and individuals. Consequently, a reshaped focus on pro-active action is required. However, there would appear to be a range of barriers hindering climate change adaptation action, which can be classified into three key sources: actors making decisions, the context (the place or system) and the exposure to risks associated with climate change (Eisenack et al. 2014). In the context of real estate, multiple climate change risks may affect property in a multitude of ways and it is the actors, of which there are many, who are the main barriers to adaptive action. In real estate, there are a plethora of actors involved in the various stages of the development process; yet, ultimately, the clients (owner, developer, investor, occupier) are the key decision-makers. They are restrained by government, and the various levels that place restraints on real estate, yet opportunity exists within these structures to take action, although greater guidance and direction by governments would likely accelerate the process. However, one of the largest considerations for real estate 'clients' is the financial implications of change and how this is seen by the market. Warren-Myers et al. (2020b) in their research investigating the capacity of the real estate industry to take action on climate change, exposed a number of barriers to action which revolved around three main themes, information validity and exchange, financial challenges and market competitiveness, and government role in leading adaptation action. At present, the current approaches for many governments is a focus on disaster recovery, rather than investing in preventative measures. This unfortunately is effectively perpetuating the problem and perhaps creating greater potential for moral hazard as a result (see for example the case of drought in Australia: Hayman and Rickards 2013). As governments continue to offer aid to affected people in a post-disaster scenario, this will, in essence, continue to encourage people to build and reside in disaster risk areas by providing this 'backup insurance' if disasters strike (Bunten and Kahn 2017).

Challenge 5: Without significant and certain actions to reduce GHG emissions, it is difficult to anticipate the type of adaptive action and level of action required to future-proof property assets.

Conclusion

This chapter has identified five challenges posed to the real estate sector in relation to climate change. We now respond to these through the identification of research needs.

Challenge 1: There is increasing need for detailed understanding of climate change implications on real estate at the local scale. This would allow more effective adaptation decision making for the sector.

Research Response 1: It would be beneficial for property stakeholders to advocate for, and contribute funds towards, conducting research to understand the climate change implications on real estate at locally relevant scales. This information should be provided in a format that is clear, and widely beneficial and applicable for all levels of decision-makers involved in the development, investment and management of property – from renters and home owners to large commercial entities, and governments.

Challenge 2: There is a diversity of sub-sectors within real estate, with heterogeneous types of real estate, characteristics, actors and associated climate change impacts. Research is needed to understand the climate change impacts across the diversity of the real estate sector, to inform decision making.

Research Response 2: Research is needed within each of the different real estate sub-sectors and across diverse locations to (1) better understand the full potential of climate change mitigation, and (2) prepare properties and their relevant stakeholders for the adaptation actions required to future proof their assets and prevent stranded asset syndrome.

Challenge 3: There is limited accessible information available about the direct impacts of climate change for the real estate sector. There is a need for an increase in the quality, reliability and sharing of data on climate change and its implications.

Research Response 3: There is a need to make research and information about climate change in the real estate sector applicable and available. There is a need to overcome perceived competitive advantage and begin sharing mitigation and adaptation strategies for the greater good.

Challenge 4: For significant GHG emission targets to be met and to limit climate change implications, further research is required on life cycle consideration of GHG emissions, and drivers and levers to generate mainstream change across the real estate industry.

Research Response 4: Research is need is to identify and implement opportunities across the real estate sector to reduce GHG emissions in line with achieving the Paris Agreement goal of 1.5°C.

Challenge 5: Without significant and certain actions to reduce GHG emissions, it is difficult to anticipate the type of adaptive action and level of action required to future-proof property assets.

Research Response 5: Research is needed to better understand the range of adaptation levels required for the real estate sector under different scenarios of warming. This would provide greater understanding and transparency of the actions required of different stakeholders, the range of investment decisions and the cost implications of these decisions and adaptive strategies.

These research responses point to areas of research needed to understand the current and future risks that climate change extremes pose. Such information will help to ensure assets are not carbon stranded; inform risk mitigation or divestment strategies; spur changes to due diligence processes and their consequences; and build knowledge and capacity to enact required changes throughout the industry. The current inadequate and limited focus on mitigation is not sufficient to avoid the catastrophic impacts of climate change and its consequences for the real estate sector. To achieve the Paris Agreement goals, action is needed across the built environment, and mitigation and adaptation need to be considered concurrently and acted upon. Mitigation actions for the real estate sector must be in proportion to the reductions in emissions needed to limit warming to 1.5°C. Adaptation actions must be aware of the impacts of warming at 1.5°C and in excess of this. There will not be a uniform approach and there will be extensive research required to identify a variety of, often unique, pathways and solutions to the challenges climate change presents. Actors in the real estate sector must adapt and adjust to climate change, in order to avoid becoming the frog in the cooking pot.

Note

1.   Real estate is 'real property' and is often referred to in some countries as property. For the purposes of this chapter real estate and property are assumed to be synonymous, where real estate is the land and any permanent improvements attached to the land whether natural or man-made.

References

Atreya, A., and Czajkowski, J. (2014). "Housing price response to the interaction of positive coastal amenities and negative flood risks (No. 329-2016-13016)." *Presented at 2014 Annual Meeting*, Minneapolis, Minnesota.

Baldauf, M., Garlappi, L., and Yannelis, C. (2020). "Does climate change affect real estate prices? Only if you believe in it." *The Review of Financial Studies*, 33(3), 1256–1295.

Beltrán, A., Maddison, D., and Elliott, R. J. (2018). "Is flood risk capitalised into property values?" *Ecological Economics*, 146, 668–685.

Bernstein, A., Gustafson, M. T., and Lewis, R. (2019). "Disaster on the horizon: The price effect of sea level rise." *Journal of Financial Economics*, 134(2), 253–272.

Betts, R. A., Alfieri, L., Bradshaw, C., Caesar, J., Feyen, L., Friedlingstein, P., Gohar, L., Koutroulis, A., Lewis, K., Morfopoulos, C., Papadimitriou, L., Richardson, K. J., Tsanis, I., and Wyser, K. (2018). "Changes in climate extremes, fresh water availability and vulnerability to food insecurity projected at 1.5°C and 2°C global warming with a higher-resolution global climate model." *Philosophical Transactions of the Royal Society A: Mathematical, Physical and Engineering Sciences*, 376(2119), 20160452.

Bienert, S. (2014). *Extreme Weather Events and Property Values: Assessing New Investment Frameworks for the Decades Ahead*. Urban Land Institute.

Bunten, D., and Kahn, M. E. (2017). "Optimal real estate capital durability and localized climate change disaster risk." *Journal of Housing Economics*, 36, 1–7.

Cambridge Institute for Sustainability Leadership (CISL). (2019). *Physical Risk Framework: Understanding the Impacts of Climate Change on Real Estate Lending and Investment Portfolios.* Cambridge: The Cambridge Institute for Sustainability Leadership.

Chastas, P., Theodosiou, T., and Bikas, D. (2016). "Embodied energy in residential buildings-towards the nearly zero energy building: A literature review." *Building and Environment*, 105, 267–282.

Connell, J. (2016). "Last days in the Carteret Islands? Climate change, livelihoods and migration on coral atolls." *Asia Pacific Viewpoint*, 57(1), 3–15.

Deloitte Access Economics. (2016). *The Economic Cost of the Social Impact of Natural Disasters.* Australian Business Roundtable for Disaster Resilience & Safer Communities.

Department of Climate Change and Energy Efficiency. (2011). "Climate change risks to coastal buildings and infrastructure: A supplement to the first pass national assessment." Available online: http://www.environment.gov.au/climate-change/ adaptation/publications/climate-change-risks-coastal-buildings (accessed on 9 January 2017).

Dixon, G., Bullock, O., and Adams, D. (2019). "Unintended effects of emphasizing the role of climate change in recent natural disasters." *Environmental Communication*, 13(2), 135–143.

Dosio, A., Mentaschi, L., Fischer, E. M., and Wyser, K. (2018). "Extreme heat waves under 1.5°C and 2°C global warming." *Environmental Research Letters*, 13(5), 054006.

Eisenack, K., Moser, S. C., Hoffmann, E., Klein, R. J., Oberlack, C., Pechan, A., Rotter, M., and Termeer, C. J. (2014). "Explaining and overcoming barriers to climate change adaptation." *Nature Climate Change*, 4(10), 867–872.

Elsner, J. B. (2020). "Continued increases in the intensity of strong tropical cyclones." *Bulletin of the American Meteorological Society.*

Elsner, J. B., Kossin, J. P., and Jagger, T. H. (2008). "The increasing intensity of the strongest tropical cyclones." *Nature*, 455(7209), 92–95.

Fuerst, F., and McAllister, P. (2011). "The impact of Energy Performance Certificates on the rental and capital values of commercial property assets." *Energy Policy*, 39(10), 6608–6614.

Fuerst, F., McAllister, P., Nanda, A., and Wyatt, P. (2015). "Does energy efficiency matter to home-buyers? An investigation of EPC ratings and transaction prices in England." *Energy Economics*, 48, 145–156.

Fuerst, F., and Warren-Myers, G. (2018). "Does voluntary disclosure create a green lemon problem? Energy-efficiency ratings and house prices." *Energy Economics*, 74, 1–12.

Fuerst, F., and Warren-Myers, G. (2021). "Pricing climate risk: Are flooding and sea level rise risk capitalised in Australian residential property?" *Climate Risk Management*, 34, 100361.

Furnnell, A. (2020). "Insuring your home may get harder and more expensive as climate change increases risks." *Future Tense*. Australian Broadcasting Corporation. Available online: https://www.abc.net.au/news/2020-05-14/home-insurance-as -climate-change-and-disasters-affect-industry/12227466 (accessed 28 August 2020).

Grafakos, S., Pacteau, C., Delgado, M., Landauer, M., Lucon, O., Driscoll, P., Wilk, D., Zambrano, C., O'Donoghue, S., and Roberts, D. (2018). "Integrating mitigation and adaptation," in C. Rosenzweig, P. Romero-Lankao, S. Mehrotra, S. Dhakal, S. Ali Ibrahim, and W. D. Solecki, (eds.), *Climate Change and Cities: Second Assessment*

Report of the Urban Climate Change Research Network. Cambridge: Cambridge University Press, pp. 101–138.

Graham, S., Barnett, J., Fincher, R., Hurlimann, A., and Waters, E. (2013). "The social values at risk from sea level rise." *Environmental Impact Assessment Review*, 41, 45–52.

Green Building Council Australia. (2018). "Global commitment for net zero carbon buildings." *Industry News*. Sydney: Green Building Council of Australia. Available online: https://new.gbca.org.au/news/industry-news/global-commitment-net-zero -carbon-buildings/ (accessed 29 August 2020).

Hamilton-Webb, A., Manning, L., Naylor, R., and Conway, J. (2017). "The relationship between risk experience and risk response: A study of farmers and climate change." *Journal of Risk Research*, 20(11), 1379–1393.

Hayman, P., and Rickards, L. (2013). "Drought, climate change, farming and science: The interaction of four privileged topics," in L. Courtenay Botterill, and G. Cockfield (eds.), *Drought, Risk Management, and Policy: Decision-Making Under Uncertainty*, CRC Press, pp. 47–69. https://doi.org/10.1201/b14918.

Hermann, E., and Kempf, W. (2017). "Climate change and the imagining of migration: Emerging discourses on Kiribati's land purchase in Fiji." *The Contemporary Pacific*, 29(2), 231–263.

Hinkel, J., Aerts, J. C. J. H., Brown, S., Jiménez, J. A., Lincke, D., Nicholls, R. J., Scussolini, P., Sanchez-Arcilla, A., Vafeidis, A., and Addo, K. A. (2018). "The ability of societies to adapt to twenty-first-century sea-level rise." *Nature Climate Change*, 8(7), 570–578.

Hurlimann, A., Browne, G., Warren-Myers, G., and Francis, V. (2018a). "Facilitating climate change adaptation in the Australian construction industry – identification of information needs." *Proceedings of the 4th Practical Responses to Climate Change Conference: "Climate Adaptation 2018: Learn, Collaborate, Act"*. Melbourne: Engineers Australia, pp. 155–163.

Hurlimann, A. C., Browne, G. R., Warren-Myers, G., and Francis, V. (2018b). "Barriers to climate change adaptation in the Australian construction industry – impetus for regulatory reform." *Building and Environment*, 137, 235–245.

Hurlimann, A., and Dolnicar, S. (2011). "Voluntary relocation – an exploration of Australian attitudes in the context of drought, recycled and desalinated water." *Global Environmental Change – Human and Policy Dimensions*, 21, 1084–1094.

Hurlimann, A. C., Warren-Myers, G., and Browne, G. R. (2019). "Is the Australian construction industry prepared for climate change?" *Building and Environment*, 153, 128–137.

Intergovernmental Panel on Climate Change. (2015). *Climate Change 2014 – Synthesis Report*, Cambridge: Cambridge University Press.

Intergovernmental Panel on Climate Change. (2018). *Global Warming of 1.5°C. An IPCC Special Report on the Impacts of Global Warming of 1.5°C Above Pre-industrial Levels and Related Global Greenhouse Gas Emission Pathways, in the Context of Strengthening the Global Response to the Threat of Climate Change, Sustainable Development, and Efforts to Eradicate Poverty*. Available online: http://www.ipcc.ch/ report/sr15/ (accessed 10 November 2018).

Investor Group on Climate Change. (2016). *Assessing Climate Change Risks and Opportunites for Investors: Property and Construction Sector*. [Online] http://igcc .org.au.

James, D. (2018). "Lost at sea: The race against time to save the Carteret Islands from climate change." *ABC News*. Available online: https://www.abc.net.au/news/

2018-08-04/the-race-against-time-to-save-the-carteret-islanders/10066958?nw=0 (accessed 30 July 2020).

Jevrejeva, S., Jackson, L. P., Grinsted, A., Lincke, D., and Marzeion, B. (2018). "Flood damage costs under the sea level rise with warming of 1.5 °C and 2 °C." *Environmental Research Letters*, 13(7), 074014.

Kron, W., Löw, P., and Kundzewicz, Z. W. (2019). "Changes in risk of extreme weather events in Europe." *Environmental Science & Policy*, 100, 74–83.

Kron, W., Steuer, M., Löw, P., and Wirtz, A. (2012). "How to deal properly with a natural catastrophe database – analysis of flood losses." *Natural Hazards and Earth Systems Science*, 12(3), 535–550.

Kulp, S. A., and Strauss, B. H. (2019). "New elevation data triple estimates of global vulnerability to sea-level rise and coastal flooding." *Nature Communications*, 10(1), 1–12.

Morris, A. (2020). "The bushfires in Australia and housing." *Housing Finance International*, 45–48.

Mueller, J., Loomis, J., and González-Cabán, A. (2009). "Do repeated wildfires change homebuyers' demand for homes in high-risk areas? A hedonic analysis of the short and long-term effects of repeated wildfires on house prices in southern California." *Journal of Real Estate Finance & Economics*, 38(2), 155–172.

Muldoon-Smith, K., and Greenhalgh, P. (2019). "Suspect foundations: Developing an understanding of climate-related stranded assets in the global real estate sector." *Energy Research & Social Science*, 54, 60–67.

Murfin. J., Spiegel, M., and Scheinkman, J. (2020). "Is the risk of sea level rise capitalized in residential real estate?" *Review of Financial Studies*, 33(3), 1217–1255.

Newell, G., MacFarlane, J., and Walker, R. (2014). "Assessing energy rating premiums in the performance of green office buildings in Australia." *Journal of Property Investment & Finance*, 32(4), 352–370.

NOAA National Centers for Environmental Information. (2020). *Billion-Dollar Weather and Climate Disasters: Overview*. Asheville: National Oceanic and Atmospheric Administration.

Queensland University of Technology. (2010). *Impacts and Adaptation Response of Infrastructure and Communities to Heatwaves: The Southern Australian Experience of 2009*. National Climate Change Adaptation Research Facility, Gold Coast.

Rasmussen, D. J., Bittermann, K., Buchanan, M. K., Kulp, S., Strauss, B. H., Kopp, R. E., and Oppenheimer, M. (2018). "Extreme sea level implications of 1.5°C, 2.0°C, and 2.5°C temperature stabilization targets in the 21st and 22nd centuries." *Environmental Research Letters*, 13(3), 034040.

Röck, M., Saade, M. R. M., Balouktsi, M., Rasmussen, F. N., Birgisdottir, H., Frischknecht, R., Habert, G., Lützkendorf, T., and Passer, A. (2020). "Embodied GHG emissions of buildings – the hidden challenge for effective climate change mitigation." *Applied Energy*, 258, 114107.

Schmidt, M., Crawford, R. H., and Warren-Myers, G. (2020). "Quantifying Australia's life cycle greenhouse gas emissions for new homes." *Energy and Buildings*, 224, 110287.

Shvidenko, A., and Schepaschenko, D. (2013). "Climate change and wildfires in Russia." *Contemporary Problems of Ecology*, 6(7), 683.

Smith, M. H. (2013). *Assessing Climate Change Risks and Opportunities for Investors: Property and Construction Sector*. Investor Group on Climate Change.

Steffen, W., Mallon, K., Kompas, T., Dean, A., and Rice, M. (2019). *Costs of Climate Change Report*. Climate Council of Australian Limited.

Strauss, B. H., Kulp, S., and Levermann, A. (2015). "Carbon choices determine US cities committed to futures below sea level." *Proceedings of the National Academy of Sciences*, 112(44), 13508.

Teicher, H. M. (2018). "Practices and pitfalls of competitive resilience: Urban adaptation as real estate firms turn climate risk to competitive advantage." *Urban Climate*, 25, 9–21.

Turco, M., Rosa-Cánovas, J. J., Bedia, J., Jerez, S., Montávez, J. P., Llasat, M. C., and Provenzale, A. (2018). "Exacerbated fires in Mediterranean Europe due to anthropogenic warming projected with non-stationary climate-fire models." *Nature Communications*, 9(1), 3821.

UN-HABITAT. (2011). *Cities and Climate Change: Global Report on Human Settlements 2011*, London: Earthscan.

United Nations. (2015). *Paris Agreement*. Available online: http://unfccc.int/files/essential_background/convention/application/pdf/english_paris_agreement.pdf (accessed 2 November 2017).

United Nations Environment Program. (2019). *Emissions Gap Report*. Nairobi: UNEP.

Urban Land Institute, and Heitman. (2019). *Climate Risk and Real Estate Investment Decision-Making*. Available online: https://europe.uli.org/climate-risk-and-real-estate-investment-decision-making/ (accessed 29 August 2020).

Victorian Bushfires Royal Commission. (2010). *2009 Bushfires Royal Commission Final Report*. Government of Victoria, Melbourne.

Walsh, K. J., McInnes, K. L., and McBride, J. L. (2012). "Climate change impacts on tropical cyclones and extreme sea levels in the South Pacific – a regional assessment." *Global and Planetary Change*, 80, 149–164.

Warren-Myers, G., Aschwanden, G., Fuerst, F., and Krause, A. (2018). "Estimating the potential risks of sea level rise for public and private property ownership, occupation and management." *Risks*, 6(2), 37.

Warren-Myers, G., Hurlimann, A., and Bush, J. (2020a). "Advancing capacity to adapt to climate change in the Australian property industry – addressing climate change information needs." *Journal of European Real Estate Research*, 13(3), 321–335.

Warren-Myers, G., Hurlimann, A., and Bush, J. (2020b). "Barriers to climate change adaption in the Australian Property industry." *Journal of Property Investment & Finance*, 38(5) 449–462.

Warren-Myers, G., Hurlimann, A., and Bush, J. (2021). "Climate change frontrunners in the Australian property sector." *Climate Risk Management*, 33, 100340.

Wessel, P. V. (2018). "A perfect storm: The ramifications of Cape Town's drought crisis." *The Journal for Transdisciplinary Research in Southern Africa*, 14(1), e1–e10.

World Green Building Council. (2020). *What is Net Zero?* World Green Building Council. Available online: https://www.worldgbc.org/advancing-net-zero/what-net-zero (accessed 30 July 2020).

Yin, J., Griffies, S. M., and Stouffer, R. J. (2010). "Spatial variability of sea level rise in twenty-first century projections." *Journal of Climate*, 23(17), 4585–4607.

Zander, K. K., Botzen, W. J. W., Oppermann, E., Kjellström, T., and Garnett, S. T. (2015). "Heat stress causes substantial labour productivity loss in Australia." *Nature Climate Change*, 5(7), 647–651.

9 The confluence of real estate and infrastructure: a research agenda

Raghu Dharmapuri Tirumala

Introduction

Real estate and infrastructure are increasingly seen as dominant sectors in global economies when measured by their volume of stock, investments, and employability (Lambrev, 2019; Shatkin, 2016). Globalization, along with cross-border transactions, is accelerating the commonalities between these two sectors, and wider financial and investment markets are making the relationship more pronounced, as witnessed in the 2007 Global Financial Crisis (GFC) (Newell & Peng, 2009). While the origins of the GFC were in the sub-prime mortgage market in the USA, the capital markets and the real economy, including infrastructure, subsequently went into recession.

Infrastructure has been considered a vital cog in the global economy, contributing to a country's productivity, ease of doing business, and competitiveness (Calderon & Serven, 2014). The research on different facets of infrastructure, including its constituents, investments, mode of delivery, policymaking, public–private partnerships, investment returns, and risk profiles, has been extensive from the 1980s, and continues to provide insights for policymaking, development, financing, and delivery of services (Beeferman & Wain, 2016a; Grigg, 2011). Infrastructure investments have a major impact on a country's comparative advantage (Yeaple & Golub, 2007) and economic development (GDP) (Aschauer, 1990). While infrastructure investments are a common theme for many nations, there is no uniform acceptance of the definition of infrastructure. Infrastructure has been perceived as a foundation (substructure, 'skeleton') for the manufacturing of goods and provision of services (Beeferman & Wain, 2016a). Infrastructure has been classified into economic and social – the economic infrastructure (comprising communication, energy, transport, and utilities) serves to increase productivity, while the social infrastructure (comprising education, health, and other civic services) provides

165

a foundation for basic services (EIB, 2010; Weber, Staub-Bisang, & Alfen, 2016).

Infrastructure is characterized by its technical and institutional traits. The technical traits comprise indivisibility, very long project life cycles, and immovable, not easily transferable, assets (Beeferman & Wain, 2016a). The institutional traits relate to the substantial influence that the public proponents have on the conceptualization and implementation of the infrastructure projects, allocation of rights to various entities, provision of regulatory mechanisms, formulating policies that affect economic aspects, including returns to investors over varying investment horizons, and development of secondary markets (Beeferman & Wain, 2016b; Newell & Peng, 2008). Most infrastructure sectors operate in monopolistic environments (Canning, 1999; EIB, 2010). An infrastructure asset's intrinsic value depends on the cash flows generated by its use, which in turn is based on capital investments and leverage (Beeferman & Wain, 2016a). The large capital expenditure requirements for developing infrastructure assets provide a natural entry barrier (Yermo, Della Croce, & Stewart, 2011). However, the operating and maintenance expenditure (O&M) is smaller than the capital expenditure (Paul, 2014). The financing of infrastructure projects is typically through non-recourse or limited recourse mechanisms (Inderst, 2016; Newell & Peng, 2008), and the valuations are based on discounted cash flow analysis, which is expected to provide an inflation hedge (Dechant & Finkenzeller, 2012). The infrastructure market is relatively opaque compared with other asset classes due to a lack of reliable data and research (Inderst & Stewart, 2014). As most infrastructure projects have a longer construction period, they have a relatively low elasticity of demand (Estache & Garsous, 2012). All these aspects imply that the private players in the infrastructure industry and the public sector stakeholders who develop a project and regulate the system need to possess higher expertise (Beeferman & Wain, 2016a).

The infrastructure sector has witnessed many cycles over the last three decades – its assets were undervalued in the 1990s, had a substantial revaluation in the 2000s, and were overheated in the wake of the global financial crisis (EIB, 2010; Weber et al., 2016). Many countries have attempted to come out of the GFC through increased spending on infrastructure, and similar sentiments are being expressed in the wake of the COVID-19 situation. The rising private participation in investment and operations in infrastructure has attracted the attention of broader financial markets. A rise in public–private partnerships fuelled by the expectations of better services and the financial stress of many governments has also generated more investment opportunities (Mause & Krumm, 2011).

The growing importance of real estate in the last four decades has shaped it as a separate asset class in an investor's portfolio. In addition, there has been financialization of the real estate domain and integration with broader financial markets, and ever-growing internationalization with exploding cross-border transactions (Seek, Sing, & Yu, 2016a; 2016b). The real estate sector shares many characteristics with the infrastructure sector, namely indivisibility, longer construction periods, valuation based on location, limited liquidity, valuation based on future cash flows, and substantial scope for capital gains. However, the two sectors also have many dissimilarities. While the usage of infrastructure assets is typically restricted to its stated purpose, real estate assets can have alternate uses in general. The real estate markets have a greater degree of information availability and transparency due to relatively better competition, they are more integrated with the capital markets, and have better secondary market avenues (through the various real estate indices in vogue across the developed markets) (Lambrev, 2019). The transfer of ownership is relatively simple in real estate; however, the regulatory and institutional frameworks in the infrastructure sector make the process quite complex (Newell & Peng, 2008) as, in many projects implemented under public–private partnership arrangements, the private sector does not have any ownership rights (Blanc-Brude, 2013). The scale of investments required in infrastructure assets is comparatively larger than required for real estate assets.

The similarities and differences between real estate and infrastructure have been a topic of interest to many researchers, particularly from the investment perspective.

Research on real estate and infrastructure interrelationships

The research content on the real estate and infrastructure sector confluence has focused on two main streams. The first stream of the research includes how the region's proximity to infrastructure or development has impacted real estate prices. The second stream of investigation constitutes whether real estate and infrastructure can be treated as distinct asset classes and the role of these two asset classes in an investment portfolio.

Real estate and infrastructure: urban planning

The exponential interest in infrastructure investments has resulted in the implementation of many projects. These developments have created enormous opportunities for real estate development in the vicinity of such developments. Researchers have used numerous hedonic price models to investigate the relationship between infrastructure projects and real estate prices (particularly the residential sector) (Adebayo, Akogwu, & Yisa, 2012). The outcome of such research provides a wealth of knowledge on the behaviour of real estate markets within and across city and regional boundaries. The general conclusion has been that infrastructure development (or lack of it) has substantially influenced urban growth, land prices, and housing prices. Typically, it has been found that proximity to urban transportation systems – such as Metro, tram and bus stations – positively impacts land prices. In contrast, the larger transportation projects, such as ports, airports, and national railway stations, have a negative impact on land prices due to elements such as noise and pollution (Al-Mosaind, Dueker, & Strathman, 1993; Bowes & Ihlanfeldt, 2001; Cervero & Landis, 1993; Forkenbrock, 2001; Martínez & Viegas, 2009; Norman, Sirmans, & Benjamin, 1995). A range of special lag and nonparametric estimation models has been used to assess the impact of infrastructure on urban land prices (Boarnet & Crane, 2001; Cohen, Cromley, & Banach, 2015; McMillen & Redfearn, 2010).

Another prominent related research theme is understanding the interaction between land use and its price based on the impact of the transportation infrastructure, more commonly known as Land-use/Transport Interaction Models (LUTI). The research on these models has substantially progressed over time as multiple methodological approaches have been adopted, including the theory of urban complexity and the simulation techniques for understanding various scenarios (Waddell, 2002).

Real estate and infrastructure allocations in a multi-asset portfolio

Real estate finance as a topic is relatively less prominent in the research agenda when compared with other themes. An analysis of the titles of papers from real estate conferences (American Real Estate Society, European Real Estate Society, American Real Estate and Urban Economics Association) between the years 2015 and 2019, indicates that the research is clustered around largely 'real estate' (overall sector), housing, investment performance, and energy efficiency (Breuer & Steininger, 2020). The words 'mortgage' and 'infrastructure' do not appear in any appreciable manner. As the development of real estate is capital intensive requiring a combination of own funds and borrowed money (Tipple, Korboe, Willis, & Garrod, 1998), the structure of finance is essential for sustainable housing and other markets (Boamah, 2010; Warnock & Warnock, 2008). The real estate finance-related topics account for a 5.6% share in the finance-related conferences from 2015 to 2020 (Breuer & Steininger, 2020).

An analysis of the returns provided by the global capital markets and global listed real estate indicates that the latter has substantially compensated the investors from 1994 to 2015. It has been noticed that the correlation between the capital markets and real estate has been increasing over time, which has reduced the diversification benefits of including real estate in a multi-asset portfolio. However, during the period 2003 to 2015, the core infrastructure assets do not seem to be highly correlated with the global capital markets, reflecting the investors' predisposition to be overweight on the infrastructure sector. Real estate represents about 6% and (private) infrastructure about 2% of the world market portfolio. Listed assets make up only about 15% of all real estate investments but about 85% of the infrastructure universe. A typical multi-asset portfolio of a balanced pension fund appears as (i) equities (domestic and international) – each between 10 and 45%; (ii) fixed income, real estate, hedge funds, private equity and infrastructure each between 0 and 30%; and (iii) private credit and cash – each between 0 and 20% (Nieuwerburgh, Stanton, Berkeley, & De Bever, 2015).

The declining yields and the shortage of good quality commercial real estate provided a trigger for real estate investors to foray into infrastructure, as the sectors are considered similar (Beeferman & Wain, 2016b; Newell & Peng, 2008). Many institutional investors keep infrastructure in their asset allocations along with the fixed income and private equity, while the real estate allocations are typically aligned with the fixed income markets. International financial investors have started looking at infrastructure as a separate asset class from the late 2000s (Inderst & Stewart, 2014; Newell & Peng, 2009). Surveys conducted by Preqin in the late 2000s have indicated that nearly 47% of investors have a separate infrastructure allocation, while 43% include private equity in their portfolio and 10% have real estate in their portfolios (Preqin, 2020). Owing to the low to medium correlation of infrastructure with other traditional asset classes, investors include infrastructure in their portfolio to have adequate diversification across various asset classes (Beeferman & Wain, 2016b; Newell & Peng, 2008). However, given the large capital requirements and the low elasticity of demand, increased allocation to infrastructure in a multi-asset portfolio could also reduce the diversification, while the allocation to real estate might increase the diversification benefits. The risk-return profile of global infrastructure assets is substantially different from that of global equities and real estate. For instance, after the GFC, the global infrastructure assets took nearly three years to recover their capital, while equities and real estate took close to six years (Weber et al., 2016).

Institutional investors consider real estate and infrastructure as good inflation hedging asset classes (Inderst & Stewart, 2014; Magweva & Sibanda, 2020; Norman et al., 1995; Yermo et al., 2011). Infrastructure is seen as a complement rather than a substitute to real estate (Dechant & Finkenzeller, 2012). More recent research has indicated that listed infrastructure (Oyedele, 2014) and direct infrastructure (Dechant & Finkenzeller, 2013) do not replace real estate but have their place in a multi-asset portfolio. The share of direct and indirect allocations to infrastructure in a multi-asset portfolio has diversification benefits, which has led to the argument that the two sectors are distinct and cannot be classified together as real estate. The pricing of infrastructure services often includes mechanisms to pass on the costs of inputs (for instance, fuel prices of power generation plants), commodities, and administrative expenses (Gallagher & Mansour, 2000). The revenues possible from typical infrastructure assets emanate from the user fees or are paid by the project proponent (budget financed) (Weber et al., 2016). Both the approaches can be linked to inflation explicitly or need not be, but, with higher pricing power, they still attain the objective of inflation hedging (Magweva & Sibanda, 2020). However, due to the very diverse nature of infrastructure sectors, not all infrastructure assets provide this hedging opportunity, as the same depends on the contractual provisions and underlying business models. For instance, if the revenue stream does not have pass-through mechanisms or inflation adjusting tariff mechanisms, the particular asset does not protect from inflationary pressures. In the regional/sub-national infrastructure sub-sectors, such as water supply, gas or energy sectors, regulators may allow adjustments based on many factors, including expenditures likely to be incurred, expanding user base, interest rates, and inflation (Wurstbauer & Schäfers, 2015). Telecommunications is a good example of the high pricing power of the infrastructure sector. Communication assets, particularly mobile towers, have strict regulations on where they can be located and are prone to objections from the local neighbourhoods. This creates a high entry barrier, which gives the owners of these assets substantial pricing power and is known to be inflation resilient (Wurstbauer & Schäfers, 2015). This aspect of research in real estate and infrastructure is largely confined to developed national markets such as the US, UK, Australia, Singapore, etc., and has not spread to the developing world (Newell, 2020).

Another topic of research interest in the real estate and infrastructure financial confluence is the importance of land value capture. With burgeoning cities and the growing expectations of its occupants, there is a tremendous strain on the finances for providing the much-needed urban infrastructure (Cai, Liu, & Cao, 2020). Many city managers are increasingly constrained on finances as the buoyancy of their taxes is limited, and the devolutions that they expect from the higher levels of the government are decelerating (Theurillat, 2017). Consequently, they are on the lookout for newer sources of funding. The sharp uptake in the real estate market has given the city managers a novel avenue of funding and has enabled them to configure numerous urban infrastructure projects with land or property as a revenue source (Tirumala & Tiwari, 2021). Multiple models of land value capture finance mechanisms that enable a portion of the increase in the land markets to be captured by the local government for funding urban infrastructure, are increasingly popular in structuring projects in developing countries (Cai et al., 2020; Tirumala & Tiwari, 2021). This method is more evident in transportation projects, for instance, in Hong Kong, Singapore, Hyderabad (India), Delhi, London, and many other larger cities in developing countries. Hong Kong has been particularly cited as a successful land value capture mechanism example through its 'Rail plus Property' (Cheung, Chan, & Kajewski, 2012). This system assumes that property values substantially increase when close to railway stations, and the value capture from this mechanism helps the public entity mitigate the infrastructure costs for developing the railway system. One more variant of the land value capture system is the New York subway to Hudson's yard (van der Veen & Korthals Altes, 2011) financed using debt and repaid through the property tax revenues from the proposed real estate development. Projects using land value capture mechanisms have also attracted considerable opposition from the residents (for example, in the case of the Nandi corridor in Karnataka, India) or when the revenue models have not worked out appropriately as the real estate demand did not materialize as anticipated (Tirumala & Tiwari, 2021).

Reconceptualising real estate and infrastructure scholarship

The scope of the interface between the real estate and infrastructure sectors is wide and opens up an array of research possibilities. As more and more data become available on the performance of the sectors and their respective constituents, additional research possibilities have emerged. Figure 9.1 sets out the broad contours of the research that could potentially be undertaken in the confluence between real estate and infrastructure, as discussed in the previous section. The relevance of research in the urban planning domain that focuses on the relative impact of prices and directional growth would be topical while the developments are being planned. Multi-asset portfolio return maximization is a topic of interest to a wide range of stakeholders. Accordingly, there is a lot of research that looks at appropriate allocations to real estate and infrastructure. With increasing fiscal stress borne by the public policymakers and city administrations, newer ways of configuring revenue models are being explored, particularly capturing uptake in land prices and using land as a revenue supplement in infrastructure projects. There is increasing synergy between the stakeholders, particularly those in the financial sector and consulting space.

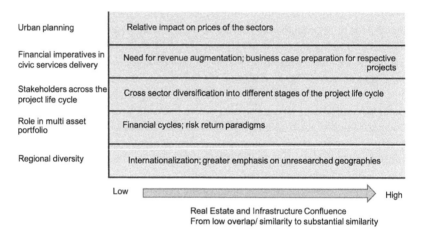

Figure 9.1   Elements of the research agenda

There has been substantial and broad-based interest in the research themes on real estate and infrastructure as set out in Figure 9.1. The big shifts that have marked the research scholarship include exploring the respective roles of the two sectors in a multi-asset portfolio (and the consequent elements) from an urban planning perspective. The internationalization of the sector and greater cross-participation of stakeholders has accelerated interest in such themes. The research emanates from a wider array of academic disciplines – construction, finance, policy and governance, law, and the more conventional urban planning sector. As these themes cut across a broad spectrum of sectoral functioning, the future research agenda will likely be focused on more rigorous and intricate analysis of these aspects, with paradigm resets occurring as and when there is a mainstreamed consensus on the outcomes of the extant research.

Financialization and internationalization

The influence of finance, particularly cross-border finance, has dramatically altered the outlook of many sectors, including real estate and infrastructure. The activities across the project life cycle are witnessing financialization, with an increasing number of traditional companies performing finance-related roles (Cooper, 2015). The financial investment community is now exerting greater influence on the activities of the organizations, which in turn needs a better understanding of the long-term risks and returns of such transformation. The research activities have an international tone, which informs the policies and responses to various circumstances. Depending on the extent of influence of real estate and infrastructure on each other across geographical markets and stakeholder ambits, the differing results would mean these topics remain contextual. Many countries, including the UK, Australia, India, China, Canada, and South Korea, are promoting private participation in infrastructure (Fleta-Asín & Muñoz, 2020; Ruiz Díaz, 2020), and are adopting more sophisticated business models that factor revenues from real estate. The policymakers would need more guidance on measuring and capturing the increase in real estate value and mechanisms to transfer the same to finance infrastructure (Tirumala & Tiwari, 2021). The changing geopolitics, accentuated with the Covid-19 situation, could have a long-term impact on the infrastructure and real estate markets (Edward & Poterba, 2020). The investment barriers across different countries are transforming, be it due to Brexit, China's status in global geopolitics, or political activities in the Southeast Asian countries. The research agenda within this subdomain will be to investigate the relative allocations in (independent or cross-border) multi-asset portfolios, investment objectives and defensive strategies, costs and returns of increased financialization in the operations, and considerations of different stages of investment life cycles.

Land value capture and land-based financing

The ever-increasing demands for better infrastructure services delivery and the growing aspirations of the civic society will continue to put pressure on countries' finances. The success of Hong Kong and Singapore in using land-based financing elements in financing their infrastructure has motivated many other countries to explore such options (Cheung et al., 2012; Hwang, Zhao, & Gay, 2013). The advent of private, commercial, and institutional finance into the emerging infrastructure sectors encourages the public sector project proponents to continuously innovate towards developing newer financial instruments. Land value capture and real estate development as a sweetener for project viability will continue to gain attention. Land has an important mention in many Sustainable Development Goals, including Goals 1, 2, 5, 7, and 11 (United Nations, 2015), and is seen as a contributor to achieving global development. There is an increased interest in the tools promoted by international forums such as the Royal Institution of Chartered Surveyors and Global Land Tool Network, which provide mechanisms for capturing the uptake in land value (Munoz-Gielen, 2011; Rics, 2012). There is also a substantial amount of research and criticism on using these land value capture methods for infrastructure development, relating to the issues of equity and unaffordability (Berrisford, Cirolia, & Palmer, 2018). The funding sources for cities are typically made of tax and non-tax sources, and their control is better on the latter, as the need for approvals is higher with regard to the tax revenues (Peterson, 2008). However, there is limited research on the mechanics of the process and how real estate and infrastructure complement each other in the development of cities, and the policy implications.

There is potential to research when and how real estate and infrastructure value enhancement happens, how to measure and capture the same equitably and sustainably, how the policies should be framed that allow for better usage of commercial mechanisms, how the revenue supplements and additionality should be accounted and shared, and how this interlinkage should be structured to enable a wider benefit across society.

Stakeholders

Real estate and infrastructure research has often been studied from the perspective of individual stakeholders, be it institutional investors, retail investors, or developers, and more particularly from the point of view of policymakers in the infrastructure domain. The research that examines a cross-sectional view and the inter-sectoral perspectives is relatively limited. With increasing participation in the two sectors from diverse stakeholders (governments, city administrations, private developers, financial institutions, consulting firms, legal and technical advisors, architects, civic society, etc.), their influence on the framing of policies and implementation requires greater understanding. The literature is scant on how the advising community or the asset managers such as Savills, Colliers, Cushman Wakefield, Jones Lang Lasselle, or the Big Four management consulting firms influence the project structures or the policy landscape. The research agenda can have multiple themes: how much and to what extent each stakeholder group affects the policy or the structuring of projects with real estate and infrastructure components? Do they recommend a certain portfolio structure based on specific geography? How do different stakeholders view the risk-return profile in different geographies/ cross-border transactions? Has the ex-post analysis of the investment portfolio yielded the same findings as the ex-ante investigation? Has the participation of various investors/stakeholders substantially varied at different stages of the project life cycle? Has the cross-border nature of transactions influenced this? The research could empirically examine the interface between the real estate and infrastructure sectors from the perspectives of different stakeholders.

Greater regional diversity

The real estate and infrastructure markets are witnessing a transformation across the globe, and with different markets following varying trajectories. There has been a substantial growth of the investment-grade markets in Asia, with China, India, Indonesia, and Malaysia emerging strongly, apart from the traditionally stronger Singapore and Japan markets. The cross-border investments in real estate have been growing rapidly, the flows between intra-Asia markets expanding at a rate much greater than that of Asia and the rest of the world (Colliers, 2021). The indirect investment route, through the REIT structures, is being envisaged in Chinese and Indian markets, while the infrastructure investments have been a priority through the budgets and national economic development agendas. There has been substantial literature on the real estate growth in the African markets, while the Middle East had booming infrastructure and real estate sectors until recently. However, the research findings on the confluence of these sectors have not been studied in these markets in as much detail as with the developed regions (America, Europe, and Australia) (Newell, 2020). There is a need to assess if the trends and findings obtained in the developed world across all the agenda items hold in other markets. While the research regarding the urban planning aspects has been picking these markets (Berrisford et al., 2018; Cai et al., 2020; Steel, van Noorloos, & Klaufus, 2017), there is a need for greater research on port-folio management and revenue management of infrastructure and real estate projects.

Summary and conclusions

This article presents the interconnection between the real estate and infra-structure sectors, the current research coverage, emerging trends, and the possibilities for future research. The early-stage research on the interlinkages has emerged from the need to assess the impact of infrastructure on real estate prices. As a result, there has been substantial work that examines how the various infrastructure projects impact the residential, commercial, and indus-trial real estate, with nuanced work on the timing, phases of project develop-ment of both the sectors (Boarnet & Crane, 2001; Cohen et al., 2015; McMillen & Redfearn, 2010). Subsequently, as the real estate sector is integrating with the broader capital markets, the research on the role and extent of weights of these two sectors in an overall investment portfolio has taken momentum (Inderst & Stewart, 2014; Magweva & Sibanda, 2020; Norman et al., 1995; Yermo et al., 2011). In addition to these subjects, this chapter has sketched four broad themes for a contemporary research agenda focusing on the interlinkages between real estate and infrastructure, namely financialization and internationalization, land value capture and land-based financing, stakeholders, and greater regional diversity. This research agenda shifts from considering these two sectors independently to a more holistic integrated theme for a larger group of researchers. The chapter also suggests more diversification of regions, particularly Asian markets, from a national or a sub-national perspective, shifting attention from the physical aspects of the projects to broader sustainable financial, institutional and social aspects.

While the extent and quality of the current research are enormous, the undercurrents transforming the real estate and infrastructure sectors mean that the interlinkages between the two sectors will be more pronounced and would continue to be a recurring theme. It is also likely that the research will prove to be highly contested, with differences and similarities being demonstrated at regional, national, and sub-national levels and from the perspectives of multiple stakeholders at different points of time in their project/investment life cycles. The transformation from a simple city/human settlement level subject to a much more complex multidisciplinary, multi-geography stakeholder involvement with associated management, governance, and regulatory interventions requires a contemporary research agenda that is incisive and theoretically robust. The recurring meta-issue that underpins the contemporary research agenda is the relationship between the markets and the stakeholders. This traverses the expectations informed by the local needs and the dialogue needed for the more effective functioning of the sectors.

References

Adebayo, C., Akogwu, G., & Yisa, E. (2012). Determinants of income diversification among farm households in Kdaduna state: Application of Tobi regression model. *Patnsuk Journal, 8*(2).

Al-Mosaind, M. A., Dueker, K. J., & Strathman, J. G. (1993). Light-rail transit stations and property values: A hedonic price approach. *Transportation Research Record*, (1400).

Aschauer, D. (1990). *Public Investment and Private Sector Growth*. Economic Policy Institute, Washington, DC.

Beeferman, L., & Wain, A. (2016a). Infrastructure: Defining matters. *SSRN Electronic Journal*. https://doi.org/10.2139/ssrn.2714308

Beeferman, L., & Wain, A. (2016b). Infrastructure: Doing what matters. *SSRN Electronic Journal*. https://doi.org/10.2139/ssrn.2714343

Berrisford, S., Cirolia, L. R., & Palmer, I. (2018). Land-based financing in sub-Saharan African cities. *Environment and Urbanization*, *1*(30), 35–52. https://doi.org/10.1177/0956247817753525

Blanc-Brude, F. (2013). Towards efficient benchmarks for infrastructure equity investments: A review of the literature on infrastructure equity investment and directions for future research. Retrieved from http://docs.edhec-risk.com/mrk/000000/Press/Towards_Efficient_Benchmarks.pdf. EDHEC-Risk Institute Publications, 88.

Boamah, N. A. (2010). Housing affordability in Ghana: A focus on Kumasi and Tamale. *Ethiopian Journal of Environmental Studies and Management*, *3*(3).

Boarnet, M., & Crane, R. C. (2001). Transit-oriented planning. In *Travel by Design*. https://doi.org/10.1093/oso/9780195123951.003.0013

Bowes, D. R., & Ihlanfeldt, K. R. (2001). Identifying the impacts of rail transit stations on residential property values. *Journal of Urban Economics*, *50*(1). https://doi.org/10.1006/juec.2001.2214

Breuer, W., & Steininger, B. I. (2020). Recent trends in real estate research: A comparison of recent working papers and publications using machine learning algorithms. *Journal of Business Economics*. https://doi.org/10.1007/s11573-020-01005-w

Cai, Z., Liu, Q., & Cao, S. (2020). Real estate supports rapid development of China's urbanization. *Land Use Policy*, *95*. https://doi.org/10.1016/j.landusepol.2020.104582

Calderon, C., & Serven, L. (2014). The effects of infrastructure development on growth and income distribution. *Annals of Economics and Finance*, *15*(2), 521–534. https://doi.org/10.1596/1813-9450-3400

Canning, D. (1999). Infrastructure's contribution to aggregate output. *Policy Research Working Paper Series*, (November).

Cervero, R., & Landis, J. (1993). Assessing the impacts of urban rail transit on local real estate markets using quasi-experimental comparisons. *Transportation Research Part A*, *27*(1). https://doi.org/10.1016/0965-8564(93)90013-B

Cheung, E., Chan, A. P. C., & Kajewski, S. (2012). Factors contributing to successful public private partnership projects: Comparing Hong Kong with Australia and the United Kingdom. *Journal of Facilities Management*, *10*(February), 45–58. https://doi.org/10.1108/14725961211200397

Cohen, J. P., Cromley, R. G., & Banach, K. T. (2015). Are homes near water bodies and wetlands worth more or less? An analysis of housing prices in one Connecticut town. *Growth and Change*, *46*(1). https://doi.org/10.1111/grow.12073

Colliers. (2021). Asia-to-global real estate investment: Singapore takes the lead. Colliers. Retrieved 23 February 2021, from https://www2.colliers.com/en-sg/news/cm-asia-real-estate-investment-capital-flows-singapore-takes-lead

Cooper, C. (2015). Accounting for the fictitious: A Marxist contribution to understanding accounting's roles in the financial crisis. *Critical Perspectives on Accounting*. https://doi.org/10.1016/j.cpa.2014.08.002

Dechant, T., & Finkenzeller, K. (2012). The role of infrastructure investments in a multi-asset portfolio – answers from dynamic asset allocation. *SSRN Electronic Journal*. https://doi.org/10.2139/ssrn.1992520

Dechant, T., & Finkenzeller, K. (2013). How much into infrastructure? Evidence from dynamic asset allocation. *Journal of Property Research*, *30*(2). https://doi.org/10.1080/09599916.2012.731075

Edward, G., & Poterba, J. (2020). *Economic Analysis and Infrastructure Investment* (No. 28215). Cambridge MA. https://doi.org/10.3386/w28215

EIB. (2010). Public and private financing of infrastructure: Evolution and economics of private infrastructure finance. *EIB Papers*, *15*(1).

Estache, A., & Garsous, G. (2012). The impact of infrastructure on growth in developing countries. *IFC Economics Notes*, (2007), 1–11.

Fleta-Asín, J., & Muñoz, F. (2020). How does risk transference to private partner impact on public-private partnerships' success? Empirical evidence from developing economies. *Socio-Economic Planning Sciences*, 72. https://doi.org/10.1016/j.seps.2020.100869

Forkenbrock, D. J. (2001). Comparison of external costs of rail and truck freight transportation. *Transportation Research Part A: Policy and Practice*, 35(4). https://doi.org/10.1016/S0965-8564(99)00061-0

Gallagher, M., & Mansour, A. (2000). An analysis of hotel real estate market dynamics. *The Journal of Real Estate Research*, 19(1), 133–164.

Grigg, N. S. (2011). *Infrastructure Finance: The Business of Infrastructure for a Sustainable Future*. https://doi.org/10.1002/9781118266182

Hwang, B. G., Zhao, X., & Gay, M. J. S. (2013). Public private partnership projects in Singapore: Factors, critical risks and preferred risk allocation from the perspective of contractors. *International Journal of Project Management*, 31(3), 424–433. https://doi.org/10.1016/j.ijproman.2012.08.003

Inderst, G. (2016). Infrastructure investment, private finance, and institutional investors: Asia from a global perspective. *SSRN Electronic Journal*. https://doi.org/10.2139/ssrn.2721577

Inderst, G., & Stewart, F. (2014). Institutional investment in infrastructure in developing countries: Introduction to potential models. *World Bank Policy Research Working Paper* (February).

Lambrev, D. (2019). Infrastructure indices: Comparative analysis of performance, risk and representation of global listed proxies. *Naše Gospodarstvo/Our Economy*, 65(3). https://doi.org/10.2478/ngoe-2019-0011

Magweva, R., & Sibanda, M. (2020). Inflation and infrastructure sector returns in emerging markets – panel ARDL approach. *Cogent Economics and Finance*, 8(1). https://doi.org/10.1080/23322039.2020.1730078

Martínez, L. M., & Viegas, J. M. (2009). Effects of transportation accessibility on residential property values. *Transportation Research Record: Journal of the Transportation Research Board*, 2115(1). https://doi.org/10.3141/2115-16

Mause, K., & Krumm, T. (2011). Public–private partnershipping as a tool of government: Exploring its determinants across German states. *German Politics*, 20(4), 527–544. https://doi.org/10.1080/09644008.2011.606313

McMillen, D. P., & Redfearn, C. L. (2010). Estimation and hypothesis testing for nonparametric hedonic house price functions. *Journal of Regional Science*, 50(3). https://doi.org/10.1111/j.1467-9787.2010.00664.x

Munoz-Gielen, D. (2011). Improving public-value capturing in urban development. *Innovative Land and Property Taxation*, 150–170.

Newell, G. (2020). The need for more research on the Asian real estate markets. *Journal of Property Investment and Finance*, 39(1). https://doi.org/10.1108/JPIF-05-2020-0059

Newell, G., & Peng, H. W. (2008). The role of U.S. infrastructure in investment portfolios. *Journal of Real Estate Portfolio Management*, 14(1). https://doi.org/10.2469/dig.v39.n1.3

Newell, G., & Peng, H. W. (2009). The impact of the global financial crisis on A-REITs. *Pacific Rim Property Research Journal*, 15(4). https://doi.org/10.1080/14445921.2009.11104291

Nieuwerburgh, S. Van, Stanton, R., Berkeley, U. C., & De Bever, L. (2015). *A Review of Real Estate and Infrastructure Investments by the Norwegian Government Pension Fund Global (GPFG).* Alberta. Retrieved from https://www.regjeringen .no/contentassets/f353169233704a55b3af6b0b36fb3129/ekspertrapport_eiendom _infrastruktur.pdf
Norman, E. J., Sirmans, S. G., & Benjamin, J. D. (1995). The historical environment of real estate returns. *Journal of Real Estate Portfolio Management, 1.*
Oyedele, J. B. (2014). Infrastructure investment and the emerging role of institutional investors: The case of pension funds and sovereign wealth funds. *Academic Journal of Interdisciplinary Studies.* https://doi.org/10.5901/ajis.2014.v3n1p43
Paul, S. (2014). Finances and governance of urban local bodies: An approach of urban development perspective from a developing country (India). *Journal of Urban and Regional Analysis, 6*(2), 181–201. https://doi.org/10.37043/jura.2014.6.2.5.
Peterson, G. E. (2008). *Unlocking Land Values to Finance Urban Infrastructure.* Washington DC: The World Bank. https://doi.org/10.1596/978-0-8213-7709-3
Preqin. (2020). Preqin | Alternative assets data, solutions and insights. Retrieved 25 February 2021, from https://www.preqin.com/
Rics. (2012). RICS Valuation - Professional Standards (Red Book). *Basis of Value.*
Ruiz Díaz, G. (2020). What drives the failure of private participation in infrastructure projects? *International Journal of Managing Projects in Business, 13*(6). https://doi .org/10.1108/IJMPB-12-2019-0298
Seek, N. H., Sing, T. F., & Yu, S. M. (2016a). Bridging the gap between capital and real estate markets. In *Singapore's Real Estate.* https://doi.org/10.1142/9789814689274 _0008
Seek, N. H., Sing, T. F., & Yu, S. M. (2016b). Real estate education. In *Singapore's Real Estate.* https://doi.org/10.1142/9789814689274_0009
Shatkin, G. (2016). The real estate turn in policy and planning: Land monetization and the political economy of peri-urbanization in Asia. *Cities, 53,* 141–149. https://doi .org/10.1016/j.cities.2015.11.015
Steel, G., van Noorloos, F., & Klaufus, C. (2017). The urban land debate in the global South: New avenues for research. *Geoforum, 83.* https://doi.org/10.1016/j.geoforum .2017.03.006
Theurillat, T. (2017). Financing urban growth in China: A case study of Qujing, a medium-sized City in Yunnan Province. *China Perspectives, 2017*(1). https://doi .org/10.4000/chinaperspectives.7203
Tipple, A. G., Korboe, D., Willis, K., & Garrod, G. (1998). Who is building what in urban Ghana? Housing supply in three towns. *Cities, 15*(6). https://doi.org/10.1016/ s0264-2751(98)00036-5
Tirumala, R. D., & Tiwari, P. (2021). Land-based financing elements in infrastructure policy formulation: A case of India. *Land, 10*(2), 133. https://doi.org/10.3390/ land10020133
United Nations. (2015). *Sustainable Development Goals and Targets.* United Nations.
van der Veen, M., & Korthals Altes, W. K. (2011). Urban development agreements: Do they meet guiding principles for a better deal? *Cities, 28*(4), 310–319. https://doi.org/ 10.1016/j.cities.2011.03.001
Waddell, P. (2002). Urbanism: Modeling urban development for land use, transportation, and environmental planning. *Journal of the American Planning Association, 68*(3). https://doi.org/10.1080/01944360208976274
Warnock, V. C., & Warnock, F. E. (2008). Markets and housing finance. *Journal of Housing Economics, 17*(3). https://doi.org/10.1016/j.jhe.2008.03.001

Weber, B., Staub-Bisang, M., & Alfen, H. W. (2016). *Infrastructure As an Asset Class: Investment Strategy, Sustainability, Project Finance and PPP* (pp. 1–392). Wiley. https://doi.org/10.1002/9781119226574

Wurstbauer, D., & Schäfers, W. (2015). Inflation hedging and protection characteristics of infrastructure and real estate assets. *Journal of Property Investment and Finance, 33*(1). https://doi.org/10.1108/JPIF-04-2014-0026

Yeaple, S. R., & Golub, S. S. (2007). International productivity differences, infrastructure, and comparative advantage. *Review of International Economics, 15*(2). https://doi.org/10.1111/j.1467-9396.2007.00667.x

Yermo, J., Della Croce, R., & Stewart, F. (2011). Promoting longer-term investment by institutional investors. *OECD Journal: Financial Market Trends, 2011*(1). https://doi.org/10.1787/fmt-2011-5kg55b0z1ktb

PART III

Institutions: behaviours, government and foreign actors

10 Local community in brownfield redevelopment: the Alphington Paper Mill Project in Melbourne

Xuqing Li, Hao Wu and Huiying (Cynthia) Hou

Introduction

With the rapid population growth and limited land supply in the urban regions, brownfield redevelopment has turned into an attractive option among developers, local government bodies and investors. US developers have recognised brownfield land as an opportunity in recent decades (Thomas 2002). Eisen (cited in Heberle and Wernstedt 2006) argues that brownfield development is an approach to reverse previously developed lands to slow down the unsustainable development trend in the US. Developing brownfields is a possible way to slow down urban sprawl by preserving industrial land, it being an environmental protection strategy while contributing to economy growth and community revitalisation (see Criterion & Apogee cited in Amekudzi, McNeil & Koutsopoulos 2003; Beriatos & Brebbia 2008; Cheng, Geertman, Kuffer & Zhan 2011; De Sousa 2003, 2005; Dixon 2007; Ganser & Williams 2007; Haslam 2009, p.153; Smith 2010; Thornton, Franz, Edwards, Pahlen & Nathanail 2007). Compared with greenfield development, brownfield development utilises existing infrastructure, which brings less external pressure to achieve higher population density (Amekudzi et al. 2003). However, the relatively short development history and the risks involved in brownfield development lead to its stakeholders facing many concerns before they can enjoy any benefit it may bring. This chapter reviews and summarises current research that relates to a community's involvement in brownfield redevelopment and its impact. There are few research focuses on this area. A significant brownfield mixed-use residential redevelopment in Melbourne, one of the most liveable global cities, is investigated through a qualitative approach. The detailed case study involves a micro-level evaluation of the conditions and underlying concerns of a community's knowledge and the engagement in local level brownfield development processes in Melbourne.

Complexity of brownfield development

Haslam (2009) defines brownfields as underutilised and contaminated infill properties due to changes of development patterns. His definition relates to the US industrial revolution when people were forced to move out of central cities. One widely cited definition of brownfields is by the United States Environmental Protection Agency: "… abandoned, idled, or under-used industrial and commercial facilities where expansion or redevelopment is complicated by real or perceived environmental contamination" (USEPA, cited in Coffin 2003; Fields cited in Geltman 2000; Lange & McNeil 2004). Later, in the 2001 *Small Business Liability Relief and Brownfields Revitalization Act*, the definition was amended to: "with certain legal exclusions and additions, the term 'brownfield site' means real property, the expansion, redevelopment, or reuse of which may be complicated by the presence or potential presence of a hazardous substance, pollutant, or contaminant" (USEPA, cited in Coffin 2003). Although funding assessment and brownfield redevelopment in the US were guided by this legal definition, their applications are due to policy, finance and case specific issues (Yount 2003). A generic definition is hard to find in the US as each state differs by market demand and land use control regime (Charles cited in Geltman 2000). Another definition that focuses on diverse stakeholder requirements that have become well-known is (Alker et al. 2000),

> … any land or premises which has previously been used or developed and is not currently fully in use, although it may be partially occupied or utilised. It may also be vacant, derelict or contaminated. Therefore, a brownfield site is not necessarily available for immediate use without intervention.

A lack of a universal definition of brownfields and brownfield development makes success of brownfield reuse difficult to evaluate. It is hard to achieve a consensus among the stakeholders. Although some common factors are agreed upon, such as previously used as industrial or commercial land, the definitions emphasise various perspectives in different circumstances or locations. Without some general consensus, brownfield practice in cities and regions remains uncertain and risky. Guided by the definition of brownfields, local government has adopted specific regulations and standards to deliver and assess brownfields development. In Australia, inadequate understanding of brownfield developments is confirmed in industry practice and academic studies to be one of the major challenges to the nation's sustainable regional and urban development (Fowler 2007; Wu & Chen 2012; Wu, Qin & Yang 2016).

Risks involving multi-parties, including the local community, are an important issue envisaged in the reuse of brownfields. A significant amount of development cost is committed to remediation, infrastructure construction or upgrade, increasing liability, and involving the local community's interests (CRDCUSCM cited in Thomas 2002).[1] In addition, the potential negativity from publicity regarding contaminated land impedes the certainty of land use, which leads to asymmetric information about the contamination and its associated stigma spreading to the whole community (Coffin 2003). Hence, brownfields development is not only risky for landowner and developers, it also affects other stakeholders, such as planning and regulatory authorities, occupiers, builders and general community members in the area (Wu & Chen 2012; Wu, Tiwari, Han & Chan 2017). It is necessary and essential to ensure a sufficient and effective communication process in brownfield development that takes into account the directly affected key stakeholders, namely those from the local community. After all, risks in brownfields development are a spatially as well as socially driven concern (Winson-Geideman, Krause, Wu & Warren-Myers 2017; Wu, Tiwari, Han & Chan 2018).

Local communities have had significant impacts on the promotion, identification and performance of brownfield development (Haslam 2009; Lange & McNeil 2004; Lange, Wang, Zhuang & Fontana 2013; Thomas 2002; Wu & Chen 2012; Wu et al. 2017). But relative to extensive studies from the developer, planner and lender's perspectives, little is known about local communities' active role from the socio-political perspective (Wu et al. 2018). Relative to the supply side influence of the private sector in brownfield projects, the local community represents an equally powerful demand-side influence due to its collective demand for lower adverse effects of land contamination. It is easier to conduct this research in a democratic society. Local communities are heavily associated in brownfield developments because they are the most immobile groups during and after the redevelopment. They are the most profoundly affected group. Establishing a sufficient and effective regulatory framework helps other stakeholders better understand the local community's concerns and to gain its support to achieve a more balanced and satisfying outcome.

To minimise negative effects due to communication failure and the absence of key parties, cities and nations establish management protocols for community participation in brownfield redevelopment. For example, Australia has developed a planning framework for land use planning and development, with legal enforcement power, to allow local communities to express opinions and to participate during urban redevelopment (Wu & Chen 2012; Wu, Qin & Yang 2016). In the United States (Florida), in the absence of local communities, the state failed to implement redevelopment policies which caused social problems (Haslam 2009). The significant role of local communities in brownfields-related socio-economic matters is clear.

Brownfields and local communities

Although generally implied by the NIMBY (Not In My Back Yard) phenomenon and extensively discussed in the urban development literature, the clear extent to which local communities are involved in the brownfield redevelopment process is often ignored. This approach is insufficient to fully appreciate the local community's role in brownfields in mature democratic societies. The literature has considered the significance of communities in the planning and development of brownfield sites. Yet, a specific micro-level study of their concerns and interactions in land redevelopment remains an under-addressed area.

The planning and development literature emphasises community welfare in land use processes and for a long time its importance has been recognised. Kaiser et al. (1995) described how to plan a method to allocate resources for public interests by balancing the diverse community objectives. Community participation is an important contributor to a progressive planning and design process, a process that also gains support when it comes to urban landscape and human needs (Matsuoka and Kaplan 2008). There is concern regarding the unique challenge of meeting a local community's needs, compared with those of other stakeholders, given their diverse and complex goals (Kelly 2012; Heberle & Wernstedt 2006). Kelly (2012) introduced multiple methods for community planning. For example, considering an objective-driven approach, large-scale public involvement is unavoidable when a planning authority adopts this approach to frame the objectives for the smaller local community groups. Other approaches include opportunity- and problem-driven approaches, showing that community participation is necessary and vital (Kelly 2012). Although the role of the local community and its participation are recognised and evaluated in land use processes in general, insufficient connection has been made with brownfield development. This isolation in community engagement is not uncommon. A similar situation has been found in the literature of community and social capital building (Manzo &

Perkins 2006). As one significant and complex land phenomenon, brownfield development can influence large-scale communities and other social activities. Therefore, a greater connection with the community should be made.

Some recent studies of brownfield developments mention communities' participation as an important contributor to the land redevelopment success. For example, the US Environmental Protection Agency has identified several themes of sustainable brownfield development based on case studies, project evaluation and review, and shown that existing knowledge of communities and associated organisations are important contributors to sustainable brownfield development (USEPA cited in Heberle & Wernstedt 2006). Notably, community involvement or participation can sometimes be a socially costly process due to the fact that community comprises different special group interests, which may result in costly collective action or inaction. Heberle and Wernstedt (2006) argue that effective community participation at the early project stage benefits other stakeholders. Community participation not only enhances the project's bottom line, but also contributes to alternative design and social opportunity (Heberle & Wernstedt 2006). Haslam (2009) considers community support to be one of the promoting factors in brownfield project success in Florida, where accessibility and community participation are promoted. Lange and McNeil (2004) make a similar argument based on the findings from a national survey conducted in the US. They identify community support as one of the variables that has a strong impact on brownfield project success. These studies recognise that most stakeholders in brownfield projects are aware of the importance of local community and the potential benefits of their participation.

As the success of brownfield development is partly aided by community participation, it is assumed that a positive overall outcome offsets the participation's negative impacts. For instance, one of the opposing views argues that community participation may increase project risk or expected cost because the community may object to a project or demand more investment to counter the uncertainty regarding contamination, its remediation, ownership issues and so on (Lange et al. 2013). As Coffin (2003) states, it is inadequate information and communication that cause negative and passive community sentiment. Landlords are concerned with the negative impacts of exposing information about their sites, such as a reduction in the market value, regulatory change and decontamination costs, which leads to information asymmetry and risk to all the involved parties (Wu et al. 2018). While effective communication and community participation may generate positive social outcomes in the decontamination of a brownfield site, communication also benefits all stakeholders by generating a plan to balance their interests, supported by the community.

In fact, the developer may benefit from having a development proposal and plan, if it effectively incorporates a community's concerns and suggestions. This plan not only gains the developer the support of the community, but also potentially saves time and effort in getting planning approval as planning authorities often take a community's support or objections seriously during the planning process (Haslam 2009). This is also demonstrated theoretically as, among other indicators, a larger weight is allocated to a community's support when the multi-attribute decision-making process in brownfield development is tested (Lange et al. 2013). It is reasonable to expect that a community's participation is an integral part of brownfield planning and redevelopment.

The brownfield development case

The case project being investigated is identified as the Alphington Paper Mill Development (also known as Yarra Bend Residential Development; hereafter: APMD) in Melbourne, Australia. Figure 10.1 shows the site's location relative to its adjacent suburbs, transportation lines, public space (e.g. parks) and so on.

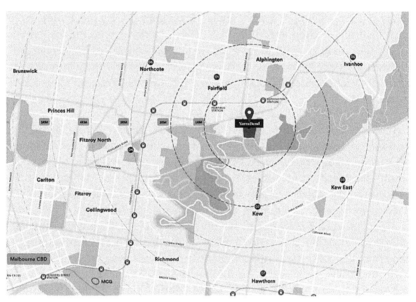

Source: Alphington Paper Mill Development Map (2019)

Figure 10.1   APMD location

The project was selected for the following reasons. First, the urban planning system and regulations that are relevant to brownfield development in Melbourne have been developed and applied in practice since the early 1990s (Wu & Chen 2012). As a former industrial city in Australia, Melbourne has a large portfolio of brownfield sites, it also has developed a comprehensive regulatory framework for their redevelopment and has implemented community engagement activities (Wu & Chen 2012; Wu et al. 2016). Meanwhile, the system allows for specific planning schemes of particular development projects to be based on local council policy. Second, the Alphington case has rich project-level information on its nature, scale and significance. It demonstrates a high level of social transparency where project details are accessible through the local Council website. The APMD site was owned by the former Alphington Paper Mill Factory, whose long-time operation has left the site with a high risk of contamination. The site is over 16-hectares, and the redevelopment has a long project timeline, high-density land use, cultural heritage complexity and significant social image. All of which contribute to its significance. The local government, City of Yarra Council, identifies the project as a major strategic redevelopment within the inner Melbourne area. A Specific Development Plan Overlay scheme was generated based on the property, which reinforced its political significance. A Community Reference Group was appointed by the Council in addition to normal community involvement processes. This qualifies the APMD as a case suitable for an inquiry into the local community's role in brownfield development. Figure 10.2 shows various perspectives of the site, including its neighbourhood and the buildings that are in use, completed or whose construction is in progress.

The case study

Brownfield sites are considered as risky locations. The underlying reasons to engage in this risky property redevelopment implies the expected social and financial benefits will exceed the costs (Heberle & Wernstedt 2006). Many of these benefits would not be achieved without knowledge of existing situations and opportunities for local communities, including the regeneration effect of brownfield sites (Heberle & Wernstedt 2006). The existing literature recognises various perspectives of a community's role in brownfield redevelopments. With a few exceptions (Winson-Geideman et al. 2017), the 'place-specific analysis' is lacking. This chapter focuses on the local communities for evidence of their engagement in a large-scale brownfield redevelopment project in Melbourne. It adopts a qualitative approach to the core question: what is the role of the local community in brownfield redevelopment in a mature suburban setting?

Notes: The rectangle in photo 1 highlights the location of the Alphington Paper Mill Development project and its distance from its nearby communities; photos 2–5 show details of the project

Source: Authors

Figure 10.2   Current conditions of the APMD project

It aims to identify local communities' perceptions, experiences and involvement. Data were collected via face-to-face interviews and with a questionnaire survey in the local community. As discussed, what is absent in brownfield research is a focus on the communities' concerns for their participation in the reuse of the brownfield land. Thus, case-based detailed studies are needed to gain such insights, despite some issues of the property-specific approach used in brownfields research (Heberle and Wernstedt 2006). As qualitative methods provide heterogeneous data, which a quantitative approach could easily ignore (Kelle 2006), a larger-scale endeavour to cover a broader area using quantitative methods could likely be used after building up insights into behavioural details regarding the subject matter (Wu & Chen 2010).

Data were collected using a questionnaire survey of the nearby communities. The purpose of the survey was to gain information about: (1) the level of the community's awareness of the APMD project; (2) their knowing channels regarding the project; (3) the background of the project; (4) personal involvement in the project; and (5) personal perception of the project. A total of 51 community members participated in the survey: 29 males and 22 females. To generate further insights, face-to-face interviews were organised with one local community club member and representatives of the developer, Glenvill. Table 10.1 gives summary statistics of the survey, showing the distribution of gender, age, and education of the survey participants. It also includes residency and home ownership status, which help to identify the likely diversity in opinions within different layers of residents in the local communities.

Analysis and evaluation

Communities' awareness and involvement

The survey results show few differences between the Alphington (suburb) residents and the non-Alphington residents. The specific survey question focuses on the awareness and involvement of local communities by their residency status and home ownership status. Fifty-seven percent (16/28) of the Alphington residents and 70% (16/23) of the non-Alphington residents were aware of the project by early 2015. This indicates that nearly 50% of the respondents were aware of the APMD project to various levels. Although its sample size may limit the prediction power of the actual level of community members' awareness of the project, the overall response regarding the public awareness of the APMD project is reasonably high across local communities.

Table 10.1   Summary of survey participants

Variable		Frequency	Percentage
Gender	Male	29	56.8
	Female	22	43.1
Age	18–34	20	39.2
	35–65	29	56.9
	65 and above	2	3.9
Education level	Senior secondary	15	29.4
	Tertiary (High Dip.)	11	21.6
	Bachelor degree	15	29.4
	Graduate	6	11.8
	Master degree	4	7.8
Residency status	Alphington resident	28	54.9
	Non-Alphington resident	23	45.1
Home ownership status	Home owner	22	43.1
	Tenant	28	54.9
	No response	1	0.6

Source: Authors

Within the local communities, further variations are found in their awareness of the APMD project.

Regarding the stated involvement in the APMD, no participant indicates his or her involvement in the project is high. Around 50% of Alphington residents and non-Alphington residents believe that their involvement in the APMD project as a community member is almost zero. This concern is investigated mainly from local vs. non-local residents (Figure 10.3) and resident owner vs. renter (Figure 10.4) perspectives. Figure 10.3 shows some signs of different levels of involvement in the APMD between Alphington residents and non-Alphington residents. The sampled local residents are moderately involved in the APMD project processes and the engagement level of the local residents is slightly higher.

Figure 10.4 shows a similar level of involvement between the participants who are home owners and tenants. It appears that a higher percentage of the participants who are tenants have a lower level of involvement in the APMD. As expected, home owners from the local communities are more actively engaged in the project's process.

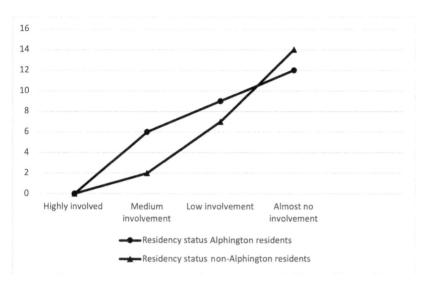

Figure 10.3   Participants' involvement by residency status

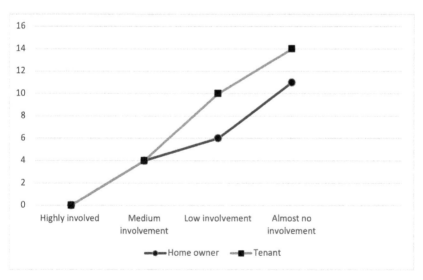

Figure 10.4   Participants' involvement by home ownership status

Among the sampled Alphington residents, it is intended to identify the timing since each of them became aware of the project. The survey results show a variation in their degrees of awareness of the APMD project. Figure 10.5 shows the results categorised by the total responses, the Alphington and the non-Alphington residents. Twenty-eight (of 51) respondents were aware of the APMD before/since the redevelopment plan was approved in 2015. Nine (of 51) were made aware since the demolition started. Only one respondent was aware of the project at the start of the formal community consultation. Among the sampled, 16 local and 11 non-local residents are found to have been aware of the project prior to its approval. The level of community awareness is moderate. Interestingly, over 50% of the Alphington residents who were aware of the project in its early stage were lightly involved in the project. The non-Alphington residents who are aware of the project in its early stage also indicated low or no involvement in the project. This triggers the question regarding why the Alphington residents lack the motivation to become actively involved.

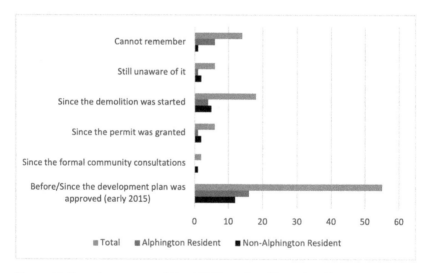

Figure 10.5   Awareness of the APMD project (Question 1)

In terms of the factors that the respondents consider negatively affect their involvement in the APMD by relevance to local residents, 46% (13 out of 28) of Alphington residents indicate their "lack of understanding of the project's impact", while 70% (16 out of 23) of non-Alphington residents suggest "not a resident in this area" as key factors. It is beyond the scope of this study to examine reasons behind the diversity of influential factors. However, a lack of project knowledge of brownfield redevelopment appears to discourage local resident participation while low social relevance is a factor affecting non-local residents' engagement. A visit to the project's display home in 2019 found that the developer had built a gallery displaying the site's industrial heritage, which serves as an educational opportunity to inform the local and the broader communities.

Perceived importance of local community impact

The survey results reveal a 'gap' between respondents' self-stated aware-ness and self-stated involvement in the APMD project. It implies that early awareness may not lead to subsequent community involvement in brownfield projects. As *awareness* normally describes the state of one's knowing certain information, it does not reveal an effort to seek further information to support action or passively take no action. *Involvement* often describes the state of being engaged in a process of activities. It does not specify the process is actively pursued or passively assigned. Survey participants stated their level of awareness and involvement in the APMD, including their perceived conse-quences of the community action. Community members' attitudes towards the APMD process is reflected by their perception of the community impact on the brownfield development processes.

It is assumed that community members' sense of the local community's impact on brownfield projects will affect their actual involvement. The survey allows the participants to rate the level of community impact on APMD. Figure 10.6 shows that participants have diverse views on the significance of the local com-munities in the APMD process, where 4% (2) consider it a strong influence and more than 42% believe it at least partially under-represented. Twenty-four percent (12/51) believe the community has participated in part of the planning process, but failed to express local residents' concerns and influence the devel-opment plan. Eighteen percent (9/51) believe the community's concerns and opinions are ignored. Thirty-nine percent (20/51) believe the local communi-ties communicate with the Council and the developer regarding their concerns during the project's planning process.

These results suggest the community's perceived role in the APMD project is consistent with its stated involvement. It appears the participants are not strongly positive about the community's overall impact on the APMD but believe that they are part of the project's land use planning process. They do not believe local communities' interest is ranked highly in a project of this nature. Some participants commented that they are disappointed that their concerns were not treated properly. For example, an interviewee at a local

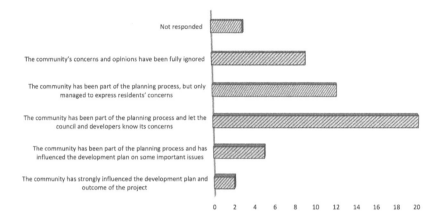

Figure 10.6   Community impact rated by the participants (Question 12)

community sports club commented, "[concerns raised by community clubs are] selected and monitored by the appointed group … before it is discussed [by council and developers] … It is really up to the developer creating things that fit into the guidelines [made by council]." This shows that brownfields stakeholders, such as the developer and the Council, have interests that differ from local communities. It is not a straightforward process for the communities' concerns to be effectively expressed and efficiently communicated among stakeholders.

Intergroup comparison

One would also recognise the diverse opinions within the local communities. The survey raises questions regarding the potential reasons for this diversity in participants' response. One question allows participants to nominate the factors they think are obstructing their involvement in the APMD. Results are presented based on two categories, i.e. local residency status and tenure. Table 10.2 shows 41% (21/51) consider their lack of understanding of the project's impact has obstructed their involvement. Within the subgroups by residency status and property tenure type, the survey results show a diverse range of opinions. Sixty-seven percent of the non-Alphington residents believe residency status affects their involvement the most. It is clear that the 'non-local' residents are not prohibited from being involved in the APMD as long as they can raise valid project-related concerns. However, living in surrounding neighbourhoods of the APMD implies a shorter 'social distance' to the project. As for survey participants who are tenants, 57% consider their lack of project knowledge obstructs their direct involvement. For home owners, their concerns are more in line with the communicative obstructions, much less on project information. This is not surprising, because local home owners are able to access the site and request information from the Council as their interests are more directly affected. Some respondents nominated additional factors. One respondent suggested they had "no faith that community concerns would be taken seriously – developer were powerful". Four respondents suggested a lack of time prevented their involvement in the APMD, which is a commitment issue. Another respondent comment, "so many developments around" – which seems to suggest the city-wide property development boom has overwhelmed some of communities' participation effort.

One further community level concern that the survey intends to discover is the factors that the respondents believe to encourage their involvement in the APMD. Table 10.3 shows 77% (39/51) of all the respondents believe that the possible impacts of the APMD will motivate them to engage in the process. In contrast to the question about where people express their concerns about asymmetric project information, the respondents recognise the potential impact of brownfield reuse may encourage their willingness to engage in the project. It appears a struggle exists between *passive responses*, due to a lack of information, and *active responses*, due to knowing the project's possibilities. This is unsurprising because information has dual effects on people's understanding and behaviour. Furthermore, residency status could influence a community member's sense of responsibility – 54% (15/28) of the Alphington residents compared with 22% (5/23) of the non-Alphington residents chose the importance of community member responsibility as an influential factor.

A few further factors are nominated by the respondents. One of the local-community level concerns is, "parking will impact on local residents' dog club". Other comments include, "my house is here" and "I am living locally and a part of a community group", and are the local community level responses to the relationship between the APMD and the livelihood of local residents.

Discussion and conclusion

This study examines a local community's engagement in a large-scale brownfield project – the APMD in Melbourne. It aims to discover the motivations and obstructions at local community level. Findings indicate that the local community responds passively to the APMD owing to some obstructing factors. In addition, there are positive motivating factors that encourage

Table 10.2   Negative factors of participants' involvement

	Residency status				Ownership status				Total	
	Alphington residents		Non-Alphington residents		Home owner		Tenant			
	No.	%	No.	%	No.	%	No.	%	No.	%
Publicity of the project	3	10.7	2	8.7	2	9.1	3	10.7	5	9.8
Difficulty of accessing information about this project	8	28.6	2	8.7	4	18.2	6	21.4	10	19.6
Difficulty of expressing opinions during the planning process (including submission of objections and being a member of the Community Reference Group)	7	25	3	13.0	6	27.3	5	17.9	11	21.6
Lack of understanding of the project's impacts	13	46.4	8	34.8	5	22.7	16	57.1	21	41.2
There is no incentive of involvement (for example money)	7	25	2	8.7	3	13.6	6	21.4	9	17.6
I am not a resident in this area	0	–	16	69.6	7	31.8	9	32.1	16	31.4
Others, please describe:	6	21.4	4	17.4	5	22.7	4	14.3	10	19.6
Total	28	–	23	–	22*	–	28	–	51	–

Note: *One respondent did not indicate his/her ownership status in the questionnaire
Source: Authors

active engagement. The negative factors are those that discourage community members progressing from the stage of project awareness to the stage of project involvement in the redevelopment process. Sorting by levels of influence in the APMD, this study finds that a lack of understanding of the project's impact is the most influential factor, followed by residency status, the difficulty of accessing information, personal issues such as commitment cost, the difficulty of expressing an opinion during the planning process, missing incentives for direct involvement, and lastly, the project's publicity. The motivations for local communities' involvement in the project include: the possible impacts of the project being the most influential factor, the local responsibility as a community member, and communities being forced to respond owing

Table 10.3   Positive factors of participants' involvement

	Residency status			Ownership status			Total			
	Alphington residents		Non-Alphington residents		Home owner		Tenant		Total	
	No.	%	No.	%	No.	%	No.	%	No.	%
The possible impacts of the development	23	82.1	16	69.6	18	81.8	20	71.4	39	76.5
The responsibility as a community member	15	53.6	5	21.7	8	36.4	12	42.9	20	39.2
I am forced to be involved, because: (please describe)	4	14.3	1	4.3	3	13.6	2	7.1	5	9.8
Others, please describe:	0	–	2	8.7	2	9.1	0	–	2	3.9
Total	28	–	23	–	22*	–	28	–	51	–

Note: *One participant did not indicate his/her ownership status in the questionnaire

to community-level negative external effects, such as pollution and disturbance. While there are some motivating factors, community members may respond passively to a brownfield project owing to some demotivating forces. Interestingly, some of the motivating factors that the study identifies are personal and community-specific.

Summarising the motivations and obstructions that influence local communities' brownfields involvement, information about the project's possible impact plays an important role. A lack of information obstructs an active community response as local communities do not know how to actively respond or engage with the process. Knowing some information could enable local communities to step forward for an active response, as they know they will be affected and so need to inform others of their concerns. But this change of responding mode requires time, effort, access and other resources for people to progress from lacking information to knowing the possible impacts. These conditions are included in the list of obstructions as personal issues.

Among the stakeholders, the developers' perspective needs some specific attention. From interviews with representatives of Glenvill, head developer of the APMD, a different perspective is noted. As one of the respondents reflects:

> I think it's important to know that we got council requirements that we have to meet ... we have to meet parking requirements, visitor parking as well ... we have requirements for each lot, we have requirements on street parking and restrictions ... we are required to do traffic management plans...

Developers are responsible for council and client requirements, which means, if not being formally contracted and enforced, a community's direct concerns may need an extra layer of effort for them to be communicated during the project process. This implies a social contract perspective may emerge out of brownfield processes. Furthermore, a passive response hardly delivers a community's concerns to the council. Communities could actively interact with the council to express their concerns. Under the existing planning scheme of brownfield development control, it is difficult and infeasible for developers to contact a community without the council's support and supervision with regard to project safety, financial feasibility and community consent. It is important for the council and the community to identify missing motivations and institutional barriers to assist in the community's active response to brownfield development process. As the existing literature argues, effective social involvement, once generated, will facilitate inclusive development and generate positive social outcomes.

This study reaches several conclusions about a local community's involvement in and impact on brownfield development. A brownfield development project that is large-scale by land size, project complexity and potential influence, is likely to attract significant attention from local and nearby communities. Local communities' awareness typically starts as a passive response and could develop into an active response that will exert influence. The two types of response are defined based on the requirements of the community member's time, effort and interaction with other stakeholders in the project process. A passive response usually remains a small-scale influence, while an active response has greater potential to result in actual influence on the brownfield development. Motivational problems and existing obstructions may discourage communities from progressing from passive to active responses. These obstructions could be information about the project's impact, personal issues, residency status and so on. Increasing local communities' knowledge about a project's potential impacts helps diminish the above-mentioned obstructions and can simultaneously encourage an active community response to environmental concerns. The APMD project appears to be successful in doing this.

The role of knowledge to help raise the community's environmental concerns in a brownfield development process is worth investigating in greater detail in the future.

Note

1. Consumers Renaissance Development Corporation & US Conference of Mayors (CRDCUSCM).

References

Alker, S., Joy, V., Roberts, P. and Smith, N., 2000. The definition of brownfield. *Journal of Environmental Planning and Management*, 43(1), pp. 49–69.

Alphington Paper Mill Development Map, 2019. Glenvill Group, viewed 28 October 2019, https://yarrabend.com.au/location

Amekudzi, A., McNeil, S. and Koutsopoulos, H.N., 2003. Assessing extra-jurisdictional and area-wide impacts of clustered brownfield developments. *Journal of Urban Planning and Development*, 129(1), pp. 27–44.

Beriatos, E. and Brebbia, C.A. (eds.), 2008. *Brownfields IV: Prevention, Assessment, Rehabilitation and Development of Brownfield Sites* (Vol. 107). WIT Press.

Cheng, F., Geertman, S., Kuffer, M. and Zhan, Q., 2011. An integrative methodology to improve brownfield redevelopment planning in Chinese cities: A case study of Futian, Shenzhen. *Computers, Environment and Urban Systems*, 35(5), pp. 388–398.

Coffin, S.L., 2003. Closing the brownfield information gap: Some practical methods for identifying brownfields. *Environmental Practice*, 5(1), pp. 34–39.

De Sousa, C., 2005. Policy performance and brownfield redevelopment in Milwaukee, Wisconsin. *The Professional Geographer*, 57(2), pp. 312–327.

De Sousa, C.A., 2003. Turning brownfields into green space in the City of Toronto. *Landscape and Urban Planning*, 62(4), pp. 181–198.

Dixon, T., 2007. The property development industry and sustainable urban brownfield regeneration in England: An analysis of case studies in Thames Gateway and Greater Manchester. *Urban Studies*, 44(12), pp. 2379–2400.

Fowler, R., 2007 (September). Site contamination law and policy in Europe, North America and Australia – trends and challenges, In *Eighth Meeting of the International Committee on Contaminated Land*, Stockholm, pp. 10–11.

Ganser, R. and Williams, K., 2007. Brownfield development: Are we using the right targets? Evidence from England and Germany. *European Planning Studies*, 15(5), pp. 603–622.

Geltman, E.G., 2000. *Recycling Land: Understanding the Legal Landscape of Brownfield Development*. University of Michigan Press.

Haslam, C., 2009. Urban redevelopment and contaminated land: Lessons from Florida's brownfield redevelopment program. *Environmental Practice*, 11(3), pp. 153–163.

Heberle, L. and Wernstedt, K., 2006. Understanding brownfields regeneration in the US. *Local Environment*, 11(5), pp. 479–497.

Kaiser, E.J., Godschalk, D.R. and Chapin, F.S., 1995. *Urban Land Use Planning* (Vol. 4). Urbana, IL: University of Illinois Press.

Kelle, U., 2006. Combining qualitative and quantitative methods in research practice: Purposes and advantages. *Qualitative Research in Psychology*, 3(4), pp. 293–311.

Kelly, E.D., 2012. *Community Planning: An Introduction to the Comprehensive Plan*. Island Press.

Lange, D. and McNeil, S., 2004. Clean it and they will come? Defining successful brownfield development. *Journal of Urban Planning and Development*, 130(2), pp. 101–108.

Lange, D., Wang, D., 'Mark' Zhuang, Z. and Fontana, W., 2013. Brownfield development selection using multi-attribute decision making. *Journal of Urban Planning and Development*, 140(2), p. 04013009.

Manzo, L.C. and Perkins, D.D., 2006. Finding common ground: The importance of place attachment to community participation and planning. *Journal of Planning Literature*, 20(4), pp. 335–350.

Matsuoka, R.H. and Kaplan, R., 2008. People needs in the urban landscape: Analysis of landscape and urban planning contributions. *Landscape and Urban Planning*, 84(1), pp. 7–19.

Smith, G., 2010. Brownfield planning: A tool for economically and socially effective sustainable urban development. In *46th ISOCARP Congress*, Nairobi, Kenya.

Thomas, M.R., 2002. A weighted, multi-attribute, site prioritization and selection process for brownfield redevelopment. *Environmental Practice*, 4(2), pp. 95–106.

Thornton, G., Franz, M., Edwards, D., Pahlen, G. and Nathanail, P., 2007. The challenge of sustainability: Incentives for brownfield regeneration in Europe. *Environmental Science & Policy*, 10(2), pp. 116–134.

Winson-Geideman, K., Krause, A., Wu, H. and Warren-Myers, G., 2017. Non-spatial contagion in real estate markets: The case of Brookland Greens. *Journal of Sustainable Real Estate*, 9(1), pp. 22–45.

Wu, H. and Chen, C., 2010. A pilot case study of brownfield high-density housing development in China. *International Journal of Housing Markets and Analysis*, 3(2), pp. 119–131.

Wu, H. and Chen, C., 2012. Urban 'brownfields': An Australian perspective. In *Proceedings of 18th Annual Pacific-Rim Real Estate Society Conference*, pp. 1–20.

Wu, H., Qin, B. and Yang, J., 2016. Regulatory system and institutional design for brownfield redevelopment in Melbourne. *Urban Planning International*, 31(4), pp. 72–78.

Wu, H., Tiwari, P., Han, S. and Chan, T., 2017. Brownfield risk communication and evaluation. *Journal of Property Research*, 34(3), pp. 233–250.

Wu, H., Tiwari, P., Han, S. and Chan, T., 2018. Risk and risk factors in brownfield development. In *Proceedings of the 21st International Symposium on Advancement of Construction Management and Real Estate*, pp. 1259–1274. Singapore: Springer.

Yount, K.R., 2003. What are brownfields? Finding a conceptual definition. *Environmental Practice*, 5(1), pp. 25–33.

11 International real estate investments: issues and research agendas

Hyung Min Kim

Introduction

International real estate investment is becoming increasingly important as a source for new development projects, property transactions, and the growth of the real estate industry that can result in both overall economic growth and inequality in property ownership. It is, in general, part of Foreign Direct Investment (FDI) activities, although indirect real estate investment is also rapidly growing. This chapter reviews key research agendas of real estate FDI which is a combined outcome of global capital/human flows, investment decisions, macro-economic dynamics, and institutional changes in both home and recipient countries. The volume of real estate FDI demonstrates the significance of this activity being expressed in economies, social relations, global links, and urban geographies. While FDI is known as one of the key drivers to urban growth – '*FDI-led urban growth*' (Kim & O'Connor, 2019, p. 2) – real estate FDI generates more direct effects on urban space due to the nature of the investment type. Real estate that involves bricks and mortar (and beyond) produces new space. In addition to developing new buildings, this activity amplifies actors in the real estate industry. As the real estate industry is wide in scope, a wide array of international real estate investment activities has been in place, involving multiple actors both in host and home countries. Despite the ever-growing volume, significance, and impacts of real estate FDI, it has attracted little academic attention. This chapter outlines what this activity is and describes key issues in carrying out research about real estate FDI, using a case study of real estate FDI in Vietnam. The data source is from the Foreign Investment Agency, Ministry of Planning and Investment, Vietnam (dataset of this research), to which all FDI projects are reported in the period 1989–2017. In total, 649 real estate FDI projects were reported in Vietnam.

What do we know about real estate FDI?

FDI is an outcome of firms' complicated decisions on offshore production in search of efficiency, new markets, and resources (OECD, 2002). In contrast to indirect investment that transfers capital only, FDI maintains the ownership of production transferring 'a package of assets' (Dunning, 1993). Although much academic attention has been paid to FDI from diverse perspectives including Dunning's eclectic paradigm (Dunning, 2000), understanding of real estate FDI is limited. The noticeable scale also calls for research into real estate FDI. Table 11.1 reports an overall scale of real estate FDI in selected economies. While precise statistics about real estate FDI worldwide are unavailable due to inconsistency in collecting FDI data, how significant this activity is in a single individual country can be noted. For instance, in the USA, of a total inward FDI of USD 296.4 billion, real estate was USD 22.1 billion (or 7.5%) in 2018 and, in Australia, real estate accounted for 10.6% of the total inward FDI, the fourth largest after mining (37.8%), manufacturing (11.1%), and financial and insurance activities (11.1%) in 2018 (Table 11.1). A more extreme example was observed in small island developing states where almost 90% of mergers and acquisitions (M&As) were for real estate investment in 2017. International interactions for real estate development are not brand new ideas as observed in European colonial cities (Ross & Telkamp, 2012) and post-cold war recon-struction cities such as Hamhung, North Korea and Vinh in Vietnam, assisted by Eastern Germany (Jang & Kim, 2021; Sin, 2017). While these former interactions were driven by imperial and military power or ideological ties, the current international real estate investment is capital-driven and profit-seeking under the prevailing influence of neoliberalism (Sellar & Pástor, 2015).

The present literature about real estate FDI has been a combination of the following four thematic approaches. First, earlier studies have paid attention to the rationale of international real estate investments from an investment performance perspective (Conner, Liang, & McIntosh, 1999). The "don't put all your eggs in one basket" principle was a prevailing motivation to geograph-ically diversify real estate investment options in an attempt to minimise invest-ment risks (Sirmans & Worzala, 2003). The notion of a *portfolio* has attracted investors into the transnational real estate industry (Newell & Worzala, 1995; Steinert & Crowe, 2001). This diversification approach has escalated the total market size of real estate first by encouraging locally-focused real estate investors into international markets and secondly by diverting non-real estate industries into real estate investment (Ziobrowski & Curcio, 1991). As a result, indirect real estate investment via various financing methods, such as REITs

Table 11.1   The share of real estate FDI in selected countries

	Total industries	Real estate	%
Australia	AUD 967.5 billion	AUD 102.9 billion	10.6
USA (New FDI expenditures), 2018	USD 296.4 billion	USD 22.1 billion	7.5
South Korea, 2018	USD 4,993.7 million	USD 1027.3 million	20.6
Vietnam, 2017	USD 22,616.9 million	USD 2398.0 million	10.6
Latin America & the Caribbean, 2017+	USD 29,535 million	USD 1,614 million	5.5
Small island developing states, 2017+*	USD 2,615 million	USD 2,322 million	88.8

Notes: + Net cross-border M&As, Sales; * Bahamas, Jamaica, Maldives, Mauritius and Fiji
Source: DFAT (2019); BEA (2019); MOTIE (2020); Dataset of this research; and UNCTAD (2018)

and real estate funds, has also emerged (Coakley, 1994; Worzala & Sirmans, 2003).

Second, key actors have been a focus due to their significant role as investors and real estate advisory service providers (LaPier, 1998). The accumulation of capital has been extended to international property markets. What is called the "secondary circuit of capital" by Harvey (1978) has become 'footloose' over national boundaries despite its careful location selectiveness. The questions here are who the investors are, where the capital is from, why they are motivated in this activity, and how these are mediated. While Japanese outward investment in real estate was noteworthy in the 1970s and the 1980s before Japan's 'lost 10 years' recession (Berry, 1994; Edgington, 1996), Chinese investment has been recently outstanding in multiple locations including Australia (Rogers, Lee, & Yan, 2015; Rogers & Wiesel, 2018; Wiesel & Levin, 2018), South Korea (Paik, 2019), London (DeVerteuil & Manley, 2017) and Canada (Ley, 2017). Multinational property firms, construction firms, financial institutions (e.g., pension funds), and (super-rich) individuals are key investor groups (Kim, 2020; Pow, 2017). FDI in real estate is often spurred by state actors who play a role in 'urban development leadership' (Kim, Miao, & Phelps, 2021). The Singapore government is a pioneering exemplar, best illustrated in the development of overseas industrial parks in south and east Asian countries such as China, Indonesia, and Vietnam (Phelps & Wu, 2009).

Among them, the Suzhou Industrial Park, borne of a collaboration between the Singaporean and Chinese governments, has attracted attention due to its large scale, the success of FDI attractions, and rapid urban transformation (Kim, 2015; Kim & Cocks, 2017, 2018). Recently, the Korean and Chinese governments have also been keen to promote their development models overseas such as the South Saad Al-Abdullah Smart City (SSAA) project in Kuwait by Korean state-owned enterprise, and Chinese industrial parks in Africa (Choi & Kim, 2021; Giannecchini & Taylor, 2018; Kim, Miao, & Phelps, 2021).

Third, recent publications have investigated the reshaping of cities by these international real estate investment activities as "much of urban development is physically realised through real estate investment" (Kim, 2020). Accordingly, the analysis of the impacts has been in conjunction with spatial patterns. These impacts include *towers of capital* in the CBDs of major global cities through office markets (Lizieri, 2009), as seen in London with over 45% of office spaces owned by non-UK firms (Lizieri & Kutsch, 2006), Pudong in Shanghai (Jiang, Chen, & Isaac, 1998; Olds, 1997; Zhu, Sim, & Zhang, 2006) and Seoul (Kim, O'Connor, & Han, 2015). It has also strengthened the establishment of *global villages* (Kim, Han, & O'Connor, 2015) and residential ethnic *enclaves* through housing markets (Cook, 2010; Kim, 2018, 2021). These investments are often borne of strong ethnic ties (Kim, 2017). In Vietnam's residential development, international real estate investors preferred the new urban areas away from the political centres of inner-city areas where domestic investors prevailed (Jung, Huynh, & Rowe, 2013). In Hanoi's case study, FDI in real estate was concentrated in new urban cores while manufacturing spread out across regional areas (Kim, 2020).

Fourth, institutional changes have been significant milestones in transnational real estate industries. Foreign land ownership and transnational business activities had been largely prohibited in strongly regulatory regimes. A radical institutional shift was observed in (former) socialist countries. The removal of institutional barriers promoted international real estate investment in Eastern European countries along with the privatisation of land ownership (Adair et al., 1999; Keivani, Parsa, & McGreal, 2001), raising new concerns about land security (Tesser, 2004). China's *open-door* policy from 1978/9 embraced inward FDI with state land ownership. Land use rights were first sold to foreign investors in the Shenzhen Economic Zone in 1987 (Lin & Ho, 2005). Vietnam's *Doi Moi* (or opening-up policy) has been in effect since 1986 and deregulatory policy measures on foreign property ownership have been applied. Despite ambiguous property rights and two-price systems (Thu & Perera, 2011), Vietnam's inward FDI in real estate has been the second-largest after manufacturing (Kim, 2020). The institutional change was also implemented in non-socialist countries. For instance, South Korea undertook an institutional change after the Asian financial crisis in 1997/8 to comply with the guidelines from the International Monetary Fund (Kim, O'Connor, & Han, 2015). Immediately after this institutional change, the share of international investors in the transaction of office buildings reached over 50% in selected years (Kim, O'Connor, & Han, 2015).

Understanding of real estate FDI

This section outlines the key issues in the study of real estate FDI addressing constraints and research themes. Attention has been paid to data of real estate FDI, the type of investment activities, local institutions for land management, and the dynamics of the local property market.

Data matters

There are challenges to fully understanding international real estate investment activities. First, in most cases, only aggregated statistics are available without the detail of FDI projects. Even aggregated statistics are inconsistent in collection methods between countries. For instance, six countries do not include the transactions in private purchase and sales in counting real estate FDI, while 28 other OECD countries do (OECD, n.d.). Second, as described in the previous section, international real estate investment can be carried out by indirect *portfolio* approaches. While indirect investment in real estate is of significance in enlarging the size of the real estate markets, statistics about real estate FDI normally do not detail it. Third, the origin of the source of investment is often hidden due to the use of tax havens such as the British Virgin Islands and the Cayman Islands, undermining the investment volume from the real origins. Fourth, there are temporal and amount discrepancies between the actually realised capital amounts and the registered capital amounts. With the government approvals offering a license that specifies the maximum amount and periods to be invested, firms make their investment decision, which is not necessarily the same as their initial plan. Fifth, reported investment within the recipient country is often based on the location of the (regional) headquarters without acknowledging the real location where the FDI project is taking place, which is more obvious for FDI projects in multiple locations. Furthermore, FDI statistics tend to overemphasise large cities in identifying the recipient cities.

Owing to limited access to data, except for only a handful of data-abundant case studies (Kim, 2020; Kim, Han, & O'Connor, 2015; Kim, O'Connor, & Han, 2015), many publications relied upon quantitative research approaches, interviewing investors and locals (Kim, 2017; Rogers et al., 2015; Wiesel & Levin, 2018). These data-related drawbacks limit precise understanding, but still offer valuable insights in understanding the trends in volume and spatial patterns.

Investment activity matters

Direct real estate FDI undertakes three inter-related activities: (1) new development, (2) purchases of existing properties, and (3) real estate services (Kim, 2020). First, real estate development projects are known for high-risks; cross-border investment adds more risks due to local politics, institutional unfamiliarity, and macro-global economies. These projects require high amounts of capital for land acquisition and construction compared with investment in real estate services. Owing to unique land policies and land tenure traditions in each country, land acquisition does not always follow a market mechanism, which is a critical barrier to investors. Often, real estate FDI is blurred by industrial and infrastructural FDI projects which inevitably require land and construction. For instance, factories are built on industrial land through manufacturing FDI projects. Firms should ensure their rights to own and/or use the land and their factory buildings which are part of the key elements in real estate industries. International real estate development projects build new international standard commercial properties and create new international real estate markets, seeding follow-up inward investment for international players. This seeding effect was especially apparent in the cities without sizeable commercial property stocks for international investors.

Second, the purchase of existing properties is common in more mature real estate markets due to established transparency, high commercial property stocks, and facilitating real estate professionals. Once cities in developing countries have more commercial properties, including the ones developed by international investors through their development projects, the purchase of properties becomes more and more pervasive. Real estate transactions require rigorous market analysis, in-depth legal and financial reviews, valuation, financing, consultation, and advertisement, leading to the growth of the real estate market. The purchase of existing properties also requires high investment amounts.

Third, FDI in real estate services is a rapidly growing industrial type to assist a wide range of real estate activities with the rise in international real estate investments. As articulated in Sassen's (2001) global city hypothesis, FDI in real estate services strengthens advanced producer services. These producer service firms might first follow large property transactions, but their business operations, in turn, facilitate further international real estate investment activities. Investors need local information about regulatory frameworks, market trends, market mechanisms, and key players for their international investment decisions. While large-scale multinational firms in real estate such as CBRE, Jones Land LaSalle, and Savills are outstanding examples, small- and medium-sized real estate producer service firms are emerging (Bagchi-Sen, 1995). They work at various stages in the real estate industry including market analysis before investment, site analysis for development, valuation for trans-actions, financing for investment, legal reviews, designing of the property, advertisements for marketing, management of properties (after the completion of development) and disposal when the investor wants to exit the market (Kim & Kent, 2019; Kim, O'Connor, & Han, 2015). While the actual investment amount for producer services in real estate is not as large as development and the purchase of existing properties, these service sectors are key to the growth in the overall real estate industry and internationalisation of the market. Their significant presence attracts new investors into the core market of well-known cities and arouses investors to look for further investment opportunities in second-tier cities, regional areas, and even other surrounding countries (Kim & Kent, 2019).

Land matters

The scope of international real estate investments is wide, involving multiple land uses such as commercial, residential, industrial, infrastructure, ware-houses, hotels, manufacturing and land. Among them, commercial properties have long been a focus due to their large-scale city-reshaping power and, recently, residential high-end properties are growing in popularity. FDI in manufacturing requires industrial sites and factory buildings which are impor-tant parts of real estate industries.

Real estate investment inevitably involves issues about land ownership. In many countries, freehold land ownership is regulated. For instance, state land ownership has been in place in Singapore on the basis of a 99-year leasehold (Han, 2005). China and Vietnam have implemented their state land ownership with long-term leasehold being a general practice for foreign and domestic investors (Han & Pannell, 1999; A. M. Kim, 2007). These countries have issued land use rights that can be traded to private sectors up to the specified duration of leasehold. Often investors undertake negotiations to purchase the land use rights with the government. Many local governments that hold land ownership have become entrepreneurial, offering incentives for the land use rights along with tax exemptions in special zones such as industrial parks and export processing zones (Yang & Wang, 2008). The leasehold agreement, in place in many parts of the world, such as Canberra in Australia, Israel, and Ghana, plays a role in controlling the unlimited influence of foreign investors in the domestic land (Benchetrit & Czamanski, 2004; Gough & Yankson, 2000).

The selection of land use is dependent upon various factors such as the economic structure and legal and institutional settings of the recipient countries and the intention and the strategies of investors. While office buildings are the most reported land use type (Kim, O'Connor, & Han, 2015; Lizieri, 2012; Lizieri & Kutsch, 2006; Zhu et al., 2006), retails, hotels, housing, and mixed-use are also favoured properties by international investors. There are also very large-scale new town development projects that contain multiple land uses and infrastructure involving real estate developers and construction firms. With more tightly integrated global flows of knowledge, people and capital, new town development via FDI is an emerging trend. The Suzhou Industrial Park is a pioneer of this kind and the SSAA, composed predominantly of housing for married couples, is the most recent example.

Property price matters

The escalation and the vulnerability of property prices are key concerns for international real estate investment in the local property market. Many recipient cities reported the concerns of locals about worsening housing affordability, notably in Canada, Australia and the UK. Office prices and vulnerability were reported in Seoul's office market immediately after the market was opened up (Kim, O'Connor, & Han, 2015). On the one hand, the activeness of international real estate investors pushes up the demand in the property sales market by placing a higher bid, resulting in the moving-up of the demand curve. On the other hand, they can be the suppliers of space if their investment is for real estate development. Their investment in development adds to the supply of properties, which may move up the supply curve leading to a lower equilibrium price. These two different forces of the local market seem to produce unknown outcomes, but, in most cases, the supply of properties by international investors results in a focus on high-end properties influenced by the international standard which is more expensive than ordinary properties in the local market. Once a building is owned by an international investor, there is a high possibility of it being sold to another international investor, as exemplified in the Daewoo headquarters building in Seoul (Kim, O'Connor, & Han, 2015) and Keangnam Landmark Tower 72 in Hanoi (Kim, 2020). The housing development is often tied up with ethnic connections and migratory networks. International developers from a certain country finance the development cost from their home country, promote their properties in the home country, sell or rent out to the migrants or the international students from the same country and manage the properties through real estate agencies from the same country (Liu & Gurran, 2017; Paik, 2019; Rogers et al., 2015). These ethnic chains strengthen inward-looking behaviours; the small market size largely bounded to the ethnic ties and limited access to local market information for new investors from the same origin sustain property prices that are high compared with the locally dominant property market. However, migration inflows do not always encourage foreign property ownership and escalate property prices. In the case study of Seoul, the influx of international low-skilled labourers appeared in a concentrated geographical fashion, but their involvement in homeownership was low, resulting in a limited impact on the local housing transaction market in those areas (Kim, Han, & O'Connor, 2015).

A case study of real estate FDI in Vietnam

This section provides an overview of real estate FDI in Vietnam outlining the recent trends, locational patterns, and major investment groups, and detailing exemplary international real estate investment projects. The case study will provide a better understanding of this emerging activity.

A trend

After Doi Moi, in 1987, the Vietnamese government enacted the Law on Foreign Investment in Vietnam, a legal foundation for inward FDI. Subsequently, the first real estate FDI project was reported in 1989 and, since then, in total, 649 real estate FDI projects (or USD 17.4 billion in terms of the realised amount) had been reported by 2017. The volume of FDI in real estate was the second largest after manufacturing, which has taken the lion's share – 57.9%. Real estate FDI is not a standalone activity. Kim (2020) observed the interlocking nature of real estate with manufacturing via ethnic connections and FDI-associated expatriate families.

Figure 11.1 shows the trend of real estate FDI up to 2017. Three investment cycles were observed and there was an exponential increase in the late-2000s. In 2008 alone, 80 real estate FDI projects were reported with USD 5.8 billion. The most recent decade saw a stable inflow of real estate FDI amounts, but the number of projects is rapidly growing, as seen in the bar graph in Figure 11.1.

Those recent projects pay more attention to real estate services rather than capital-intensive development projects (see Table 11.1).

Spatial patterns and land uses

Table 11.2 reports the top five recipient provinces. Not surprisingly, Ho Chi Minh City (HCMC), Vietnam's economic hub, and Hanoi, Vietnam's political centre, are the two prominent provincial-level recipient cities. In addition to development projects, real estate service firms were highly concentrated in HCMC; more than half of real estate service firms were established there (52.2%), corresponding to the spatial pattern of producer service firms in global cities. In HCMC and Hanoi, residential and commercial properties were the two development types favoured by international investors. Residential developments such as Ciputra and Hyundai Hillstate in Hanoi have supplied high-end housing targeting expatriate workers and better-off Vietnamese households in new urban cores away from the political centre (Jung et al., 2013). Commercial development has contributed to building 'towers of capital' in the central business areas of these two top-tier cities (Lizieri, 2009). Often these two property types were integrated into one project as mixed-use development, such as the Lotte Centre, both in Hanoi and HCMC and notably Keangnam Landmark Tower 72 in Hanoi, re-shaping the landscape, the skyline, and the function of the city (Kim, 2020).

Industrial and infrastructure developments were rare in these two top-tier cities, while HCMC also attracted recreational property developers by virtue of its natural attributes. Binh Duong and Dong Nai are regional areas of HCMC and Da Nang is located in the middle of Vietnam along the Pacific Ocean. Most of the real estate FDI in these provinces is directed to the development of mixed-use recreational properties, such as resorts, golf courses, hotels, and entertainment parks, along with apartment development.

Key investor groups

Tax havens have been actively employed by investors, as seen in high numbers of investment projects from the British Virgin Islands and the Cayman Islands. In fact, the British Virgin Islands is the top origin of investment, accounting for 28.2%, followed by Singapore, South Korea, and Japan (see Table 11.3). Investment via the Cayman Islands was highly concentrated in HCMC – 23 out of 27 real estate projects. Unfortunately, as discussed above, details about these projects via the tax havens are unavailable in official documents. Singapore real estate investment has been active in diverse locations, but Korean investment predominantly favoured Hanoi due to the presence of Korean multinationals,

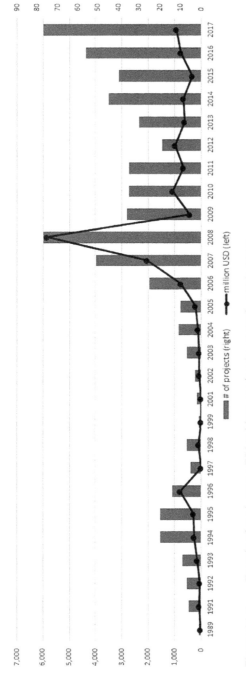

Figure 11.1   Trends of real estate FDI in Vietnam (realised FDI), 1989–2017

Table 11.2   Top 10 locations of real estate FDI in Vietnam, 1989–2017

Province	Realised FDI billion USD (%)	Total num. of RE FDI projects	Residential	Commercial	Recreational	Industrial	Infrastructure	RE services
			Land use (inclusive of mixed use)					
HCMC	3.7 (21.5%)	269 (41.4%)	83 (50.6%)	85 (45.2%)	22 (27.5%)	3 (4.8%)	0 (0.0%)	141 (52.2%)
Hanoi	3.1 (17.7%)	122 (18.8%)	24 (14.6%)	44 (23.4%)	7 (8.8%)	2 (3.2%)	2 (28.6%)	59 (21.9%)
Binh Duong	2.1 (12.3%)	36 (5.5%)	6 (3.7%)	6 (3.2%)	3 (3.8%)	2 (3.2%)	0 (0.0%)	20 (7.4%)
Dong Nai	1.9 (11.1%)	26 (4.0%)	11 (6.7%)	9 (4.8%)	4 (5.0%)	4 (6.5%)	0 (0.0%)	11 (4.1%)
Da Nang	1.7 (9.8%)	40 (6.2%)	10 (6.1%)	10 (5.3%)	16 (20.0%)	1 (1.6%)	0 (0.0%)	15 (5.6%)
Others	4.8 (27.7%)	156 (24.0%)	30 (18.3%)	34 (18.1%)	28 (35.0%)	50 (80.6%)	5 (71.4%)	24 (8.9%)
Total	17.4 (100.0%)	649	164	188	80	62	7	270

Source: Modified from Kim (2019)

Table 11.3   Top origins of real estate FDI in Vietnam (realised FDI), 1989–2017

Origin country	N	million USD	%
British Virgin Islands	87	4,893	28.2
Singapore	122	3,691	21.2
Korea	120	3,129	18.0
Japan	63	977	5.6
Cayman Islands	27	956	5.5
United Kingdom	15	586	3.4
The rest	215	3,146	18.1
Total	649	17,378	100.0

such as Samsung, and their associated expatriate families (Kim, 2020, 2021). Other than the tax havens, the top three origins of investment were from Asia – Singapore, Korea, and Japan, showing inter-Asia interactions. These countries have established sizeable real estate industries while undertaking urbanisation processes. The property market has been central to their modern economies and they were often called '*property states*' (Haila, 2017; Joo, 2018). The expansion of their real estate industries reflects a keen interest in offshore real estate investment. Vietnam has been a battlefield for these three property states. Chinese investment has not yet been as large as these three countries, but its volume is gradually growing. Western countries are rather inactive to date; the UK was ranked only sixth in Vietnam. The small involvement of French investors (0.9%) implies the extent of post-colonial (rather than colonial), post-Doi Moi economic interactions with Vietnam.

Example projects

Table 11.4 reports the top ten real estate FDI projects in terms of the registered (licensed) amount. Simply due to the scale, all the top ten projects were to develop and construct mixed-use multiple complexes including housing, offices, hotels, shopping malls, and entertainment parks. While Nos. 1, 2, 5, and 9 were leisure-oriented resort development projects (such as casinos, entertainment parks, golf courses, and hotels), the rest were planned to develop large-scale residential and commercial properties. The earliest project of this kind was Hanoi's Ciputra (No. 3), with an FDI licence approval in 1996 and its construction commencement in 2002. Its primary function is residential, but it includes shops and golf courses, located in the northwest of Ho Tay. It used

Table 11.4   Top 10 real estate FDI projects in Vietnam, 1989–2017

No.	Year	Investor	Amount*	Origin of investor	Province	Current status[+]
1	2008	ASIAN Coast Development	4.2	Canada	Ba Ria-Vung Tau	UC
2	2010	VinaCapital	4.0	Singapore	Quang Nam	UC
3	1996	Development Planning Investment	2.0	Singapore	Hanoi	UC
4	2009	Luster Development; Smart Dragon Development	1.7	Samoa	Binh Duong	C
5	2008	Starbay Holdings	1.6	BVI	Kien Giang	UC
6	2012	Tokyu Corporation	1.2	Japan	Binh Duong	UC
7	2015	Denver Power; Corredance	1.2	BVI	HCMC	NYC
8	2007	Keangnam	1.1	South Korea	Hanoi	C
9	2012	New City Properties Development; Sunrise Vietnam	1.0	South Korea	Phu Yen	UC
10	2008	Berjaya Leisure	0.9	Cayman Islands	HCMC	NYC

Notes: * Registered capital in billion USD; + UC means under construction; C means completed, and NYC means not yet commenced, in May 2020

Source: Dataset of this research

to be agricultural land on the outskirts of Hanoi in the 1990s, but currently it accommodates large foreign national communities and is Hanoi's first gated community.

Four projects drew investment from the tax havens (Nos. 4, 5, 7, and 10), but their capital was from somewhere else. For instance, the investor of No. 10, Berjaya Leisure, was officially from the Cayman Islands, but Berjaya was known as a Malaysian investor;[1] Denver Power of Project No. 7 (officially from the British Virgin Islands) is part of GAO Capital, one of Hong Kong's largest real estate companies. The slow progress of some of these large-scale real estate projects may reflect the high risks of executing real estate FDI. Owing to the noticeable scale, the progress of these projects is newsworthy in the media. An online search showed No. 7 has been sluggish, due to difficulties in land acquisition, finalising planning approval and conflict with locals;[2] after delays in construction, Project No. 10 was sold to the largest Vietnamese developer, Vinhomes, in 2018. Project No. 5, by Hong Kong investor Starbay Holdings, via the British Virgin Islands, was granted approval in 2008, but construction did not start until almost a decade later.[3] Project No. 9 commenced construction, but this has halted due to failure to secure planning approval for the development of forest land.[4] These projects are undertaken over a long-term period with high business risks, including time to undertake the land acquisition, planning approval, negotiations with local residents, and construction. Projects can, therefore, be susceptible to economic and political changes of fortune that may arise over such a lengthy time frame.

Conclusion: research agendas

As reviewed in this chapter, real estate FDI is an under-researched topic in urban studies, real estate disciplines and the globalisation literature, although it is becoming a 'business-as-usual' activity in many cities. As seen in Vietnam's case, the volume of real estate FDI has seen an unprecedented increase, along with economic cycles. Development projects dominated at the initial phase when international standard commercial properties were rare in stock. However, those development projects have contributed to building large-scale high-end commercial properties that, in turn, further bring in international real estate investment – a shift to a more mature stage of the internationalised real estate market. In tandem with this shift, advanced producer services in real estate are also growing to assist real estate development and sales, which contributes to the establishment and the growth of the real estate industry both locally and globally.

As analysed in the FDI literature, why, who, where, and how questions can be also applied to studies about real estate FDI specifically. How international real estate investors overcome local regulatory, institutional barriers, where they prefer to invest in, who the investors are, and why the investors make an investment decision on location and timing are all unknown or, at best, only partially analysed in the literature. Also, the effects that real estate FDI can and will create remain an interesting research agenda. Research from multiple perspectives is valid, such as

- Institutional effects from a regulatory perspective: what urban outcomes have institutional changes generated?
- Spatial effects from a geographical perspective: where do international investors prefer to invest, and why? What spatial outcomes have been generated by real estate FDI?
- Market effects from an economic perspective: what changes have been made to the local real estate market as a result of real estate FDI?
- Linkage effects from a relational perspective: how does real estate FDI strengthen the links and the relations between home and recipient countries?
- Polarisation effects from an equity perspective: how has real estate FDI worsened housing affordability, homeownership, and inequality in recipient countries?

Those effects are likely to last a long time because real estate investment is an expression of 'long-term commitments' in the recipient location (Kim, Han, & O'Connor, 2015). Also, in line with the growth of international real estate markets, a more complicated investment structure is expected, which is an interesting research area for real estate market analysts, urban economists, urban planners, property owners, and policymakers.

This chapter paid attention to data before the spread of COVID-19. It will be an important research focus to analyse how FDI activities have changed during and after COVID-19. Given regulated human mobility, the volume of FDI flows might shrink and post-pandemic international investment activities might need to take more risks than before.

Acknowledgements

I would like to express my appreciation to Dr Ha Thai for his research assistance and Dr Anthony Kent for his careful edits. Any remaining errors are the responsibility of the author.

Notes

1. https://www.thestar.com.my/business/business-news/2018/06/05/berjaya-land -sells-stake-in-vietnam-firm-for-rm155mil (viewed on 5 February 2020).
2. https://bizlive.vn/dia-oc/de-nghi-truy-thu-du-an-khu-phuc-hop-thap-quan-sat -empire-city-3512365.html (in Vietnamese viewed on 5 February 2020).
3. https://baodautu.vn/co-chu-moi-du-an-bai-dai-resort-van-i-ach-d61845.html andhttps://www.doisongphapluat.com/kinh-doanh/mikgroup-ky-ket-thoa-thuan -hop-tac-toan-dien-voi-viettinbank-a212279.html (in Vietnamese viewed on 5 February 2020).
4. https://tbck.vn/phu-yen-tam-dung-du-an-cao-cap-new-city-34191.html (in Vietnamese viewed on 5 February 2020).

References

Adair, A., Berry, J., McGreal, S., Sýkora, L., Parsa, A. G., & Redding, B. (1999). Globalization of real estate markets in central Europe. *European Planning Studies*, *7*(3), 295–305.

Bagchi-Sen, S. (1995). FDI in U.S. producer services: A temporal analysis of foreign direct investment in the finance, insurance and real estate sectors. *Regional Studies*, 159–170. Retrieved from https://search.ebscohost.com/login.aspx?direct=true&db= 23h&AN=33863316&site=ehost-live

BEA. (2019). New Foreign Direct Investment in the United States, 2018. Retrieved from https://www.bea.gov/news/2019/new-foreign-direct-investment-united-states-2018

Benchetrit, G., & Czamanski, D. (2004). The gradual abolition of the public leasehold system in Israel and Canberra: What lessons can be learned? *Land Use Policy*, *21*(1), 45–57.

Berry, M. (1994). Japanese property development in Australia. *Progress in planning*, *41*(2), 113–201.

Choi, J., & Kim, H. M. (2021). State-of-the-art of Korean Smart Cities: A critical review of the Sejong Smart City Plan. In H. M. Kim, S. Sabri, & A. Kent (Eds.), *Smart Cities for Technological and Social Innovation* (pp. 51–72). London; San Diego; Cambridge; Oxford: Academic Press.

Coakley, J. (1994). The integration of property and financial markets. *Environment and Planning A*, *26*(5), 697–713.

Conner, P., Liang, Y., & McIntosh, W. (1999). Myths and realities of international real estate investing. *Prudential Real Estate Investors* (November), 2–11.

Cook, A. (2010). The expatriate real estate complex: Creative destruction and the production of luxury in post-socialist Prague. *International Journal of Urban & Regional Research, 34*, 611–628. doi:10.1111/j.1468-2427.2010.00912.x

DeVerteuil, G., & Manley, D. (2017). Overseas investment into London: Imprint, impact and pied-à-terre urbanism. *Environment & Planning A, 49*(6), 1308–1323. doi:10.1177/0308518X17694361

DFAT. (2019). Australian industries and foreign direct investment. *Foreign Investment Statistics.* Retrieved from https://dfat.gov.au/trade/resources/investment-statistics/Pages/australian-industries-and-foreign-investment.aspx

Dunning, J. H. (1993). *Multinational Enterprises and the Global Economy.* Wokingham, UK; Reading, MA: Addison-Wesley.

Dunning, J. H. (2000). The eclectic paradigm as an envelope for economic and business theories of MNE activity. *International Business Review, 9*, 163–190.

Edgington, D. W. (1996). Japanese real estate investment in Canadian cities and regions, 1985–1993. *The Canadian Geographer, 40*(4), 292–305.

Giannecchini, P., & Taylor, I. (2018). The eastern industrial zone in Ethiopia: Catalyst for development? *Geoforum, 88*, 28–35.

Gough, K. V., & Yankson, P. W. (2000). Land markets in African cities: The case of peri-urban Accra, Ghana. *Urban Studies, 37*(13), 2485–2500.

Haila, A. (2017). Institutionalization of 'the property mind'. *International Journal of Urban and Regional Research, 41*(3), 500–507.

Han, S. S. (2005). Global city making in Singapore: A real estate perspective. *Progress in Planning, 64*, 69–175.

Han, S. S., & Pannell, C. W. (1999). The geography of privatization in China, 1978–1996. *Economic Geography, 75*(3), 272–296.

Harvey, D. (1978). The urban process under capitalism: A framework for analysis. *International Journal of Urban & Regional Research, 2*(1), 101–131. doi:10.1111/j.1468-2427.1978.tb00738.x

Jang, K. S., & Kim, H. M. (2021). Hamhung, the second-largest North Korean city: Dynasty urbanism, colonial urbanism and socialist urbanism. *Cities, 114*(103191), 1–14. doi:https://doi.org/10.1016/j.cities.2021.103191

Jiang, D., Chen, J. J., & Isaac, D. (1998). The effect of foreign investment on the real estate industry in China. *Urban Studies, 35*(11), 2101–2110. doi:10.1080/0042098984024

Joo, Y.-M. (2018). *Megacity Seoul: Urbanization and the Development of Modern South Korea.* Oxon; New York: Routledge.

Jung, S., Huynh, D., & Rowe, P. G. (2013). The pattern of foreign property investment in Vietnam: The apartment market in Ho Chi Minh City. *Habitat International, 39*, 105–113.

Keivani, R., Parsa, A., & McGreal, S. (2001). Globalisation, institutional structures and real estate markets in central European cities. *Urban Studies, 38*(13), 2457–2476.

Kim, A. M. (2007). North versus south: The impact of social norms in the market pricing of private property rights in Vietnam. *World Development, 35*(12), 2079–2095. Retrieved from https://ezp.lib.unimelb.edu.au/login?url=https://search.ebscohost.com/login.aspx?direct=true&db=bas&AN=BAS354874&site=eds-live&scope=site

Kim, H. M. (2015). The role of foreign firms in China's urban transformation: A case study of Suzhou. In T.-C. Wong, S. S. Han, & H. Zhang (Eds.), *Population Mobility, Urban Planning and Management in China* (pp. 127–143). London: Springer.

Kim, H. M. (2017). Ethnic connections, foreign housing investment, and locality: A case study of Seoul. *International Journal of Housing Policy, 17*(1), 120–144. doi: http://dx.doi.org/10.1080/14616718.2016.1189683

Kim, H. M. (2018). The influx of high-income foreign nationals and the housing market in a developing country: A case study of Suzhou Industrial Park, China. *Journal of Housing and the Built Environment, 33*(4), 767–788.

Kim, H. M. (2019). *Real Estate Foreign Direct Investment in Vietnam: Global Forces to New Urban Development.* Paper presented at the 25th Pacific Rim Real Estate Society Conference, Melbourne.

Kim, H. M. (2020). International real estate investment and urban development: An analysis of Korean Activities in Hanoi, Vietnam. *Land Use Policy, 94*(104486), 1–10. doi:doi.org/10.1016/j.landusepol.2020.104486

Kim, H. M. (2021). Foreign Direct Investment, enclaves and liveability: A case study of Korean activities in Hanoi, Vietnam. *International Development Planning Review, 43*(3), 369–392.

Kim, H. M., & Cocks, M. (2017). The role of Quality of Place factors in expatriate international relocation decisions: A case study of Suzhou, a globally-focused Chinese city. *Geoforum, 81*, 1–10.

Kim, H. M., & Cocks, M. (2018). Urbanisation and globalisation: An overview of modern Suzhou development. In S. S. Han & W. Lin (Eds.), *Healthy Future Cities* (pp. 379–395). Beijing: China Architecture Industry Press.

Kim, H. M., Han, S. S., & O'Connor, K. B. (2015). Foreign housing investment in Seoul: Origin of investors and location of investment. *Cities, 42*, 212–223.

Kim, H. M., & Kent, A. (2019). The emergence of international urban planning and design firms in China from an OLI perspective. *Journal of Regional and City Planning, 30*(2), 123–139.

Kim, H. M., Miao, J., & Phelps, N. (2021). International urban development leadership: Singapore, China and South Korea compared. In S. H. Park, H. B. Shin, & H. S. Kang (Eds.), *Exporting Urban Korea? Reconsidering the Korean Urban Development Experience* (pp. 131–146). Oxon; New York: Routledge.

Kim, H. M., & O'Connor, K. (2019). Foreign Direct Investment flows and urban dynamics in a developing country: A case study of Korean activities in Suzhou, China. *International Planning Studies, 24*(2), 125–139.

Kim, H. M., O'Connor, K. B., & Han, S. S. (2015). The spatial characteristics of Global Property Investment in Seoul: A case study of the office market. *Progress in Planning, 97*, 1–42.

LaPier, T. (1998). *Competition, Growth Strategies, and the Globalization of Services: Real Estate Advisory Services in Japan, Europe, and the United States.* London; New York: Routledge.

Ley, D. (2017). Global China and the making of Vancouver's residential property market. *International Journal of Housing Policy, 17*, 15–34.

Lin, G. C. S., & Ho, S. P. S. (2005). The state, land system, and land development processes in contemporary China. *Annals of the Association of American Geographers, 95*(2), 411–436.

Liu, S., & Gurran, N. (2017). Chinese investment in Australian housing: Push and pull factors and implications for understanding international housing demand. *International Journal of Housing Policy, 17*(4), 489–511. doi:10.1080/19491247.2017.1307655

Lizieri, C. (2009). *Towers of Capital: Office Markets & International Financial Services.* Chichester, UK; Ames, Iowa: Wiley-Blackwell.

Lizieri, C. (2012). Global cities, office markets and capital flows. In B. Derudder, M. Hoyler, P. J. Taylor, & F. Witlox (Eds.), *International Handbook of Globalization and World Cities*: Cheltenham: Edward Elgar Publishing.

Lizieri, C., & Kutsch, N. (2006). *Who Owns the City 2006: Office Ownership in the City of London*. London: University of Reading Business School and Development Securities plc.

MOTIE. (2020). Foreign Direct Investment Statistics. Retrieved from https://www .motie.go.kr/motie/py/sa/investstatse/investstats.jsp

Newell, G., & Worzala, E. (1995). The role of international property in investment portfolios. *Journal of Property Finance*, 6(1), 55–63.

OECD. (2002). *Foreign Direct Investment for Development: Maximising Benefits, Minimising Costs*. Paris: OECD.

OECD. (n.d.). Foreign Direct Investment statistics metadata. Retrieved from https:// qdd.oecd.org/data/FDI_Metadata_ComparativeTables/Q15+C_Q15_EXC.

Olds, K. (1997). Globalizing Shanghai: The 'global intelligence corps' and the building of Pudong. *Cities*, 14(2), 109–123.

Paik, W. (2019). Chinese investment in foreign real estate and its interactions with the host state and society: The case of Jeju, South Korea. *Pacific Affairs*, 92(1), 49–70.

Phelps, N. A., & Wu, F. (2009). Capital's search for order: Foreign direct investment in Singapore's overseas parks in Southeast and East Asia. *Political Geography*, 28, 44–54.

Pow, C. P. (2017). Courting the 'rich and restless': Globalisation of real estate and the new spatial fixities of the super-rich in Singapore. *International Journal of Housing Policy*, 17(1), 56–74.

Rogers, D., Lee, C. L., & Yan, D. (2015). The politics of foreign investment in Australian housing: Chinese investors, translocal sales agents and local resistance. *Housing Studies*, 30(5), 730–748.

Rogers, D., & Wiesel, I. (2018). Australian urban geographies of housing in the context of the rise of China in the 'Asian Century'. *Geographical Research*, 56(4), 393–400.

Ross, R. J., & Telkamp, G. J. (2012). *Colonial Cities: Essays on Urbanism in a Colonial Context* (Vol. 5). Springer Science & Business Media.

Sassen, S. (2001). *The Global City: New York, London, Tokyo* (2nd ed.). Princeton, NJ: Princeton University Press.

Sellar, C., & Pástor, R. (2015). Mutating neoliberalism: The promotion of Italian investors in Slovakia before and after the Global Financial Crisis. *International Journal of Urban & Regional Research*, 39(2), 342–360. doi:10.1111/1468-2427.12210

Sin, D. S. (2017). The planning of the reconstruction of the cities of Hamhung and Hungnam in North Korea by the DAG urban planning brigade of the GDR from 1955–1962 – a treatise on urban development from the perspective of a contemporary witness. (PhD) Hafen City University (in German), Hamburg.

Sirmans, C. F., & Worzala, E. (2003). International direct real estate investment: A review of the literature. *Urban Studies*, 40(5–6), 1081–1114.

Steinert, M., & Crowe, S. (2001). Global real estate investment: Characteristics, optimal portfolio allocation and future trends. *Pacific Rim Property Research Journal*, 7(4), 223–239.

Tesser, L. M. (2004). East-central Europe's new security concern: Foreign land ownership. *Communist and Post-communist Studies*, 37, 213–239.

Thu, T. T., & Perera, R. (2011). Consequences of the two-price system for land in the land and housing market in Ho Chi Minh City, Vietnam. *Habitat International*, 35(1), 30–39.

UNCTAD. (2018). *World Investment Report 2018: Investment and New Industrial Policies* (9211129265). Retrieved from Geneva: https://unctad.org/en/PublicationsLibrary/wir2018_en.pdf

Wiesel, I., & Levin, I. (2018). Cohesion and differentiation in Australia's elite suburbs. *Geographical Research, 56*(4), 410–420.

Worzala, E., & Sirmans, C. F. (2003). Investing in international real estate stocks: A review of the literature. *Urban Studies, 40*(5–6), 1115–1149.

Yang, D. Y.-R., & Wang, H.-K. (2008). Dilemmas of local governance under the development zone fever in China: A case study of the Suzhou region. *Urban Studies, 45*(5–6), 1037–1054. doi:10.1177/0042098008089852

Zhu, J., Sim, L.-L., & Zhang, X.-Q. (2006). Global real estate investments and local cultural capital in the making of Shanghai's new office locations. *Habitat International, 30*(3), 462–481.

Ziobrowski, A. J., & Curcio, R. J. (1991). Diversification benefits of U.S. real estate to foreign investors. *Journal of Real Estate Research, 6*(2), 119–142. Retrieved from https://search.ebscohost.com/login.aspx?direct=true&db=23h&AN=4475294&site=ehost-live

12 Neoliberalization in urban governance at the real estate turn: perspective from urban redevelopment in China

Xiang Li

Introduction: understanding the neoliberalizing orientation in a real estate turn

Rapid urban development characterized by massive land monetization and space production demonstrates a remarkable real estate turn in Asia's urban politics (Shatkin, 2017). This turn is triggered by the neoliberalizing orientation in urban governance demonstrated by the establishment of an open, competitive and unregulated market associated with the liberation of state intervention for economic and urban development (Brenner & Theodore, 2002; Harvey, 1989). The development of neoliberalism is accompanied by a localization process that brings localities back to the centre of political regimes to amend the distressed condition caused by the managerialism of national states (Brenner & Theodore, 2002; Macleod, 2002).

Urban redevelopment thus becomes one key arena to understand the neoliberal orientation because it unifies local institutional transformation with global neoliberalization to form disparate urban political and governance changes throughout the transformation (Jessop, 2002; Weber, 2002). In this regard, fundamental shifts occur encompassing a range of reforms in redevelopment governance, land management, and state–community relations for real estate construction (Wu, 2010). Local authorities become increasingly interested in monetizing dilapidated urban land for power enhancement and capital generation through the engagement of real estate actors. Neoliberalism serves to play an instrumental role in the justification and legitimization of the state policy.

Distinct waves of neoliberalism have been identified in urban redevelopment across the globe, such as re-neoliberalism (Peck, Theodore, & Brenner, 2009) and post-neoliberalism (Peck, Theodore, & Brenner, 2010). Current studies, however, fail to distinguish between different historical waves of neoliberalism embedded in urban redevelopment in the Global South, especially in the Chinese context. In attempting to bridge the gap, this chapter examines the implications of neoliberal policies in urban redevelopment to understand the neoliberal transformation in urban China. The discussion contributes to understanding the variation and localization of neoliberalism in China, as a response to the critical discourse of "Chinese neoliberalism" – a variegated process with differing spatial and political manifestation (Lim, 2014). To achieve the above objective, this chapter addresses the following questions: What policy instruments did the Chinese state use in addressing social crisis in different waves of neoliberalization? What impacts have the policies had on institutions as a result of the change in governance structure in each wave? What are the continuities and alterations between the consecutive waves of transformations?

Through a comprehensive review of the related policies and existing studies on urban redevelopment in contemporary China, we argue that the Chinese state used two waves of policy mobility and institutional changes to initiate and deepen this neoliberalization of urban redevelopment. The first wave was characterized by land monetization and property-led development initiated through top-down reformative policies and collective actions to meet the elusive goals of urban modernization and economic growth. In this process, the real estate construction was to assume one of the leading thrusts (He & Wu, 2009). However, the growth-first regime resulted in widespread contestations and severe social conflicts. In response to the social crisis, a participatory institutional reform has been launched involving significant changes in the property rights regime, a new land transfer approach and a new procedure for interest distribution. These reform efforts have triggered substantial restructuring in power relations among the state, the developer, and the sitting land users in urban redevelopment. This institutional restructuring of the deregulation on property markets in China concur with the worldwide revision of neoliberalism, especially the urban transformation trajectory in the Global South (Eraydin & Taşan-Kok, 2014; Gautreau & Bruslé, 2019; Sader, 2009).

Marketization and property-led redevelopment from the 1980s to the 2000s

To retrieve the flagging society under the centrally planned governing structure, the Chinese Central Government promulgated an array of policies to launch a marketization reform in urban areas from the 1980s to the 2000s. These marketization policies initiated a property-led redevelopment period featuring decentralized state power and mounting market power that facilitated real estate development.

Policy transformation to marketization and property-led redevelopment

By establishing the land leasehold market in 1987, the central government introduced market value to urban land in order to rationalize land allocation and improve land use efficiency (Han, 2000; Yeh & Wu, 1996). However, the presence of price differentials between the administrative allocation and commercial land transfer generated prevalent speculative behaviours. Some public institutions thus obtained land through state allocation and sold it at a higher price in the newly created land market to acquire substantial profit (Yeh & Wu, 1996; Zhang, 2002). In 1991, the central policy institutionalized the government's monopoly in the primary land market: any potential land users should purchase land use rights from local governments and land transfer between potential and sitting users was forbidden (Yeh & Wu, 1996).

Simultaneously, the central state decentralized the administrative power to the local state to promote local development efficiency and incentives. Through the enactment of the Urban Planning Act in 1989, the central government authorized municipalities with powers to plan land use and issue land use permits (He & Wu, 2009). In 1994, a tax-sharing system was promulgated by the central state to enhance the financial autonomy of the local government by redistributing the revenue between itself and the local government (Oi, 1992). According to the new system, the central government took a large portion of non-land-based tax-related revenue whilst the local government kept the remaining balance. Meanwhile, all the land-based taxes[1] were kept by the local state (Wong, 2000). The reduction of financial support from the superior government and increase of fiscal autonomy at the local level incentivized the local government to play an entrepreneurial role and take charge of profits and losses (Harvey, 2002). Land leasing associated with space production in land-related (re)development thus has become the principal approach to amplifying the revenue of the municipalities (Hsing, 2010).

Housing reform was another neoliberal transformation through the commercialization and privatization of public housing provision. The year 1988 marked the beginning of housing reform when the State Council promulgated a policy to initiate the commercialization of public housing (He & Wu, 2009). In the 1990s, a series of reform policies launched a housing provident fund system to increase employees' wages for housing purposes and gradually eliminated the welfare housing system (Wang, 2001; Wang & Murie, 1996). Since then, the responsibility of housing provision gradually transferred to the housing market while the government and work units were no longer required to meet the housing requirements of their employees. In 1999, the central state published a milestone document that encouraged the local housing authority to sell public housing to the sitting tenant for public housing privatization (Miao & Maclennan, 2017; Wang, Shao, Murie, & Cheng, 2012).

As a response to market transferrable land and commercialized housing, a real estate market has been created and real estate development soon became one of the major growth poles in urban development (Ding & Knaap, 2005; Shin, 2009). Municipal governments commenced initiating large-scale urban redevelopment projects in the built-up area, not only aiming to activate the commercial value of the inner city area but also to restructure the urban functions for luring greater resources in the local competition (Hsing, 2010; Wu, 2004). However, the emphasis on in-kind compensation resulted in the low incentive of the developer to initiate urban redevelopment (Dowall, 1994). In attempting to deal with this, policies were promulgated to accelerate urban redevelopment for rapid capital circulation. In 2001, a demolition permit scheme was established by the central state to retain the local government's authority for compulsory demolition and move from resettlement provision to monetary compensation (Fang & Zhang, 2003). This policy contributed to an enforced relocation institution that strengthened the local state entrepreneurship in urban redevelopment.

Power relations in property-led redevelopment

The neoliberal policies increased the autonomy of local governments and enabled them to take control of the urban redevelopment process, regarding the assembly of finance, land, and building resources for property-led urban construction (Yeh & Wu, 1996). Meanwhile, these policies removed the supply side constraints of the private sectors and empowered them to play an important role in urban development (Wu, 1996; Yeh & Wu, 1996). The power relations among the main stakeholders, which nested in urban redevelopment, were thus restructured. When facing a dearth of financial and other resources, the local government tended to form a growth coalition with other resource-rich actors such as developers and state-owned enterprises (SOEs) to dominate the decision-making process (He & Wu, 2005). Each actor came to power in differing redevelopment practices, forming three patterns of power relations: government-led, SOEs-led and developer-led – characterizing the property-led redevelopment period.

The local government played a dominant role in most urban redevelopment cases because of its land ownership and administrative jurisdictions on land use and development intensity. In Shanghai, the district government established a pro-growth coalition to facilitate urban (re)development with non-public sectors (foreign investors, managers of enterprises of various ownership, etc.) (Zhang, 2002). In this coalition, the local government took the leadership, whilst the non-public sectors deployed mounting power to require the local government to take their interests into account. In Chongqing, the local government played a dominant role with the most substantial influence on land redevelopment (Han & Wang, 2003). Developers assumed the role of the initiator to form the project, which had to unconditionally follow governments' decisions and develop a good relationship with the latter to strengthen their power. After the establishment of affordable housing provision policies in 2000 in Beijing, the local government began to play a proactive and dominant role in residential redevelopment (Shin, 2009). It provided funding to projects and transformed its affiliations into a development corporation as a public agency. With the authorized decision-making power, the agency dominated the redevelopment process, ranging from planning and land assembly to construction and relocation.

Although the local government was configured with notable power in decision-making, the SOEs with land ownership holdings in hand were able to deploy strong power to influence, even change, the government's decisions in some cases. In Shenzhen, the municipal government granted the full status of a developer to some SOEs construction companies which possessed abundant land resources (Zhu, 1999). These SOE-affiliated developers had the power to conduct land transfers and make decisions on development plans. They transformed to a market-oriented role in pursuit of economic interest through commanding their land assets in urban (re)development (Zhu, 2002). With limited financial resources, the local government was only able to utilize land subsidies as an instrument to lever market sectors. In Beijing, in order to avoid sharing interest with the central government, local governments deliberately allocated land to SOE developers for redevelopment at a price far below the market rate (Fang & Zhang, 2003). In this process, the municipalities and SOEs who monopolized the inner-city land in the primary land market were able to seek massive monetary profit from the residential redevelopment project by trading the allocated land to private developers. Based on their land resources and a close relationship with the local government, SOEs were powerful enough to lobby the governments to change land use and overturn zoning and building codes to enlarge the profit-seeking space for developers. In Chongqing, SOEs, who occupied a large proportion of urban land, played the role of land provider in some urban redevelopment projects (Han & Wang, 2003). Being short of capital but rich in administratively allocated land, they either built up their own development companies or cooperated with private developers to accomplish and enormously profit from the property development.

Facing increasing constraints of financial resources in the rapid urbanization process, the local government had to facilitate the deployment of market sectors after the marketization reform (Wu, 2004). Private developers, especially the international real estate companies, sometimes even outweighed the local government in the redevelopment process, modifying the involved participants and the governance structures. In a landmark redevelopment case in Shanghai, the international developer came to power to take over the redevelopment process, from investment and design to construction and management, based on its ample capital, expertise and development experiences (He & Wu, 2005). The local government played the role of a facilitator to set up the redevelopment project as a hallmark with political objectives, and mobilized massive administrative resources to smooth the way for the project. In Beijing, a joint venture between the international developer and government-owned development company was established to conduct the redevelopment project (Shin, 2009). The foreign developer was configured with strong power to influence the decision-making process owing to its vast majority investment share in the joint venture. With a small portion of investment through a state-owned real estate company, the local government was able to participate in the entire decision-making process and played a co-operator role. The local government played a facilitating role by not only building up the alliance between foreign and local developers but also arranging the land lease through negotiation rather than public auction.

Subordinated stakeholders, including state banks and professional demolition companies, have been identified in current studies. The real estate companies relied heavily on loans from state banks to initiate the redevelopment project (Han & Wang, 2003; Wu, 2004). The real estate companies assigned the work to specialized demolition companies to force residents to move out, as a result of the complexity and difficulty of demolition work (Wu, 2004).

However, the community, which was configured without any evident power, played a marginalized role (Shin, 2009; Yang & Chang, 2007). Although residents tended to find space for mobilization within policy gaps and resorted to diverse strategies according to their interpretation and anticipation of state actions, such as individual or collective lawsuits, petitions, violent confrontations and cross-neighbourhood mobilization (Hsing, 2010), the individual and mobilized resistances they adopted proved to be futile when facing the powerful coalition between developers and local governments, because no public agent was representing their interests (Shin, 2009; Zhang, 2002).

Consequences

Under the influence of the neoliberal policies, urban redevelopment became a means of growth promotion to stimulate rapid land-centred capital accumulation and extraction for the economically powerful players (He & Wu, 2009; Julie, 2019). The state shifted its role from being a social welfare provider to an interventionist to regulate market operation, whilst the obligation of housing provision changed from the municipal governments or work units to private sectors. The low level of public participation in the decision-making process and unfair interest distribution triggered intensive social resistance, which resulted in violent conflicts and severe social instability (Ye, 2011).

The aggressive promotion of urban (re)development at the local level also caused tensions between the central and local governments (He & Wu, 2009). At the central level, the market-oriented reform was a trial-and-error experiment to decentralize the development pressure and improve land use efficiency. However, the local government attempted to seek short-term returns and extract value from the urban redevelopment process. Speculative and corrupt practices were not rare (He & Wu, 2009). The issues and contradictions of the efficiency-oriented redevelopment need to be addressed.

Deregulation and participatory redevelopment from the 2000s to the 2010s

In endeavouring to address the country-wide mobilizations and contestations associated with severe social instability, the central government proposed policies to launch a participatory reform by inviting sitting land users to join in the decision-making process to share their interests with the economically powerful actors (Li, Han, & Wu, 2019; Li & Liu, 2017; Tian & Yao, 2018). These policies initiated a participatory redevelopment period characterized by restrained state power and the mounting bargaining power of the residents from the 2000s to the 2010s.

Policy reform towards deregulation and participatory redevelopment

With increasingly strict constraints on rural land conversion from the central government, a participatory institutional reform was initiated in the early

2000s to encourage urban redevelopment in Chinese cities, especially in the mega-cities where acute land scarcity emerged to hinder further urban expansion. The institutional reform resulted in significant changes in multiple aspects, including the institutionalization of property rights, a new land transfer approach and a fairer interest distribution mechanism.

Since the country transformed from a centrally planned economy to a market economy, pure public ownership was diversified into the coexistence of multi-ownerships, calling for the recognition and protection of property rights. In 2004, the amendment to the 1982 Constitution conceded that when residents' properties were expropriated, they had the power to obtain fair compensation (He & Wu, 2009). In 2007, the central government released the Property Right Law to formally grant the 'inviolability' of private property rights to property owners (National People's Congress, 2007). The issuance of the property right law not only legalizes the rights and obligations, but also conceptualizes the cultural and moral notion that people have a right to oppose a development they perceive as unfair (Abramson, 2011). However, the property right reform set no specific requirement or procedures to guarantee a just implementation process for the housing expropriation, and the definition of the public interest was still ambiguous (Zhang, 2008). The lack of public participation and the consequently distributive inequality in the state-led redevelopment triggered increasingly fierce resistance from the residents who were empowered by the clearly defined property right (Mertha, 2009). The immense social protestation has been the most significant barrier to urban redevelopment proceeding (Lin, 2015).

In endeavouring to incentivize the sitting land users to engage in urban redevelopment, in 2009 the Guangdong government established the *Sai Jiu Gai Zao* (three old redevelopment, in English) policy for the experiment of a market-led approach to facilitate urban redevelopment (Guangdong Provincial Government, 2009). The policy restricts the dominance of the local government, delegates certain powers to existing land users and reallocates the land value increment between the state and existing landowners (Tian & Yao, 2018). It waives the traditional rule that land use transfer for commercial use has to go through a process in which local government assembles fragmented land use rights from the sitting users and auctions the acquired site to developers for redevelopment. The direct land use rights transfer between the new land users (normally private developers) and the existing land users is allowed. The original property owners thus have the power to choose, negotiate and share interests with the involved developer in the transfer process (Lin, 2015).

In 2011, the state council issued a policy to abolish the demolition permit institution, so ensuring a just and participatory redevelopment process (The State Council, 2011). The policy stipulates that compulsory housing expropriation only applies to the public interest purpose, and only the local government should take charge of the acquisition process. In terms of a fair decision-making process and transparent outcome, the policy encourages more public participation in the formal institutional arrangements.

Power relations in participatory redevelopment

These central policies, on one hand, constrain the direct involvement of the local government and encourage the state to play a facilitating and regulatory role in urban consolidation. On the other hand, the community is empowered to play a significant role in decision-making by arguing with the economically powerful stakeholders (Li & Liu, 2017; Tian & Yao, 2018). Developers are also authorized redevelopment rights through a direct land transfer mechanism (Li, Han, & Wu, 2019; Li, Wu, & Han, 2019). The traditionally powerful actors, such as the local government and developers, as well as the newly empowered property owners, thus have influences in various ways, leading to three patterns of power relations in urban redevelopment – namely, government-led, developer-led, and owner-led redevelopment.

In some redevelopment cases, the local government played a dominant role while residents were configured with increasing power to counteract the influences of the local government. In Fangzhicheng, Xi'an, by forming a coalition with a developer, the local government intended to undermine the interests of the affected residents and forcefully implement the redevelopment (Cheng, 2012). Residents, despite being without formal property deeds, mobilized and resisted the repression from the local authorities and developers coalition. As the forceful measures failed to achieve the land assembly, the local government had to adopt a collaborative attitude to break the collective resistance and retain support from the affected residents. On completion of agreements from the majority of the affected residents, it was able to initiate the demolition. In a historic Muslim community in Xi'an, after proposing a redevelopment plan, the local government strived to create a market environment to attract private investment for its prompt implementation (Zhai & Ng, 2013). Affected residents organized and mobilized to resist the local government, whilst representatives repeatedly submitted collective petitions to higher-level governments for political assistance. As a response, the Ministry of Construction delegated investigators to inspect the legitimacy of the redevelopment plan at the local level. The intervention of the central government successfully prevented the implementation of the demolition plan. To lift the land value of the central city in Beijing, the local government formed a coalition with a SOE, the de facto landowner, to redevelop the Jiuxianqiao area (Zhang, Chen, & Tochen, 2016). Residents established a self-organized committee to mobilize collective resistance against the alliance, generating social instability. To facilitate the Olympic Games in Beijing, the central government pressurized the local government to prioritize social stability. The latter thus organized a public vote to collect residents' opinions and suspended the redevelopment based on the result of the public vote. Two years later, the local government restarted the redevelopment and allowed residents to participate in the decision-making process. An inclusive governance was thus formed to facilitate the redevelopment implementation.

Although existing residents were significantly empowered to argue with the economically powerful parties, with the cooperation of the local government, the developer sometimes played a leading role in urban redevelopment. In Foshan, the local government excluded other competitors in the land auction to protect the involvement of a reputable international developer (Cheng, 2012). Once obtaining the land redevelopment rights, the developer was authorized to play a critical role in the redevelopment process, taking control of the procedures from establishing a redevelopment plan and design to construction and sale. The local government played a facilitating role, on one hand, to revise the redevelopment plan according to the developer's requirement, and, on the other hand, it pressurized the affected residents to relocate in order to prepare the land for redevelopment. The affected residents, holding the legal ownership, had a stronger arguing power to negotiate with the government to obtain fair compensation. In the market-oriented residential redevelopment in Shenzhen, where the state intervention was largely contained, developers played a pivotal role in initiating redevelopment by directly negotiating with the sitting residents, who were configured with strong arguing power (Li, Han, & Wu, 2019). However, the requirement of the support of all the residents resulted in power asymmetry between residents and the developer, causing violent intra-conflicts and, consequently, project delay (Li, Han, & Wu, 2019; Li, Wu, & Han, 2019).

Empowered by their collective land ownership, the urban village collective was authorized with self-redevelopment rights to initiate the owner-led redevelopment after the participatory reform, whilst the state was able to share a small portion of the value-added from the project. In the redevelopment of Wenchong village, Guangzhou, the local government became less dominant and transformed into a facilitator (Cheng, 2012). To smooth the process of urban village redevelopment, it delegated full administrative and approval power to the village collective company and gave the latter the critical role of negotiating with the developer. The village collective company thus played a dual role in the process. On one hand, it negotiated with the developer to raise compensation levels for the village collective and individual villagers; on the other hand, it strived to convince all the villagers to sign the agreement to facilitate the redevelopment. In this process, villagers' requests were adequately responded to, such as raising compensation standards and replacing the previous developer with a larger one with a greater capacity and reputation. In Xinxiang village, Guangzhou, native villagers formed a Village Joint Venture Enterprise (VJVE) as a collective representative of the village to negotiate with the local government and developer in the redevelopment process (Chung, 2013). As the legal landowner, the VJVE, on one hand, played the part of a local government power broker to fight for the interests for both individual villagers and the collective. On the other hand, it undertook an entrepreneurial role by not only forming a partnership with the private developer for extracting profit but also striving to persuade individual villagers to follow its growth-oriented redevelopment plan. In this process, the local government deployed its administrative power to conciliate the confrontation between the village collective and uncooperative residents to facilitate the redevelopment, while the developer utilized its capitalist power to seek profit from the redevelopment process. In Liede village, Guangzhou, an urban village close to the new CBD area, the local government established a government-led redevelopment plan to obtain the village land to prepare for the 2010 Asian Games (Zhou, 2014). Under the inspiration of the *San Jiu Gai Zao* policy, the VJVE refused the government's redevelopment scheme and proposed a self-redevelopment agenda. The local government approved the self-redevelopment agenda and began to play a facilitating role. The VJVE formed a collaborative partnership with the local authority and developers to complete the redevelopment.

Since urban land can be transferred through private negotiation between developers and existing land users, the requirement on developers' financial strength has been reduced. This is because developers are not required to pay enormous sums of money as land use fees to the local government to initiate the redevelopment project. The level of a developer's reliance on a loan from banking institutions has thus been diminished (Li & Li, 2011). The demolition company becomes more technically oriented by focusing on providing a professional demolition service rather than compelling existing residents to expedite the relocation, because of the empowerment of the residents (Li, Han, & Wu, 2019).

Consequences

With an increasingly collaborative institutional transformation, the local government's power was constrained by the mounting community power (Zhai & Ng, 2013; Zhang et al., 2016). The changing urban redevelopment mechanisms profoundly transformed the power relations into an increasingly inclusive and collaborative partnership and facilitated the implementation of urban redevelopment in urban village redevelopment. However, the empowerment of the affected residents created substantial barriers to the residential redevelopment process. With increasing numbers of residents joining in decision-making, the consequent heterogeneous interests and fragmented property rights add to the complexity of residential redevelopment (Li, Han, & Wu, 2019). Different from urban villages, there is no collective association to internalize the task of land assembly in residential redevelopments. The local government and developers thus have to negotiate with a large number of involved households, escalating the transaction costs. In this regard, the local government, equipped with housing expropriation power, can address the uncooperative residents' resistance to finalize the redevelopment. Without the endorsement of the local government, the developer can fail to counteract the uncooperative residents' power, resulting in pervasive speculative behaviours and mounting compensation in residential redevelopment. Housing affordability has been negatively influenced because of the spill-over effect of escalating compensation and social cost on housing prices (He, Zhang, & Wei, 2019). The significantly increased development density places a heavy burden on infrastructure and increases the project's social costs (Shenzhen Urban Planning Research Centre, 2015). All these negative externalities trigger social conflicts and contradictions, prolong the negotiation process between the initiators and affected residents, and eventually add to the transaction costs of the residential redevelopment projects.

Participatory policy was initiated by the central government to promote a more just and fair redevelopment process, because of the country-wide resistance and mobilization associated with economic and environmental considerations (Wu, 2019). However, it fails to counteract the neoliberal essence in the current urban planning policy framework but facilitates the dominance of market mechanisms in redistribution in a more decentralized and localized neoliberal political system. Without land ownership, residents' participation is, in a highly structured way, shaped by the state, which prioritizes a public growth-oriented agenda rather than the improvement of social welfare (Xu & Lin, 2019). Residents' participation merely improves the compensation terms but fails to alter the government's decision of dispossession.

Through the participatory institutional reform, the central government works as an external force from the upper level to overcome the institutional separation and stimulate cross-boundary cooperation at the local level (Schoon & Altrock, 2014). Municipal governments have had to redirect the development approach from promoting continuous spatial expansion to leading a fair, interest-sharing scheme of a spatial upgrade in a specific area (Lin, 2015). However, the participatory reform fails to resolve the structural contradiction between the central and local governments in policy implementation. Local governments still pay more attention to short-term benefits and ignore long-term effects and social equity.

Discussion

The first neoliberal institutional transformation characterized by marketization was to solve the economic issues of low cost-effectiveness and incentives in the socialist period. With the decentralized power from the central government, local governments developed strong motivations for profit-seeking from urban (re)development in order to prioritize economic development and process efficiency. They were inclined to take charge of the development process by forming alliances with actors who could bring direct economic benefits and smooth the way for demolition and relocation (Li, Wang, & Day, 2020). Residents, alongside their requirements and petitions, were regarded as barriers to the capital circulation by the growth-oriented coalition and were thus excluded from decision-making. These practices contributed to the unprecedented rapid urbanization featuring real estate development but resulted in the politics of exclusion and social instability.

As a response to the social crisis, the second neoliberal reconfiguration characterized by deregulation was to underline the role of the market mechanism to improve redistributive justice and process efficiency (Feng & Chapman, 2020). The state transforms into a facilitator and regulator role with restrained power to interfere in the decision-making process. Rather than direct interventions characterized by forceful actions, the local government commences utilizing more legislative instruments, such as policies and regulations, to realize its domination in local interactions. Residents are empowered to participate in decision-making by negotiating with economically powerful actors, such as the government and developers. The decision-making process has become more inclusive and participatory since power in urban redevelopment was no longer controlled by a single, coherent elite but began to be distributed to more involved social groups (Zhang, Lin, Hooimeijer, & Geertman, 2020).

Institutional change also has important implications for the interest redistribution mechanism. In property-led redevelopment, through space creation and capital circulation, developers gained immense revenues from the sale of commodity housing whilst the governments obtained improved public infrastructure free of charge and gained considerable profit through land use fees and relevant taxes (Zhou, Lin, & Zhang, 2018). Residents were either provided with in-situ housing in the urban fringe or monetary reimbursement, which was far below the price of the newly constructed on-site apartments (Yang & Chang, 2007). The participatory reform restructured the reallocation of development profits. The communities are empowered to join in the decision-making process and share the land conveyance income previously monopolized by the state (Li & Liu, 2017; Schoon, 2014). The compensation of sitting land users, including residents and villagers, has risen to be in accordance with the housing price in adjacent areas in terms of in-kind housing or monetary recompense. In contrast, local governments have reduced their dependence on direct land value increments, and have turned instead to requiring a small portion of the land and public facilities from the redevelopment.

However, these welfare-related measures are merely to pacify social resistance towards demolition and relocation, in order to facilitate urban redevelopment rather than to revert to the egalitarian planning system of the socialist period (Li & Liu, 2017). This is because local state entrepreneurship is still retained to make urban redevelopment a pivotal instrument in revitalizing underutilized land for consistent capital accumulation without having to incur any immediate burden in the form of costs or budgets (Wu, 2017). The institutional transformations neither change the evaluation system for local official promotion nor change the means of profit for local governments (Li, Han, & Wu, 2019; Li, Wu, & Han, 2019). Real estate development assumes a substantial role in meeting ambitious goals of urban modernization and creating new growth in urban (re)development (Shatkin, 2017). Commodification of land that has neoliberal components in urban (re)development assumes, as a technology of governing, a strategy of accumulation and a tactic of rent-seeking by the government. Therefore, these neoliberal transformations ultimately contribute to enhancing state power over urban land and development. This echoes the argument of Sheng and Webber (2019) that the Chinese state manifests strong selectivity in adopting neoliberal instruments to smooth the way for urban (re)development in a relativist manner, rather than accepting neoliberalism as a ruling ideology.

What is noteworthy is that the transformation of power relations brought by neoliberal policy changes in urban China are consistent with post-neoliberalism in south America, which is conceptualized as an adjustment rather than a departure from neoliberalism (Gautreau & Bruslé, 2019; Peck et al., 2010; Sader, 2009). This is because the reforms reveal the flexibility and adaptability of neoliberalism in the real estate domain, which are not aimed at radically breaking away from neoliberal frameworks. However, it is different from re-neoliberalism, which emphasizes neoliberalism as a ruling mindset in a rigid way based on the belief that self-regulating markets will generate an optimal allocation of investments and resources (Peck et al., 2009). In China, the state still plays a pivotal role by shaping the power configuration and dictating the interest redistribution in redevelopment governing (Wu, 2017; Wu, He, & Webster, 2010).

Conclusion: a research agenda

This chapter contributes to understanding the implications of neoliberal policies on urban politics by identifying two waves of neoliberal transformation in urban redevelopment in China. We argue that the most recent transformation towards a participatory governance structure in urban redevelopment can be regarded as a flexible neoliberal settlement to manage the contradiction and secure ongoing legitimacy of neoliberalism through explicit forms of political management and intervention. Associated with the mobilization and extension of markets and market logics, neoliberalism is increasingly connected with new modes of power configuration, concerned specifically with the deregulation and involvement of those residents dispossessed by the neoliberalization of the marketization in the 1980s to 2000s. This process is a regulatory restructuring of the social and urban planning spectrum rather than a collapse of an entire institutional and political complex (Peck et al., 2010).

After the global economic crisis in 2008, worldwide reflections on the severe consequences of neoliberalism have emerged to counteract the issues caused by the first wave of neoliberal political practice, including social polarization and segregation, and intensification of uneven development across the globe (Peck et al., 2010). The innovative and participatory governance approaches were promulgated in the Global South to reverse the eroding social welfare state (Duménil & Levy, 2009; Eraydin & Taşan-Kok, 2014). It is widely observed that state actors use market norms, alongside authoritarian logics of governing, wherever it suits their interests in facilitating capital accumulation and enhancing social stability. These new phenomena generate interesting questions for future studies. How do we conceptualize the recalibration of a neoliberalism mindset as a worldwide theorization at the global level? How does neoliberal transformation restructure the governance dynamics in differing locations with cultural, political, and spatial specificities? Or, more radically and aggressively, is neoliberalism per se still powerful enough to function as a lens to investigate and explain the variegated and localized urbanization?

Acknowledgement

I would like to express my appreciation to my supervisor Professor Sun Sheng Han for his suggestions and editing of an early draft of this chapter. Any remaining errors are the responsibility of the author.

Note

1.   Land-based resources include tax on urban land use and occupancy of rural land, incremental tax on land value, housing property tax, urban construction and maintenance tax and so on (Wong, 2000).

References

Abramson, D. (2011). Transitional property rights and local developmental history in China. *Urban Studies, 48*(3), 553–568.
Brenner, N., & Theodore, N. (2002). Cities and the geographies of 'actually existing neoliberalism'. *Antipode, 34*(3), 349–379.
Cheng, Z. (2012). The changing and different patterns of urban redevelopment in China: A study of three inner-city neighborhoods. *Community Development, 43*(4), 430–450. doi:10.1080/15575330.2012.711763
Chung, H. (2013). The spatial dimension of negotiated power relations and social justice in the redevelopment of villages-in-the-city in China. *Environment and Planning A, 45*(10), 2459–2476. doi:10.1068/a45416
Ding, C., & Knaap, G. (2005). Urban land policy reform in China's transitional economy. *Emerging Land and Housing Markets in China, 2*, 32.
Dowall, D. E. (1994). Urban residential redevelopment in the People's Republic of China. *Urban Studies, 31*(9), 1497–1516.
Duménil, G., & Levy, D. (2009). The nature and contradictions of neoliberalism. *Socialist Register, 38*(38).
Eraydin, A., & Taşan-Kok, T. (2014). State response to contemporary urban movements in Turkey: A critical overview of state entrepreneurialism and authoritarian interventions. *Antipode, 46*(1), 110–129.
Fang, K., & Zhang, Y. (2003). Plan and market mismatch: Urban redevelopment in Beijing during a period of transition. *Asia Pacific Viewpoint, 44*(2), 149–162.

Feng, X., & Chapman, K. (2020). 'The tiger's leap': The role of history in legitimating the authority of modern Chinese planners. *Urban Studies*. doi:10.1177/0042098019882913

Gautreau, P., & Bruslé, L. P. (2019). Forest management in Bolivia under Evo Morales: The challenges of post-neoliberalism. *Political Geography*, 68, 110–121. doi:10.1016/j.polgeo.2018.12.003

Guangdong Provincial Government. (2009). *Several Opinions of the Guangdong Province Government to Promote Three Old Redevelopment for Urban Land Use Consolidation*. Retrieved from http://www.gd.gov.cn/zwgk/wjk/zcfgk/content/post_2532575.html

Han, S. S. (2000). Shanghai between state and market in urban transformation. *Urban Studies*, 37(11), 2091–2112. doi:10.1080/713707226

Han, S. S., & Wang, Y. (2003). The institutional structure of a property market in inland China: Chongqing. *Urban Studies*, 40(1), 91–112.

Harvey, D. (1989). From managerialism to entrepreneurialism: The transformation in urban governance in late capitalism. *Geografiska Annaler: Series B, Human Geography*, 71(1), 3–17.

Harvey, D. (2002). From managerialism to entrepreneurialism: The transformation of urban governance in late capitalism. *The Blackwell City Reader*, 456–463.

He, S., & Wu, F. (2009). China's emerging neoliberal urbanism: Perspectives from urban redevelopment. *Antipode*, 41(2), 282–304. doi:10.1111/j.1467-8330.2009.00673.x

He, S. J., & Wu, F. L. (2005). Property-led redevelopment in post-reform China: A case study of Xintiandi redevelopment project in Shanghai. *Journal of Urban Affairs*, 27(1), 1–23. doi:10.1111/j.0735-2166.2005.00222.x

He, S., Zhang, M., & Wei, Z. (2019). The state project of crisis management: China's Shantytown Redevelopment Schemes under state-led financialization. *Environment and Planning A: Economy and Space*, 0308518X19882427.

Hsing, Y.-t. (2010). *The Great Urban Transformation: Politics of Land and Property in China*. Oxford University Press. doi:10.1093/acprof:oso/9780199568048.001.0001

Jessop, B. (2002). Liberalism, neoliberalism, and urban governance: A state–theoretical perspective. *Antipode*, 34(3), 452–472.

Julie, T. M. (2019). Planning particularities: Reinterpreting urban planning in China with the case of Chengdu. *Planning Theory & Practice*, 20(4), 512–536. doi:10.1080/14649357.2019.164

Li, B., & Liu, C. (2017). Emerging selective regimes in a fragmented authoritarian environment: The 'three old redevelopment' policy in Guangzhou, China from 2009 to 2014. *Urban Studies*, 0042098017716846.

Li, C., Wang, M. Y., & Day, J. (2020). Reconfiguration of state–society relations: The making of uncompromising nail households in urban housing demolition and relocation in Dalian, China. *Urban Studies*, doi:10.1177/0042098020912151

Li, L., & Li, X. (2011). Redevelopment of urban villages in Shenzhen, China – An analysis of power relations and urban coalitions. *Habitat International*, 35(3), 426–434. doi:10.1016/j.habitatint.2010.12.001

Li, X., Han, S. S., & Wu, H. (2019). Urban consolidation, power relations, and dilapidated residential redevelopment in Mutoulong, Shenzhen, China. *Urban Studies*, 56(13), 2802–2819.

Li, X., Wu, H., & Han, S. S. (2019). Institutional analysis of market-led residential development in Shenzhen: A transaction cost perspective. Paper presented at the *Twenty Fifth Annual Pacific-Rim Real Estate Society Conference*, Melbourne.

Lim, K. F. (2014). 'Socialism with Chinese characteristics'. Uneven development, varie-gated neoliberalisation and the dialectical differentiation of state spatiality. *Progress in Human Geography*, *38*(2), 221–247.

Lin, G. C. S. (2015). The redevelopment of China's construction land: Practising land property rights in cities through renewals. *The China Quarterly*, *224*, 865–887.

MacLeod, G. (2002). From urban entrepreneurialism to a 'revanchist city'? On the spatial injustices of Glasgow's renaissance. *Antipode*, *34*(3), 602–624.

Mertha, A. (2009). 'Fragmented authoritarianism 2.0': Political pluralization in the Chinese policy process. *The China Quarterly*, *200*, 995–1012.

Miao, J. T., & Maclennan, D. (2017). Exploring the 'middle ground' between state and market: The example of China. *Housing Studies*, *32*(1), 73–94. doi:10.1080/02673037.2016.1181723

National People's Congress. (2007). *Property Right Law*. Retrieved from http://www.gov.cn/ziliao/flfg/2007-03/19/content_554452.htm

Oi, J. C. (1992). Fiscal reform and the economic foundations of local state corporatism in China. *World Politics*, *45*(1), 99–126.

Peck, J., Theodore, N., & Brenner, N. (2009). Neoliberal urbanism: Models, moments, mutations. *SAIS Review of International Affairs*, *29*(1), 49–66.

Peck, J., Theodore, N., & Brenner, N. (2010). Postneoliberalism and its malcontents. *Antipode*, *41*(s1), 94–116. doi:10.1111/j.1467-8330.2009.00718.x

Sader, E. (2009). Postneoliberalism in Latin America. *Development Dialogue*, *51*(1), 171–179.

Schoon, S. (2014). Three olds: Experimental urban restructuring with Chinese char-acteristics, Guangzhou and Shenzhen in comparison. In *Maturing Megacities* (pp. 105–121). Springer.

Schoon, S., & Altrock, U. (2014). Conceded informality. Scopes of informal urban restructuring in the Pearl River Delta. *Habitat International*, *43*, 214–220.

Shatkin, G. (2017). *Cities for Profit: The Real Estate Turn in Asia's Urban Politics*: Cornell University Press.

Sheng, J., & Webber, M. (2019). Governance rescaling and neoliberalisation of China's water governance: The case of China's South–North Water Transfer project. *Environment and Planning A: Economy and Space*, 0308518X19866839.

Shenzhen Urban Planning Research Centre. (2015). *Compilation and Suggestions for Urban Consolidation Policies in Shenzhen from 2012 to 2015*. Internal report.

Shin, H. B. (2009). Residential redevelopment and the entrepreneurial local state: The implications of Beijing's shifting emphasis on urban redevelopment policies. *Urban Studies*, *46*(13), 2815–2839.

The State Council. (2011). *Regulation on the Expropriation of Buildings on State-owned Land and Compensation*. Retrieved from http://www.gov.cn/zwgk/2011-01/21/content_1790111.htm

Tian, L., & Yao, Z. (2018). From state-dominant to bottom-up redevelopment: Can institutional change facilitate urban and rural redevelopment in China. *Cities*, *76*, 72–83.

Wang, Y. P. (2001). Urban housing reform and finance in China: A case study of Beijing. *Urban Affairs Review*, *36*(5), 620–645.

Wang, Y. P., & Murie, A. (1996). The process of commercialisation of urban housing in China. *Urban Studies*, *33*(6), 971–989.

Wang, Y. P., Shao, L., Murie, A., & Cheng, J. (2012). The maturation of the neo-liberal housing market in urban China. *Housing Studies*, *27*(3), 343–359.

Weber, R. (2002). Extracting value from the city: Neoliberalism and urban redevelopment. *Antipode, 34*(3), 519–540.

Wong, C. P. (2000). Central-local relations revisited the 1994 tax-sharing reform and public expenditure management in China. *China Perspectives*, 52–63.

Wu, F. (1996). Changes in the structure of public housing provision in urban China. *Urban Studies, 33*(9), 1601–1627.

Wu, F. (2004). Residential relocation under market-oriented redevelopment: The process and outcomes in urban China. *Geoforum, 35*(4), 453–470.

Wu, F. (2010). How neoliberal is China's reform? The origins of change during transition. *Eurasian Geography and Economics, 51*(5), 619–631.

Wu, F. (2017). Planning centrality, market instruments: Governing Chinese urban transformation under state entrepreneurialism. *Urban Studies*, 0042098017721828.

Wu, F. (2019). Adding new narratives to the urban imagination: An introduction to 'New directions of urban studies in China'. *Urban Studies*, 0042098019898137.

Wu, F., He, S., & Webster, C. (2010). Path dependency and the neighbourhood effect: Urban poverty in impoverished neighbourhoods in Chinese cities. *Environment and Planning A, 42*(1), 134–152.

Xu, Z., & Lin, G. C. (2019). Participatory urban redevelopment in Chinese cities amid accelerated urbanization: Symbolic urban governance in globalizing Shanghai. *Journal of Urban Affairs, 41*(6), 756–775.

Yang, Y.-R., & Chang, C.-H. (2007). An urban regeneration regime in China: A case study of urban redevelopment in Shanghai's Taipingqiao area. *Urban Studies, 44*(9), 1809–1826. doi:10.1080/00420980701507787

Ye, L. (2011). Urban regeneration in China: Policy, development, and issues. *Local Economy, 26*(5), 337–347. doi:10.1177/0269094211409117

Yeh, A. G., & Wu, F. L. (1996). The new land development process and urban development in Chinese cities. *International Journal of Urban and Regional Research, 20*(2), 330.

Zhai, B., & Ng, M. K. (2013). Urban regeneration and social capital in China: A case study of the Drum Tower Muslim District in Xi'an. *Cities, 35*, 14–25.

Zhang, L., Chen, J., & Tochen, R. M. (2016). Shifts in governance modes in urban redevelopment: A case study of Beijing's Jiuxianqiao Area. *Cities, 53*, 61–69. doi:10.1016/j.cities.2016.01.001

Zhang, L., Lin, Y., Hooimeijer, P., & Geertman, S. (2020). Heterogeneity of public participation in urban redevelopment in Chinese cities: Beijing versus Guangzhou. *Urban Studies*. doi:10.1177/0042098019862192

Zhang, M. (2008). From public to private: The newly enacted Chinese property law and the protection of property rights in China. *Berkeley Business Law Journal, 5*, 317.

Zhang, T. (2002). Urban development and a socialist pro-growth coalition in Shanghai. *Urban Affairs Review, 37*(4), 475–499. doi:10.1177/10780870222185432

Zhou, Y., Lin, G. C., & Zhang, J. (2018). Urban China through the lens of neoliberalism: Is a conceptual twist enough? *Urban Studies*, 0042098018775367.

Zhou, Z. (2014). Towards collaborative approach? Investigating the regeneration of urban village in Guangzhou, China. *Habitat International, 44*, 297–305.

Zhu, J. (1999). Local growth coalition: The context and implications of China's gradualist urban land reforms. *International Journal of Urban and Regional Research, 23*(3), 534–548.

Zhu, J. (2002). Urban development under ambiguous property rights: A case of China's transition economy. *International Journal of Urban and Regional Research, 26*(1), 41–57.

13 Institutional governance of innovation adoption in residential developments: future research directions

Godwin Kavaarpuo

Introduction

Technological innovations to the developer-builder in housing delivery are essential to improve residential developers' profitability and competitiveness, resolve growing sustainability concerns, stimulate economic growth, and to address the enormous housing deficits that developing countries, in particular, face. Despite the recognised benefits of residential innovations, whether green building materials, technologies, construction techniques, smart building, property technologies (Proptech) or administrative processes that are new (real or perceived) to the developer, the sector's overall innovation performance, in both developed and developing economies, has been unsatisfactory (Dickinson et al., 2005; Van Oorschot et al., 2020; Wolfe, 1994). Reluctant innovation interest contradicts the Schumpeterian expectations that profit-maximising residential developers must innovate, partially or entirely replacing existing production functions through creative destruction to remain in business.

So far, many studies have diagnosed the limited innovation in residential developments from the neoclassical economics viewpoint and as the sub-optimal allocation of scarce resources – the choice theoretic lens. In price theory, the rational developer and builder, for example, logically evaluate and choose optimal production functions and, accordingly, allocate scarce resources to maximise profits. The price mechanism circulates information about demand and supply and guides resource allocation. Since technological housebuilding innovations typically have superior attributes relative to conventional building, limited developer interest is interpreted as choice-constrained decisions that innovation policy should resolve. From the lens of choice, identifying adoption barriers and determinants of innovation adoption in housing gains significance. Studies have reported high investment costs, regulatory barriers,

245

knowledge and awareness deficiencies, limited financial incentives, inconsistent government support, unavailability of materials, limited data on green building technologies, low market demand and cultural inertia as curtailing the adoption-diffusion of housebuilding innovations (see, for example, Dickinson et al., 2005; Sexton & Barrett, 2003; Van Oorschot et al., 2020; Wolfe, 1994 for reviews). Ball (2003) argued that innovation reluctance in property development is linked to the industry's structure and market characteristics.

While relevant, the predominance of the science of choice leaves developers' economic organisation of innovation less understood (Buchanan, 2001; Van Oorschot et al., 2020). Indeed, such studies assume a priori that the innovation adoption opportunity already exists and is known to developers and builders. Nevertheless, as Andelin et al. (2015), Hayek (1945) and Sarasvathy (2009) have shown, the bits of information with potentially viable entrepreneurial opportunities to adopt an innovation from an exogenous source are scattered throughout the economy. These dispersed bits of information must first be coordinated and harmonised to discover any innovation adoption opportunities. The entrepreneur's central problem is coordinating scattered information with uncertain value (Hayek, 1945; von Hayek, 1989). Buchanan (1975, 2001) further argued that the science of exchange is fundamental to the understanding of exchanges, economic organisations of production and institutions. Voluntary exchanges of valuable information, property rights, products and services are impractical without institutions (North, 1992, 1994).

A growing literature (on construction in general rather than housing-specific literature) recognises the role of transaction costs in developers' production decisions and observes that transaction costs are consistently higher in innovation than conventional developments (Gooding & Gul, 2016; Kiss, 2016; Ürge-Vorsatz et al., 2012). Kiss (2016) and Kiss and Mundaca (2013) and Mundaca et al. (2013) conclude that severe uncertainties, idiosyncratic assets, asymmetric information, and bounded rationality heighten the institutional costs in innovation adoption in residential developments. Notwithstanding, the absence of an agreed definition and taxonomy of transaction costs in housing developments and innovation adoption, in particular, weakens the utility of direct quantification of transaction costs. Transaction costs may be the cost of regulations (Wong et al., 2011); the cost of using institutions (Buitelaar, 2004, 2008); the cost of running the economic system (Arrow, 1969); the cost of information search, contract specification, negotiation and dispute resolutions (Coase, 1960; Williamson, 1979). Transaction costs measure the valuable attributes of the product or bundle of property rights being exchanged, protecting rights, policing and enforcing contracts (North, 1990). Coase (1937, 1960) originally conceived transaction costs as the cost of using the price mechanism. Niehans (1969) extended transaction costs to include transport costs. Transaction costs tend to be agent-specific rather than transaction-specific (Wang, 2003). Agents in the same industry can have drastically different transaction costs for similar transactions (see, for example, Akerlof & Kranton, 2000). In housing developments, non-market transaction costs further complicate direct measurements and comparisons of the transaction costs of housebuilding innovations across developers and markets. Consequently, a comprehensive framework for understanding developers' economic organisation of innovation is still lacking.

The objectives of this chapter are three-fold. It seeks to highlight the utility of the science of contracts both as a complement but also as a substitute to the science of choice in understanding developers' innovation behaviour and generating insights for responsive innovation policy formulation. Drawing from transaction cost and entrepreneurial theory, it introduces the developers' innovation problem as a governance problem. It further provides a framework for analytical inquiries into the governance of housebuilding innovation behaviour and an outline for future research.

Understanding innovations as transactions

Innovation adoption is both the decision and actual implementation of an idea or product (Rogers, 2003), technological process (Garcia & Calantone, 2002) or new production combinations (Schumpeter, 1934), which is new (real or perceived) to the developer or builder. According to OECD/Eurostat (OECD/Eurostat, 2005, p. 46), it is "the implementation of a new or significantly improved product (good or service), or process...". Toole (1998, p. 323) defined housing innovation as the

> application of technology that is new to an organisation and that significantly; 1. improves the design and construction of living space by decreasing installed cost increasing installed performance; 2. improves the business process, e.g., reduces lead time or increases flexibility.

Inferentially, housing innovations may be administrative or organisational; construction techniques; products such as sustainable building materials, green building materials, eco-friendly materials; services; and information technology-based technologies if new to the adopter.

The essential descriptor of innovation is "newness" (real or perceived) and "non-trivial change", which Slaughter (1993) classified as at least 25% of the existing opportunity to use the innovation. Second, innovations can either be originated by the organisation itself – bottom-up oriented (Slaughter, 1993) or adopted – top-down oriented (Rogers, 2003), or collaborative – jointly developed. Joint innovation adoption is not a typical model in the property sector and is not considered further.

Innovations are distinct from inventions. To invent is to originate new products, processes or new combinations of factors of production; innovation is the decision and implementation of an invention by an agent besides the inventor (Schumpeter, 1947, p. 151). Inventions typically have no endogenous economic value until an entrepreneur applies the same within the production process to generate profit (Rosenberg, 1974). This chapter adopts this distinction while admitting that delineating precise analytical boundaries between invention and innovations is problematic. In similar regards, Ruttan (1959, p. 605) concludes that inventions are "an institutionally defined subset of technical innovations".

A transaction, on the other hand, occurs when a "good, service, [information or property rights] is transferred across a technologically separable interface. One stage of activity terminates, and another begins" (Williamson, 1985, p. 1). Strictly speaking, decision-making is also transacting. The power to decide can be transferred to another agent, within or outside of the firm's boundaries. Commons (1932) emphasised that transactions involved the transfer of property rights and liberties and not commodities. This transaction (whether involving goods, services, information, property rights, liberties), Commons (1932) says, has three fundamental attributes: conflict, order, and mutuality. What Commons recognised is that for mutual compensation to be realised in voluntary exchanges, conflicts (including divergent agent interests) must be minimised, and order created using appropriate institutional governance mechanisms. In other words, the nature of economic transfers and agents involved necessitates the use of institutions.

According to Wallis and North (1986), the use of institutions constitutes transaction costs. Institutions are necessary for valuing the attributes of that which is being exchanged, to protect agent interests, information assembly, police and enforce contracts and resolve disputes (North, 1990). Transaction costs add no value to the production of goods or services. However, they are the inevitable and often unanticipated costs that emerge from contracting activities essential in trading goods and services (Coase, 1960). In Williamson's (1979, 1985) view, extending Coasian transaction costs, the scale of transaction costs is a function of opportunism, bounded rationality, asset specificity, uncertainty, and frequency. Transacting agents do not quantify these trans-action costs. Instead, "transactions which differ in their attributes, are aligned with governance structures which vary in their cost and competence, to effect a (mainly) transaction cost economising result" (Williamson, 2003, p. 926). Since trading parties are self-seeking and boundedly rational, the resulting unavoidably incomplete contracts worsen the ex-ante and ex-post contractual hazards in innovation adoption.

Cascading innovation with transaction makes evident that to innovate is to transact. The two cannot be decoupled. Innovation is not just a new product or service, as the science of choice conceives. Innovation adoption constitutes a complex series of transactions. Innovation must be: (1) "applied" in an economically beneficial way by an entrepreneur; and (2) "transferred across a technologically separate interface". From this understanding, building tech-nologies are not substitutes as found in prototype studies and hypothetical cost comparisons of building technologies (see, for example, Adam & Agib, 2001; Didel et al., 2014; Ogundiran & Adedeji, 2012; Raheem et al., 2012). Market prices may be compared, but each material involves different supply chains, actors, stakeholder interests, expertise, and regulatory compliances. How development is organised in each case is also distinct.

The series of innovation transactions are not limited to developer–builder and technology supply relations and project design and implementation. Housing development involves several relationships with different stakeholders who have different interests. Innovation adoption disrupts and misaligns these interests and the existing relations through which housing developments occurred. Furthermore, the developer, as the capitalist entrepreneur and coordinator of the development process, must realise that a financially viable innovation opportunity exists in the first place before decision making. The information that entrepreneurs require to discover entrepreneurial opportu-nities exist as bits of information with uncertain value scattered throughout the economy (Hayek, 1945). Coordinating dispersed information is similarly transacting.

The developers' governance problem

Conceiving innovations as transactions reveals the overlooked governance problem of innovation. Again, innovations have the inherent attributes of conflict, order, and mutuality, and exchanges range from simple personal

Table 13.1   Attributes of three modes of governance

Governance structures	Governance attributes		
	Incentive intensity	Administrative control	Contract law regime
Spot market	++	0	++
Hybrid	+	+	+
Hierarchy	0	++	0

Notes: Present in significant degree +; presumed to be absent = 0
Source: Williamson (2003)

exchanges to complex, impersonal exchanges of commodities, property rights or information, which have non-zero transaction costs and hazards. Non-standardised transactions, typically associated with innovation adoption, require third-party governance mechanisms to enforce contracts and resolve disputes (North, 1991, p. 97). In a world of perfect information, benevolent rational economic agents, and inexhaustible time to determine a priori all conditions that will require future contract adaptation, contracts are complete and subsequent adaptation needless. Real-world contracts are, however, inherently incomplete and require governance to secure agent interest. Mazé & Ménard (2010), McMillan & Woodruff (2000), and Richman (2004) show that entrepreneurs do not organise transactions in a way that relies on public institutions to enforce contracts and resolve disputes. Transacting parties design transactions that avoid reliance on ex-post courts' enforcement (Richman, 2004). Even if public institutions were well developed, as in some advanced countries, private governance mechanisms are still more efficient (Richman, 2004). Consequently, transacting parties align incentives and secure transactions better in extra-legal governance structures – private ordering mechanisms – rather than rely on public institutions (Williamson, 2003) (Table 13.1).

Similarly, innovations are inherently idiosyncratic assets with high levels of uncertainty. Innovations may, for example, be site-specific, physical-asset specific, human-asset specific, temporal specific or dedicated assets (Williamson, 1991). As asset idiosyncrasy increases, the developer/builder's sunk and switching costs increase (Klein, 1988; Williamson, 1991). Associated uncertainties, on the other hand, could be primary, competitive and supplier uncertainties (Williamson, 1985). Primary uncertainties are exogenous of the transaction – natural events (including disasters), acts of terror/insecurity, changes in homebuyers' taste and preferences, government regulations and policies, among others. The likelihood of opportunistic behaviour, cost of information search costs, negotiation, and dispute resolution increases with uncertainties.

Arguably, there are four significant identifiable innovation transactions: discovery of the entrepreneurial opportunity to innovate, adoption decision-making, developer/builder relationship with the technology supplier and the associated technology supply chain, and the shifts in existing production function/economic organisation of housing development due to the adoption. The extent of the developer's production function's shift depends on whether, relative to the existing economic organisation of residential development, the innovation is an incremental, modular, architectural, system, or radical innovation (Slaughter, 1998). Radical innovations shift the existing development processes and business model the most, requiring the developer to form new (contractual) relationships and alter existing ones. Production function shifts are associated with elevated uncertainty, both in discovering and implementing new opportunities. Likewise, asset specificity is inversely related to the developers' extant knowledge to economise the associated transaction costs of the technology exchange. The often-cited inadequate knowledge/skills barrier to innovation adoption, for example, is relative. The fundamental problem is why acquire additional knowledge and skills, given that developers do not seek to maximise profit but are rather profit satisficing? How should that new knowledge/information/skills be obtained – using markets, firms, hybrids? More importantly, why expend resources to acquire additional knowledge/skills when the entrepreneurial opportunity is not ex-ante knowable? All these questions are governance-related questions. Compounding the comparative governance problem is that, at the early stages of innovation adoption in a market, the efficacy of these institutional mechanisms is unknown (Lachmann, 1971).

Owing to the ex-ante unknowability that innovation investments will yield profitable outcomes, high levels of uncertainty and risks inundate innovation investments, which primarily large-scale firms (large-scale developers) can internalise. Furthermore, a "perfectly frictionless competitive market, with no barriers to the use of information, will provide no research and development investment" (Romano, 1989, p. 863). Outputs of innovation investments in creating specialised knowledge can be imitated by others, limiting investors' ability to retrieve sunk costs. Arrow (1972) concedes that in such markets, innovation investments will also cause the marginal production cost to exceed the marginal revenue of the firm, disincentivising innovation.

Linked to the production function shifts is the discovery of entrepreneurial opportunities. How does the capitalist developer identify viable innovation opportunities? The Schumpeterian entrepreneur creates actionable

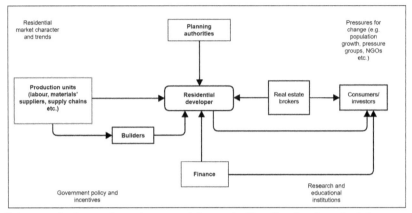

Notes: ↔ In discovering entrepreneurial opportunities, the direction of relations becomes bidirectional; ☐ Source of technological innovation
Source: Author's construct (2021), based on Drewett (1973)

Figure 13.1   Relations between the developer and other significant stakeholders in innovation adoption

entrepreneurial opportunities through the creative destruction process. The Kirznerian entrepreneur, on the other hand, is alert to entrepreneurial opportunities in the economy unnoticed by others and exploits them before others. The entrepreneur interprets experiential information and that circulated by the price mechanism to discover profitable entrepreneurial opportunities (Kirzner, 1997). In the context of innovation, the price mechanism cannot coordinate price and non-price information since a market is yet to emerge. Any "price information fails to provide information on how new markets could be served" (Eckhardt & Shane, 2003, p. 166).

To discover profitable innovation opportunities requires the alert Kirznerian entrepreneur to coordinate bits of information scattered throughout the economy (Hayek, 1937). It is when information on the greenbuilding technology's attributes, suppliers' loyalty, the interests and roles of stakeholders, national and local governments sustainability goals, residents' living expectations and affordability concerns, among others are coordinated and synthesised that entrepreneurial opportunities may emerge (Hu et al., 2014). Since scattered bits of information have uncertain value until coordinated and different actors possess different information sets, information exchanges are hazardous and require appropriately designed governance mechanisms. Disproportionate information access engenders opportunistic behaviours (see, for example, Akerlof, 1978). Large-scale developers, for example, may attempt autarky, and discover the innovation opportunity alone.

From the microanalytical unit, i.e. the transaction, one can further differentiate between transactions for which the developer/builder is the direct consumer, e.g. the acquisition of new software or IT-based solutions. There are also transactions for which the developer is an indirect consumer, e.g. new building materials and construction technologies. In the case of the latter, adoption decisions are linked to anticipated consumer reaction to the technology.

From Figure 13.1, each relationship requires a transaction cost minimising the governance mechanism. Different governance mechanisms – firms, markets, hybrids – have different efficacies in minimising different transaction costs (Shelanski & Klein, 1995; Williamson, 2003). Innovation success depends on the efficacy of the governance mechanism relative to transaction characteristics. The developer's problem of innovation becomes one of comparative governance mechanisms. Which governance mechanisms secure their interests (fairly or unfairly) and minimise their exposure to moral and contractual hazards?

An institutional approach to developers' innovation adoption behaviour

Nature of the housebuilding innovation adopters: developers and builders

Studies should recognise that human actors' attributes in the real world differ from those in economics orthodoxy regarding self-interest, cognition, and foresight. Self-interest, which is the basis for voluntary economic exchanges, also gives rise to opportunistic tendencies among trading partners. In the absence of opportunism, exchange parties could ex-ante promise to adapt contracts if, subsequently, misalignments of the initial contract's incentives become apparent.

Second, human decisions are boundedly rational (Simon, 1955). Choices are satisficing instead of maximising and may be emotional rather than logically evaluated. Limited hindsight and foresight, exacerbated by dispersed information, make complex contracts inevitably incomplete. The attributes of human activities have implications for contracting and innovation adoption decisions. (1) Developers and builders do not necessarily want to innovate irrespective of the benefits: current production arrangements and outputs may be good enough. (2) Making innovation adoption decisions can lead to irrational decisions. They are influenced by adopter(s) biases and sentiments. (3) Bounded rationality and dispersed information make complex contracts inevitably incomplete, and these elevate opportunistic tendencies in transacting.

Governance of innovation discovery and exchanges

Arguably, the first stage of innovation adoption is the developer identifying a financially viable innovation adoption opportunity. This is the focus of the Austrian entrepreneurship theories integrated with transaction cost economics as introduced in this chapter. The Austrian school focuses on the coordination of knowledge and the discovery of actionable entrepreneurial opportunities (Hayek, 1945; Kirzner, 1997, 1999; Sandye, 1999). It shifts the economic problem of innovation to the stage where the developer is unaware that an opportunity exists. The developer must gather and harmonise the scattered price and non-price information on market potentials. Since different agents possess different information with uncertain value, coordination of such information is open to the opportunistic behaviour of other parties. More importantly, why invest in such information coordination when both the value and probability of such efforts yielding economically viable opportunities are not ex-ante known? Discovering Kirznerian entrepreneurial opportunities involves information and knowledge coordination and decision-making under conditions of severe uncertainties. Such conditions in a competitive market disincentivise innovation and require public policy intervention to provide the missing innovation investments (Arrow, 1972; Romano, 1989).

Furthermore, transactions associated with conventional materials and technologies are distinct from innovative materials and technologies. In the case of the former, an established market as a governance structure exists – an arrangement where "faceless buyers and sellers ... meet ... for an instant to exchange standardised goods at equilibrium prices" (cited from Williamson, 1979). For recurrent and infrequent transactions involving conventional materials, numerous buyers and sellers exist. The continuity of a transaction relation is not essential in market transactions, and there are few or no switching costs for buyers who can switch to alternative sellers. Specialised knowledge is not necessary to retrieve mutual gains and minimise opportunistic behaviour: buyers respond autonomously to information transmitted by the price system (Hayek, 1945).

Innovations, on the other hand, are different. The costs incurred to discover and compare potential trade partners (technology suppliers), entrepreneurial opportunities, innovation prices, supplier loyalty, to measure the attributes of the technology, supply chain efficacies, among others, are different from conventional materials. Both conventional materials and innovations have transaction costs. Those of conventional materials are minimal due to standardisation and are known mainly based on experience. Associated transaction costs of innovation are largely ex-ante unknowable. When discovered, they are higher than those incurred in conventional transactions (see, for example, Kiss, 2016). This situation engenders the need for additional (specialised) knowledge.

Drawing from North (1990), determining the actual value of all goods and services associated with innovation is a severe problem for adopters. The disproportionate knowledge between the buyer (developer) and the seller (technology supplier) makes the transaction hazardous and susceptible, particularly to the ex-post contractual opportunistic behaviour of the latter. The efficacy of the developer's existing knowledge to economise transaction costs decreases as asset specificity increases. A housebuilding innovation could be site-specific, physical-asset specific, human-asset specific, temporal specific or have dedicated assets (Williamson, 1991, p. 281). The cost of due diligence, bargaining and contract monitoring and enforcement increases accordingly.

Similarly, the uncertainties associated with innovating are different from conventional materials. These uncertainties extend from discovering information about sustainable building technology, value, trading partners, supply chain, potential financial performance, customer demand, regulatory requirements, and labour requirements, among others. Indeed, innovation adoption decision outcomes are more unpredictable than conventional ones. The actions of potential partners are ex-ante unpredictable. Williamson (1985) distinguished between primary, competitive and supplier uncertainties.

Discovery/creation of institutions

Hazardous transactions require commensurate governance mechanisms to align transaction attributes better, transacting parties' interests, and to minimise ex-ante and ex-post contractual hazards. Applied to housing development, the developer chooses which development activities and professional services to coordinate internally, outsource or use institutional hybrids. Put differently, "transactions which differ in their attributes, are aligned with governance structures which vary in their cost and competence, to effect a (mainly) transaction cost economising result" (Williamson, 2003, p. 926).

Institutions (formal or informal) ensure certainty in voluntary exchanges by constraining self-seeking transacting agents' behaviour. Furthermore, regardless of the level of development of public institutions, transacting parties opt to align better incentives and secure transactions in extra-legal governance structures – private ordering – due to the latter's efficiency (Williamson, 2003).

Institutions determine the costs of economic organisation. Institutional transaction costs are prominent in housing developments, so much so that informal builders, contractors, self-help landlords and householders build outside of the statutory building and regulatory zoning frameworks to avoid them (Berner, 2000, 2001). Regulatory costs, on the other hand, impact the development costs of residential developers (Buitelaar, 2004).

In innovation, especially where a market is undeveloped or non-existent, developers have incomplete information about particular governance mechanisms' efficacy. "Successful plans ... gradually crystallise into institutions ... institutions are [often] relics of the *pioneering* efforts of former generations" (Lachmann, 1971, p. 68; emphasis added). What Lachmann highlights is not only the significance of institutions in economic exchanges but also institutions that could either be created or discovered. This logic presupposes that the developer-innovator has successfully governed the adoption transactions. An inefficient governance mechanism relative to transaction hazards will result in costly ex-post transaction costs resulting in project failure and likely subsequent discontinuity of adoption. Meanwhile, at the time of decision-making regarding potential adoption, the efficacy of possible private ordering mechanisms is unknown to the adopter, primarily where no "pioneers" exist in the local market. It is when the pioneer completes the adoption that the efficacy of the governance mechanism used is tested and established, and such information is available to others.

Developers do not only use institutions: "humanly devised constraints (formal or informal) that structure economic, social, and political interactions" (North, 1991, p. 97). They actively contribute to co-creating and adapting these rules through unintentional actions in the pursuance of self-interest, or lobbying of statutory agencies to enact new or alter existing rules (P. G. Klein, 2016; Lachmann, 1971). Institutions facilitate, shape, or hinder entrepreneurial decisions. Entrepreneurs' behaviours are sensitive to regulatory uncertainties. Regulatory uncertainties engender a wide range of entrepreneurial responses; abide by, evade, alter, or even exit a set of institutional frameworks. Indeed, existing rules of the game may structure developers' production decisions to specific coordination mechanisms and organisation of housing developments in ways antithetical to innovation.

Wallis and North (1986, p. 260) concluded: "if you want to realise the potential of modern technology, you cannot do with the state, but you cannot do without it either." Conceiving innovations in contractual terms highlights institutions' significance (private or public ordering) as facilitators or hindrances to innovation behaviour. It is less reasonable to expect developers to innovate if the political economy within which they operate incentivises their production decisions to conventional materials and technologies.

Crucial interdependencies

The housing development process is complicated. It involves multiple interdependent processes and activities and actors and agencies with different self-interests. The interests of the developers, customers, financiers, contractors, builders, artisans, planning authorities, landowners, various product suppliers, among others, are all negotiated within the development process. More importantly, the stakeholders' interests and goals often deviate from one another. Planners and policymakers' sustainability targets do not directly benefit developers if these targets do not result in increased developer profits (Graaskamp, 1992).

Similarly, homebuyers' interest is in energy-efficient housing, with good ventilation and other quality physical housing attributes. These are properties developers do not directly enjoy. Innovating introduces tension and uncertainties into existing relationships, stakeholders' interests, and the economic organisation of housing development. Green building technology adoption often requires new partnerships and procurement. It shifts the developer from the predictable behaviour of stakeholders to uncertainty. Will banks, for example, finance the project? Multiple interdependencies make the transaction hazards of housebuilding innovation particularly damaging.

Furthermore, innovation adoption has sunk costs: design changes to accommodate the innovation, procurement of new builders or tradespeople, and the learning curve of existing contractors and designers. Designing a green building consumes an additional 20% of the time compared with a similar but conventional one (Deng et al., 2018).

Future research outlook

Barrier studies, while helpful, focus on innovation as a suboptimal investment problem owing to scarce resources. This chapter does not intend to replace this investment problem of innovation. Instead, it draws attention to researchers' pro-adoption biases. More importantly, due to the preoccupation of existing literature on barriers, some phenomena on innovation have gone unnoticed, while others are poorly understood, resulting in public policy errors (Williamson, 2003). The transaction as the unit of analysis is critical to understanding housing developers' innovation behaviour – the perspective that existing research has often overlooked. This chapter has argued for a shift to this micro-analytical unit – the transaction – to improve the comprehension of developers' and builders' innovation behaviour and inform policy design. Buchanan and Williamson further strengthen this proposal. The economy is a social organisation (Buchanan, 1975, p. 225) which should be examined to discover "how alternative arrangements will work in practice" (Williamson, 2003, p. 439), as institutions are prerequisites for trade/complex exchanges (Buchanan, 1975).

This chapter, developed theoretically from transaction costs economics and entrepreneurship theory, has demonstrated the neglected aspects of innovations in residential developments. Future studies situated within the economic organisation of property development, governance mechanisms and institutions will generate pragmatic insights to accelerate innovation adoption and diffusion. Empirical studies on innovation adoption failures are necessary. Why do developers discontinue adoption? How do developers coordinate price and non-price information on innovative technologies? How do developers discover entrepreneurial opportunities to innovate? Studies that establish the relationship between innovation asset specificities, uncertainties, and adoption tendencies are essential. How do developers solve their governance problem of innovation adoption? How developers transact innovation exchanges, deal with transaction hazards and institutional governance mechanisms will illuminate the current understanding of the role institutions play in entrepreneurial decision-making.

Asymmetric information elevates the uncertainties and risks of exchanges and adoption decisions. How do developers economise uncertainties associated with innovation? What are these uncertainties? Developers' investment sentiments, biases, and information sources are other areas of further investigation. Cross-country comparisons of innovation policies, housing development institutions, regulatory frameworks, and government structures will yield valuable insights to guide policy response in order to stimulate innovation adoption and diffusion in the housing sector. Housing innovation studies should extend to the political economy within which innovation occurs.

References

Adam, E. A., & Agib, A. R. A. (2001). Compressed stabilised earth block manufacture in Sudan. France, Paris: Printed by Graphoprint for UNESCO.

Akerlof, G. A. (1978). The market for "lemons": Quality uncertainty and the market mechanism. In *Uncertainty in Economics* (pp. 235–251). Elsevier.

Akerlof, G. A., & Kranton, R. E. (2000). Economics and Identity. *The Quarterly Journal of Economics, 115*(3), 715–753. https://doi.org/10/fxdw82

Andelin, M., Sarasoja, A.-L., Ventovuori, T., & Junnila, S. (2015). Breaking the circle of blame for sustainable buildings – evidence from Nordic countries. *Journal of Corporate Real Estate.* https://doi.org/10.1108/JCRE-05-2014-0013

Arrow, K. J. (1969). The organization of economic activity: Issues pertinent to the choice of market versus nonmarket allocation. *The Analysis and Evaluation of Public Expenditure: The PPB System, 1,* 59–73.

Arrow, K. J. (1972). Economic welfare and the allocation of resources for invention. In *Readings in Industrial Economics* (pp. 219–236). Springer.

Ball, M. (2003). Markets and the structure of the housebuilding industry: An international perspective. *Urban Studies, 40*(5–6), 897–916. https://doi.org/10/fhvgjh

Berner, E. (2000). Informal developers, patrons, and the state: Institutions and regulatory mechanisms in popular housing. *Naerus Conference ESF/N-AERUS Workshop on "Coping with Informality and Illegality in Human Settlements in Developing Countries",* Leuven, Belgium, 23, 23–36.

Berner, E. (2001). Learning from informal markets: Innovative approaches to land and housing provision. *Development in Practice, 11*(2–3), 292–307. https://doi.org/10.1080/09614520120056423

Buchanan, J. M. (1975). A contractarian paradigm for applying economic theory. *The American Economic Review, 65*(2), 225–230.

Buchanan, J. M. (2001). Game theory, mathematics, and economics. *Journal of Economic Methodology, 8*(1), 27–32.

Buitelaar, E. (2004). A transaction-cost analysis of the land development process. *Urban Studies, 41*(13), 2539–2553. https://doi.org/10.1080/0042098042000294556

Buitelaar, E. (2008). *The cost of land use decisions: Applying transaction cost economics to planning and development.* John Wiley & Sons.

Coase, R. H. (1937). The nature of the firm. *Economica, 4*(16), 386–405. https://doi.org/10.1111/j.1468-0335.1937.tb00002.x

Coase, R. H. (1960). The problem of social cost. In *Classic Papers in Natural Resource Economics* (pp. 87–137). Springer.

Commons, J. R. (1932). The problem of correlating law, economics and ethics. *Wisconsin Law Review, 8,* 3–26.

Deng, W., Yang, T., Tang, L., & Tang, Y.-T. (2018). Barriers and policy recommendations for developing green buildings from local government perspective: A case study of Ningbo China. *Intelligent Buildings International, 10*(2), 61–77.

Dickinson, M., Cooper, R., McDermott, P., & Eaton, D. (2005). An analysis of construction innovation literature. *5th International Postgraduate Research Conference,* 14–15 April.

Didel, M. J., Matawal, D. S., & Ojo, E. B. (2014). Comparative cost analysis of compressed stabilised blocks and sandcrete blocks in affordable housing delivery in Nigeria. *Proceedings of International Inclusive City Growth and the Poor: Policies, Challenges and Prospects, 203.*

Drewett, R. (1973). The developers: Decision processes. *The Containment of Urban England*, 2, 163–194.

Eckhardt, J. T., & Shane, S. A. (2003). Opportunities and entrepreneurship. *Journal of Management*, 29(3), 333–349.

Garcia, R., & Calantone, R. (2002). A critical look at technological innovation typology and innovativeness terminology: A literature review. *Journal of Product Innovation Management: An International Publication of the Product Development & Management Association*, 19(2), 110–132.

Gooding, L., & Gul, M. S. (2016). Energy efficiency retrofitting services supply chains: A review of evolving demands from housing policy. *Energy Strategy Reviews*, 11, 29–40.

Graaskamp, J. A. (1992). Fundamentals of real estate development. *Journal of Property Valuation and Investment*, 10(3), 619–639. https://doi.org/10.1108/14635789210031253

Hayek, F. A. (1937). Economics and knowledge. *Economica*, 4(13), 33–54. https://doi.org/10.2307/2548786

Hayek, F. A. (1945). The use of knowledge in society. *The American Economic Review*, 35(4), 519–530.

Hu, H., Geertman, S., & Hooimeijer, P. (2014). Green apartments in Nanjing China: Do developers and planners understand the valuation by residents? *Housing Studies*, 29(1), 26–43. https://doi.org/10/gkzcpn

Kirzner, I. M. (1997). Entrepreneurial discovery and the competitive market process: An Austrian approach. *Journal of Economic Literature*, 35(1), 60–85.

Kirzner, I. M. (1999). Creativity and/or alertness: A reconsideration of the Schumpeterian entrepreneur. *Review of Austrian Economics*, 11(1–2), 5–17. https://doi.org/10.1023/A:1007719905868

Kiss, B. (2016). Exploring transaction costs in passive house-oriented retrofitting. *Journal of Cleaner Production*, 123, 65–76. https://doi.org/10.1016/j.jclepro.2015.09.035

Kiss, B., & Mundaca, L. (2013). Transaction costs of energy efficiency in buildings – an overview. *IAEE Energy Forum, 2nd Quarter*, 31–32.

Klein, B. (1988). Vertical integration as organizational ownership: The Fisher Body-General Motors relationship revisited. *Journal of Law, Economics, & Organization*, 4(1), 199–213.

Klein, P. G. (2016). Why entrepreneurs need firms, and the theory of the firm needs entrepreneurship theory. *Revista de Administração*, 51(3), 323–326. https://doi.org/10.1016/j.rausp.2016.06.007

Lachmann, L. M. (1971). *The Legacy of Max Weber*. Ludwig von Mises Institute.

Mazé, A., & Ménard, C. (2010). Private ordering, collective action, and the self-enforcing range of contracts. *European Journal of Law and Economics*, 29(1), 131–153. https://doi.org/10.1007/s10657-009-9114-x

McMillan, J., & Woodruff, C. (2000). Private order under dysfunctional public order. *Michigan Law Review*, 2421–2458. https://doi.org/10.2307/1290349

Mundaca T, L., Mansoz, M., Neij, L., Timilsina, G. R. (2013). Transaction costs analysis of low-carbon technologies. *Climate Policy*, 3062. https://doi.org/10.1080/14693062.2013.781452

Niehans, J. (1969). Money in a static theory of optimal payment arrangements. *Journal of Money, Credit and Banking*, 1(4), 706–726. https://doi.org/10.2307/1991447

North, D. C. (1990). *Institutions, Institutional Change and Economic Performance*. Cambridge University Press.

North, D. C. (1991). Institutions. *The Journal of Economic Perspectives*, 5(1), 97–112.
North, D. C. (1992). *Transaction Costs, Institutions, and Economic Performance*. San Francisco, CA: ICS Press.
North, D. C. (1994). Constraints on institutional innovation: Transaction costs, incentive compatibility, and historical considerations. *Agriculture, Environment and Health: Sustainable Development in the 21st Century*. Minneapolis: University of Minnesota Press, pp. 48–70.
OECD/Eurostat. (2005). *Oslo Manual: Guidelines for Collecting and Interpreting Innovation Data* (3rd ed.). OECD Publishing. https://doi.org/10.1787/9789264013100-en
Ogundiran, I. A., & Adedeji, Y. M. D. (2012). Urban housing delivery: Expanded polystyrene panels initiative in Abuja, Nigeria. *Proceedings of the 4th West Africa Built Environment Research (WABER) Conference*, 1033–1042.
Raheem, A. A., Momoh, A. K., & Soyingbe, A. A. (2012). Comparative analysis of sandcrete hollow blocks and laterite interlocking blocks as walling elements. *International Journal of Sustainable Construction Engineering and Technology*, 3(1), 79–88.
Richman, B. D. (2004). Firms, courts, and reputation mechanisms: Towards a positive theory of private ordering. *Columbia Law Review*, 104, 2328–2328. https://doi.org/10.2307/4099361
Rogers, E. M. (2003). *Diffusion of Innovations*, 5th Edition. Free Press.
Romano, R. E. (1989). Aspects of R&D subsidization. *The Quarterly Journal of Economics*, 104(4), 863–873. https://doi.org/10.2307/2937871
Rosenberg, N. (1974). Science, invention and economic growth. *Economic Journal*, 84(333), 90–108. https://doi.org/10/bgbnq7
Ruttan, V. W. (1959). Usher and Schumpeter on invention, innovation, and technological change. *The Quarterly Journal of Economics*, 73(4), 596–606. https://doi.org/10/dmsfvj
Sandye, G.-P. (1999). *The Evolution of Austrian Economics: From Menger to Lachmann*. Routledge.
Sarasvathy, S. D. (2009). *Effectuation: Elements of Entrepreneurial Expertise*. Cheltenham, UK and Northampton, MA, USA: Edward Elgar Publishing.
Schumpeter, J. A. (1934). *The Theory of Economic Development: An Inquiry into Profits, Capital, Credit, Interest, and the Business Cycle* (trans. Redvers Opie). Harvard University Press.
Schumpeter, J. A. (1947). The creative response in economic history. *The Journal of Economic History*, 7(2), 149–159.
Sexton, M., & Barrett, P. (2003). A literature synthesis of innovation in small construction firms: Insights, ambiguities and questions. *Construction Management and Economics*, 21(6), 613–622. https://doi.org/10.1080/0144619032000134147
Shelanski, H. A., & Klein, P. G. (1995). Empirical research in transaction cost economics: A review and assessment. *Journal of Law, Economics, & Organization*, 335–361.
Simon, H. A. (1955). A behavioral model of rational choice. *The Quarterly Journal of Economics*. https://doi.org/10.2307/1884852
Slaughter, E. S. (1993). Builders as sources of construction innovation. *Journal of Construction Engineering and Management*. https://doi.org/10.1061/(asce)0733-9364(1993)119:3(532)
Slaughter, E. S. (1998). Models of construction innovation. *Journal of Construction Engineering and Management*, 124(3), 226–231.

Toole, T. M. (1998). Uncertainty and home builders' adoption of technological innovations. *Journal of Construction Engineering and Management*, *124*(4), 323–332. https://doi.org/10.1061/(ASCE)0733-9364(1998)124:4(323)

Ürge-Vorsatz, D., Eyre, N., Graham, P., Harvey, D., Hertwich, E., Jiang, Y., Kornevall, C., Majumdar, M., McMahon, J. E., Mirasgedis, S., Murakami, S., Novikova, A., Janda, K., Masera, O., McNeil, M., Petrichenko, K., Herrero, S. T., & Jochem, E. (2012). Energy end-use: Buildings. In T. B. Johansson, N. Nakicenovic, A. Patwardhan, & L. Gomez-Echeverri (Eds.), *Global Energy Assessment (GEA)* (pp. 649–760). Cambridge University Press. https://doi.org/10.1017/CBO9780511793677.016

Van Oorschot, J. A. W. H., Halman, J. I. M., & Hofman, E. (2020). Getting innovations adopted in the housing sector. *Construction Innovation*, *20*(2), 285–318. https://doi.org/10.1108/CI-11-2018-0095

von Hayek, F. A. (1989). The pretence of knowledge. *The American Economic Review*, *79*(6), 3–7.

Wallis, J. J., & North, D. (1986). Measuring the transaction sector in the American economy, 1870-1970. In *Long-term Factors in American Economic Growth* (pp. 95–162). University of Chicago Press.

Wang, N. (2003). Measuring transaction costs: An incomplete survey. *Ronald Coase Institute, Working Paper*, *2*.

Williamson, O. E. (1979). Transaction-cost economics: The governance of contractual relations. *The Journal of Law and Economics*, *22*(2), 233–261.

Williamson, O. E. (1985). *The Economic Institutions of Capitalism: Firms, Markets, Relational Contracting*. The Free Press.

Williamson, O. E. (1991). Comparative economic organization: The analysis of discrete structural alternatives. *Administrative Science Quarterly*, *36*(2), 269–296. https://doi.org/10.2307/2393356

Williamson, O. E. (2003). Examining economic organization through the lens of contract. *Industrial and Corporate Change*, *12*(4), 917–942.

Wolfe, R. A. (1994). Organizational innovation: Review, critique and suggested research directions. *Journal of Management Studies*, *31*(3), 405–431.

Wong, F. W. H., Chan, E. H. W., & Yu, A. T. W. (2011). Property developers' major cost concerns arising from planning regulations under a high land-price policy. *Journal of Urban Planning and Development*, *137*(2), 112–120.

Index